NATURE IS C

For Detlef Kantowsky
on the occasion
of his 60th birthday

NATURE IS CULTURE

*Indigenous knowledge
and socio-cultural aspects of trees and
forests in non-European cultures*

Edited by
KLAUS SEELAND

INTERMEDIATE TECHNOLOGY PUBLICATIONS 1997

Intermediate Technology Publications Ltd
103–105 Southampton Row, London WC1B 4HH, UK

© this selection, Klaus Seeland 1997

A CIP record for this book is available from the British Library

ISBN 1 85339 410 6

Typeset by Dorwyn Ltd, Rowlands Castle, Hants
Printed in the UK by SRP, Exeter

Contents

Foreword   vii
FRANZ SCHMITHÜSEN

1. Introduction   1
   KLAUS SEELAND

2. Culturing trees: socialized knowledge in the political ecology of Kissia and Kuranko forest islands of Guinea   7
   JAMES FAIRHEAD AND MELISSA LEACH

3. The perceived environment as a system of knowledge and meaning: a study of the Mewahang Rai of eastern Nepal   19
   BARUN GURUNG

4. *Tatari:* livelihood and danger in upland Japan   28
   JOHN KNIGHT

5. Forests and trees in the cultural landscape of Lawa swidden farmers in northern Thailand   44
   DIETRICH SCHMIDT-VOGT

6. Tree marriage in India   51
   ROBERT PARKIN

7. The influence of religious beliefs and rituals on forest conservation in Nepal   57
   ANDREW W. INGLES

8. The Huaorani and their trees: managing and imagining the Ecuadorian rain forest   67
   LAURA RIVAL

9. Where trees do matter for society: the socio-cultural aspects of sal (*Shorea robusta*) and salap (*Caryota urens L.*) in the Similipal hills of Orissa, India   79
   MIHIR KUMAR JENA, KLAUS SEELAND AND KAMALA KUMARI PATNAIK

10. War, forests and the future: the environmental understanding of the young in Sierra Leone   90
    PAUL RICHARDS

11. Indigenous knowledge of trees and forests in non-European societies   101
    KLAUS SEELAND

12. Forests and trees in the world of two Tamang villages in
     central Nepal: observations with special reference to the
     role of Tamang women in forest management   113
     BETTINA MAAG

     Appendix to Chapter 12   130

     Notes on contributors   136

     Notes   138

     Bibliography   142

Foreword

FRANZ SCHMITHÜSEN

THE MEANING OF a forest is reflected in its cultural perception and, over the ages societies have developed their notions of what forests mean to them. Whatever the particular representations of forests are for the members of one society, they would certainly have a different relevance to what others see and understand in the dimensions of their own culture. The forests of today show how people have been and still are dependent on them, and how they make use of and interpret their environment in terms of survival and social advancement. The transformation of forest vegetation that we observe, indicates specific social needs, cultural values, and changing economic and technological processes. Forests represent a legacy and they are a testimony of the evolution of societies and their respective perceptions of nature.

Human activities influence forests but their impact is difficult to assess. Some of the changes are immediate and occur in the short term. Others, and often the more important ones, are indirect and are to be understood in a historical perspective. The spatial distribution of forests, and the degree of their transformation by man are the result of physical conditions and of varying cultural patterns. This applies not only to forests that have been intensively used over centuries, but also to forests which still appear to be in a natural state. They may have been spared from human intervention due to physical inaccessibility and economic considerations, or because they represent the particular spiritual values of a society. The border between intensively used forests and those showing little or no trace of human interference reflects social rules, economic options and political decisions. In this respect, all forests, including those which we still consider as natural, are cultural phenomena.

The United Nations Conference on Environment and Development in 1992 put forests and forestry on the political agenda of the world community. The preparatory stages, as well as the follow-up processes, represented by the work of the UN Commission on Sustainable Development, show that there is still considerable disagreement on many issues – in spite of growing public awareness – to regard forests as a common heritage. Large-scale deforestation in the tropics and sub-tropics both leads to and results from the social and economic problems of many people living in these regions. Protection of forests, sustainable use, and preservation of biodiversity are the challenges facing many industrialized countries in the boreal and temperate zones. The ensuing conflicts are part of fundamental controversies about social justice, self-determination and sovereignty, local political participation and democratic decision-making, as well as symptoms of the unbalanced economic development in different parts of the world.

It is in this context that research on indigenous knowledge, and on the meaning of trees and forests in different cultures, matters. It is necessary in order to demonstrate the many needs and values associated with forests in a given locality, and the importance of forested areas for the survival of indigenous people and their cultures. Research findings bring forward concrete facts which should be considered when political decisions on the utilization of natural resources are made, and they are the basis of a strong argument both for increased efforts in protecting forested areas and considering local uses. They also demonstrate the conflict between traditional practices in sustainable resource management –

vii

developed from experience and modified for difficult living conditions – and the development activities of modern states.

Investigations into the perceptions and attitudes of individuals and local communities in relation to the conservation of trees and forests play an increasing role in forestry development and policy. They provide the opportunity for an improved understanding of existing management practices under their specific social and cultural conditions, as well as the potential for adaptation to a changing economic environment. Research on the important intercultural dimensions of trees and forests requires professional foresters to integrate social and cultural information to manage forests and other scarce natural resources appropriately and sustainably. Forest research has to emphasize more the manifold ways in which man performs in his environment. This calls for new and more intensive co-operation and collaboration between the social and cultural sciences, and international research in applied natural sciences and forestry research. And it implies a more intensive exchange of ideas between researchers who emphasize the social dimensions of forestry, and those who, in practice, are responsible for resource protection and development.

This book – the result of an effort with just such a common perspective – originated within the scientific network of the International Union of Forestry Research Organizations (IUFRO). The contributors come from many scientific disciplines and various national and cultural backgrounds. Their investigations provide results which are of interest to many scientific disciplines and further academic research, as well as to foresters and other professionals engaged in natural resources management. My thanks go to the authors and to the editor who have co-operated patiently in producing this inspiring and informative collection of papers demonstrating the ingenuity, cultural uniqueness and social usefulness in which different groups of people represent their environment through their lives. We all hope that this co-operation continues in order to improve our understanding of the role of forests in societies and of the possibilities for their use and conservation.

Note

The author is a member of IUFRO Division 6: Social, Economic, Information, and Policy Sciences.

1   Introduction

KLAUS SEELAND

NOWADAYS IN THE Western world, nature is commonly perceived as separate from human culture and civilization, and as something fragile to be cared for. The notion of nature being an independent principle of species living according to their own patterns and interacting with other living beings of their surroundings is, likewise, common sense. The separation of the world into natural habitats, man-made environments and civilization, however, bypasses the perception of local communities living a more or less traditional lifestyle, where both nature and culture amalgamate into a reality where material, social and spiritual aspects merge into an encompassing view. Wherever plants, animals and human beings constitute an integrated whole, it is this specific culture that makes sense by ordering natural and social phenomena into a structured world. Strictly speaking, this structured world is an entity of natural phenomena and man-made achievements, and represents time-bound selections of experiences and notions which are amalgamations of nature and culture.

Cultural diversity is reflected in the natural bounty of a local setting where one or more societies define their material needs, and their spiritual world-views shape the habitat as well as does their respective technological power, which is at their disposal. Nature and culture can never be looked at separately for reasons of scientific analysis without losing those essentials that characterize a culture. Configurations of natural phenomena in a social perspective indicate how societies perform in a geographical region over a certain time. It is this performance that gives a culture its unique features. European, as well as non-European cultures are constituting processes to appropriate nature through their social capacities to recognize and make use of its potential. From this point of view, the trees and forests discussed in this volume are perceived as examples of particular modes of appropriation in different geographical settings. A natural space always appears as a cultural landscape, because it is a socially appropriated space.

The first contribution, by John Fairhead and Melissa Leach, focuses on indigenous knowledge as an aspect of the political ecology of forest islands in selected areas of the Republic of Guinea. It gives both an account of the Kissia population and its relationship with trees and forest, and an excellent overview of the sociality through which these are planted, enriched, used in daily consumption, and destroyed when a forest village is transferred to another location. Ethnicity matters in this part of West Africa in the preservation and management of trees and forests. The Kissia are a vivid example of a tribal population whose lifestyle is characterized by dependence on trees and forests and their products. Other tribes in the same region, however, are not at all affected by forests in the same way, and try to reduce them wherever possible. This shows that it cannot be taken for granted that 'indigenousness' necessarily implies a close relationship with trees or forests. National or regional politics within the country do reflect these contradictions between the ways different ethnic groups perform their social life and culture through one natural setting or another.

Barun Gurung draws the reader's attention to an ethnic group's perception of its environment in East Nepal. In his study of particular aspects of indigenous knowledge, he investigates the Mewahang Rai mountain farmers' views on and

1

approaches to erosion control and weed control practices, soil fertility and pest management, and genetic-resource management. As the Rai do not distinguish between the sacred and the secular, nature is appropriated by them discursively in its material as well as its spiritual dimension.

Rural livelihoods, particularly hunting, in the mountain forests of the Kii Peninsula in Japan are investigated in John Knight's contribution. In the past, the mountain forests of this region were the sole resource relied upon by inhabitants for their meagre living, and this necessitated exposure to its material and spiritual dangers. One of the important key terms is the kuyō rite, a moral category of regret for taking the lives of plants and animals and annoying the spirits inhabiting the environment. The hunters and the hunted sometimes share a similar fate, particularly when they have transgressed the ethical codes of conduct and are thus cursed by the spirits of the animals they have killed. Nowadays, the cultural, religious and emotional attachment of the local villagers has become lore of a far and distant world which is, however, morally still relevant for them. The kuyō sensibility is likely to continue under conditions of modernity, because of a cultural recognition of a commonality between humans, animals and plants.

The human geographer Dietrich Schmidt-Vogt provides an account of shifting cultivation, one of the classical topics of social anthropology. The cultural landscape of Lawa swidden farmers who live in the mountains of northern Thailand is characterized by a patchwork pattern of irrigated areas, dryland cultivation on slash-and-burn plots, and forests in different stages of plant succession. The way in which the Lawa practise swidden agriculture leads to an alteration of the plant composition in those forests that have been burned and, subsequently, used to grow crops. Thus the features of the Lawa landscape are not only shaped according to their land use pattern, but the secondary forest that usually grows approximately five years after the primary forest has been burned displays a greater variety of plant species and, thus, enriches the range of available plants to be used as food and for medical treatment. Together with the remaining patches of primary forests, these secondary forests represent an optimum of plants made available through slash-and-burn agriculture in the Lawa environment. Nature's potential is actively altered by their cultural concepts of forest management into several types of forests containing valuable forest produce within their multifold environment.

The nexus between nature and culture becomes most obvious when a natural phenomenon is involved in a custom. Tree marriage is a remarkable feature of many Hindu communities and tribal cultures throughout India, and even outside the Indian sub-continent. Robert Parkin's inquiry into the rationale of humans marrying trees gives lucid examples of the amalgamation of natural and cultural phenomena to maintain social norms, as well as to attain spiritual salvation. Marriage between humans and trees may thus be reasonable either to facilitate marriage between human beings in order to bypass religious restrictions, or as a fertility cult to facilitate the reincarnation of souls. In the tribal world of India, tree marriage, or marriage to other aspects of nature, is linked with the continuity of the kinship system, with *karma* theodicy, and social status in Hinduism. In the cultural setting of South Asia, trees have a social eligibility which is a core aspect of human identity – to be a match for a human being.

The impact of religiousness on forest management and conservation in Nepal is the focus of Andrew Ingles' contribution. A forester, he worked for some years in the Nepal-Australia Community Forestry Project and gained intimate knowledge of Nepal's religious forests. A religious forest can either be a site covered with trees, surrounding a temple or a shrine of a goddess, or it can be a sacred grove. Religious forests are sometimes managed in order to produce fuelwood for cremation, or to be sold to raise funds for charity. The author admits that the conservational value of such sites may be not very significant in terms of their size, compared to 'secular' forests. But the fact that these forms of co-operative management represent established social institutions (*guthi*, translated literally, means 'common trust') makes them, perhaps, starting points to encourage the local population to follow a similar management pattern for the sustainable use of their 'secular' forests. In addition, religious forests are claimed to be areas of great biodiversity. In his examples, Ingles shows that the degree of social organization reflects sustainability, and it is this mode of organized appropriation on the basis of religious consent that safeguards religious forests. Their benefits are shared among all Hindus of the respective community, and this is the legitimization to restrict the access of other people and any other purpose than religious. This management pattern demonstrates the role of social obligations for conservation and sustainability, once religious matters are directing its rationale.

Laura Rival did extensive research in the Ecuadorian rain forest; she provides an interesting example of the way the Huaorani, a tribe living in the Amazon rain forest, perceive and manage the peach palm (*Bactris gasipaes*). A comparatively small and isolated group, the Huaorani maintain a self-sustained life of hunting, foraging, and manioc cultivation. They are semi-nomads and roam through a large forest territory. Huaorani mythology is centred around a giant ceibo tree (*Ceibo pentranda*), which represents life, and their cosmology stresses the importance of trees and vegetation; the core of what Rival calls the Amazon ecosystem. The peach palm is the highly valued source for the Huaorani's diet and, perhaps, the tree is propagated – for the sake of cooking and consuming its fruits – to a greater extent than would be the case if people ignored the plant. It could be claimed, therefore, that man is not only taking advantage of the bounty of forest and nature, but has been actively involved in its processes, such as the diffusion of this species, since the beginnings of life. Neither naturally grown nor cultivated in a strict sense, the peach palm's propagation and its hybridization through domestication are a product of Huaorani food habits and sociality. The palm groves are the abode of the ancestors, where the Huaorani gather to celebrate their marriages. In this case, man acts as a mediator, as he represents both the characteristics of nature and culture. Undisturbed or natural forests, and cultural forests whose floral composition represent anthropogenic changes both contribute to the well-being of the forest dwellers.

Jena, Seeland, and Patnaik's investigation into the nature and economy of the sal tree (*Shorea robusta*) and the sago palm (*Caryota urens, L.*) in the tribal community of the Hill Kharia and Kuttia Kondh of Orissa (India) are further examples of the importance of certain tree species which are essential for the tribes' food supply. Their honey supply is largely dependent on tall sal trees and a wide range of flowering forest plants. The degradation of old sal forests in several parts of the area where the Hill Kharia live, has reduced the quantity of this important high quality food and valued source of cash income. Reafforestation of the degraded forest could not restore an adequate environment and equally rich varieties of plants to consolidate decreasing honey yields. The Kuttia Kondh's use and management of sago trees for palm-wine (*toddy*) production is an indispensable part of their economy and social life. Sago-palm trees are privately owned, and the people believe there is an emotional and supernatural nexus between a tree and its owner. Matters of social importance are discussed in sago-palm groves. The yield of a deceased owner's tree indicates to his community the degree of his common sense and thus his social position is evaluated posthumously. Sago-palms are inherited by the Kuttia Kondh only with the consent of their ancestral spirits. This social, material and spiritual dependence of both the tribes on these trees is a great incentive for taking good care of them by conservation through need and management.

How young people in the west African nation of Sierra Leone perceive and understand their environment is explored by Paul Richards, who carried out a sociological survey among 400 young people in three localities. The results show a more or less homogeneous picture of the distribution of knowledge on issues such as environmental resource management and forest conservation. Minor forest produce is an essential contribution to the subsistence economy of young people all over Sierra Leone. In his survey, in which Richards investigated the availability of household implements, food, fuel and building materials made out of forest products, he discovered that people were finding it increasingly difficult to procure some of these items, to cope with the rising prices and uncontrolled bush fires. Most of the young respondents displayed a good knowledge of forest environments and, although many perceived the forest to be decreasing, they were optimistic about their own and their country's future. The long-term war in Sierra Leone has had an impact on young people's attitudes towards large-scale forest-clearing in order to deny the guerilla his opportunities for ambush and hiding. The author emphasizes that deforestation, reafforestation and environmental conservation are issues of great concern to the country's youth, and the interviewees are outspoken and impassioned, demonstrating what might be called environmental consciousness.

My own contribution in this volume tries to shed some light on indigenous knowledge about trees and forests in non-European societies. To understand the roles of indigenous and modern knowledge in different cultures requires both theories of cross-cultural comparison and the role of knowledge in social change. Traditional forest-dwelling tribal societies base their knowledge on their local world. Humans, trees and other forms of plant and animal life constitute forests as interconnections of nature and culture; as an 'inter-species' form of social life. Thus, social life reflects the state of a natural, yet anthropogenically shaped, forest environment. The appropriation of nature as culture is a social process including all forms of life that share common surroundings. Scientific approaches to record and investigate indigenous knowledge features are a basic of ethnosciences. All knowledge of plant and animal species, for example, indicates certain social performances. Unknown species, however, represent unappropriated nature. It is in the social and cultural context that nature is revealed as culture, mostly through the transfer of metaphors. By their use, phenomena which are already known can be transferred to new phenomena. Examples from the names given to forests and hills by the Kuttia Kondh show just how interwoven their landscape, plant and animal life, their myths and spiritual world are with a specific epistemology.

The forests and trees in the world of two Tamang villages in Central Nepal are highlighted by Bettina Maag. She conducted research in two settings which differ in terms of the wealth of natural resources, and economic situation. In one village, the environmental situation is fairly good and its forests have been managed independently without any government supervision, whereas in the other the forest has been under the control of the government and overexploited for several decades, and today it is still under severe pressure due to its high population density. In religious matters, Tamang society is an amalgamation of animistic and ancestral cults, shamanism, the Lamaïst form of Buddhism, and is also partly influenced by Hinduism. Their forests are valuable resources of fuelwood, fodder, timber, medicinal plants, and many other minor forest products as well as being perceived as being haunted by goddesses, ghosts, and demons. The social concept of forest management and decision-making in both villages shows a gender-specific division of labour based on a different perception of forests. Tamang women care for the forest, as it provides their household with many of the everyday items they need in caring for their families. Mutual co-operation is a must if the women are to feel secure while working in the forest; work which affords them much of their social life. They are the most aware of the condition of a forest, as they have known it since early childhood, and can detect changes easily. Tamang women are the backbone of social cohesion in their village society and the rationale of management is reflected in the way they use their forests. The examples given by Maag show that, despite their role as 'guardians of the forests', Tamang women as well as their fellow villagers are susceptible to the political and market influences which, ultimately, decide the fate of their forests. The socio-political set-up defines the conditions for the margins that indigenous forest and natural resource management have in remote rural areas.

In times of more or less rapid social change due to economic development and population growth, questions about the future prospects of non-European forest communities arise. One of the most challenging may be whether the cultures of forest dwellers as distinct socio-cultural units will vanish with the decline and degradation of the physical features of, say, a 'home forest', in and with which a community would live for generations. Transitional social processes may or may not spare indigenous peoples from being integrated into the mainstream of modernization. It can be stated with some certainty, however, that they cannot escape change once exposed to lifestyles which alienate them from their traditions, and present them with a new outlook on a previously unknown, modern world. By going through processes of adaptation, tribes practically give up both their environment and nature and their cultural identity. There is no better way to show that nature is culture, than when both merge, and take on the shape of a subsistent community, entirely dependent on the natural resources accessible in its local surroundings. Culture as well as nature in their specific configuration may deteriorate with the expropriation of a people's habitat, or may be transformed by alienation through social change. Once the traditional habitat of a self-sustained community can no longer provide all the necessary resources, undergoing a process of self-transformation becomes essential for survival. Migration and the displacement of a community, for example, are disruptions from its habitat and, likewise, the beginning of a process of cultural transformation and adaptation to the social mainstream. More often than not, this process leads to the creation of an underclass who will become more and more dependent on the state or welfare institutions.

Almost every contributor to this volume emphasizes that any particular culture, representing the social features of a natural surrounding and vice versa, maintains a physical space, where different forms of life create distinct, but somehow interlinked worlds. From a social science, as well as an international and national forest policy point of view, the sustainable use of land in the future depends on resource management incorporating both local and modern scientific knowledge. The goal of contributing to the maintenance of a people's authentic vitality is important; the vitality of local cultures illustrates the genuine interest of indigenous peoples in remaining in their habitats and keeping their cultural identities. Self-reliance is represented at its best in indigenous knowledge, and its application in facing the environmental challenges of the twenty-first century will show its limitations. Only where the need is obvious, should modern scientific and technological know-how intervene.

I would like to express my sincere thanks to Professor Franz Schmithüsen, Chair of Forest Policy and Forest Economics at the Swiss Federal Institute of Technology in Zurich, for his support which made this publication possible. My gratitude also goes to Christina Giesch, Marielle Ebner-Rijke, Beat Brunner and Martin Spinnler who assisted me in editing the contributions.

2 Culturing trees: socialized knowledge in the political ecology of Kissia and Kuranko forest islands of Guinea[1]

JAMES FAIRHEAD and MELISSA LEACH

SINCE FORESTERS AND botanists first saw the forest patches which surround the villages in Kissidougou Prefecture of Guinea, they have considered them, quite literally, as 'nature': the last vestiges of the Upper Guinean forest block's northern extension. Supposing that the soils and climate of the region should support forest, they assume that it once did and that today's forest patches are relics of this past forest cover: a heritage which has survived the savannization wrought elsewhere by local inhabitants (Chevalier, 1933; Adam, 1948; Aubréville 1949; Schnell 1952; République de Guinée, 1988). In contrast, for the region's Kissia and Kuranko[2] inhabitants, these forest patches are, quite literally, cultured: encouraged to form through habitation and management, and the focus of cultural practice and social memories.

The forest patches for Kissia and Kuranko do not, however, have a single significance shared by those who live in and use them. They are not merely community forests managed for their produce by community institutions, nor are they merely community-sacred forests existing for their religious significance, although they embody elements of these. Rather, they are invested with diverse and changing meanings as different people use, value and represent them – and their constituent places and trees – in different ways. Thus, although they are 'culture' in every sense of the word, we do not seek here to identify a particular, 'authentic' cultural vision and knowledge of these forests and their trees. Instead, we want to expose the field of interests and discourses within which they are represented. Just as when foresters consider these forests as 'natural relics' they construct them as international and national heritage over which their institutions claim custodianship, so local land and tree rights and claims can be contested partly through struggles over cultural meanings (Berry, 1989; Moore, 1993). Furthermore, the cultural meanings of trees can become resources in wider social and political struggles. Taking account of how local representations articulate with modernization and globalization processes, this perspective avoids casting these forests as relics of an indigenous culture in the modern world, in which forest conservation depends on the conservation of a particular culture (Clad, 1985; Wilson, 1993).

Settled islands in savannah

Most of Kissidougou's 800 or more villages lie in open clearings in the middle of dense, semi-deciduous forest patches. These patches are small, relative to the area of the surrounding savannah, within which they lie as distinctive islands (see Plate 1). That the distribution of forest islands follows the distribution of settlement provides a strong spatial image of a basic local principle: that settled social life promotes forest establishment. To the Kissia and Kuranko, settlements are the safe, and the only proper, location for human reproduction in contrast with the land beyond in which animals and crops reproduce. The needs and activities associated with habitation create reasons and enabling conditions both for

7

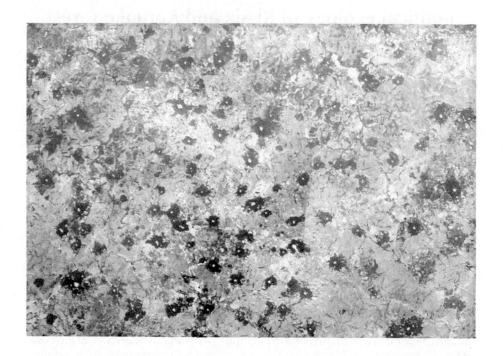

Plate 1: *Mosaic of forest islands in savannah in Eastern Kissidougou Prefecture. Dark patches indicate forest encircling white village clearings; shades of grey between the forest islands indicate more or less woody savannah and fields.*
Reproduced from aerial photomosaic, Institut de Topographie et Cartographie, Conakry.

eliminating fire, and for concentrating fertility and woody resources around settlements, thus promoting the establishment of forest in previously savannah conditions.

Forest patches are also associated with once-inhabited village and farm-hamlet sites (in Kuranko *tombondu*; in Kissie *ce pomdo*) where they exist today as the legacy of the everyday lives of past inhabitants. The Kissia and Kuranko observation that human settlement enables forest contrasts sharply with the dominant perceptions of foresters and ecologists, here as elsewhere in the forest-savannah transition zone, that human activity has only a destructive or, at best, benign effect on forest cover (Furley *et al.*, 1992).

Forest-patch distribution also follows the distribution of water in the landscape: villagers recognize that, just as living promotes forest formation, so does water-flow. Sometimes settlements are established by a rocky outcrop which concentrates water, or beside a stream, using and extending its strip of gallery (riparian) forest to form an encircling island. In other cases, water-related forest patches exist separately from village sites: in the network of gallery and inland valley swamp forests which dissect the landscape, and in the small edaphic forest patches on rocky hills.

Villagers also recognize how certain forms of land use improve soil/water relations by promoting water infiltration and storage, thus encouraging the establishment of dense vegetation. Such changes result, in particular, from the long-term
application of gardening-like cultivation techniques in savannahs (Leach and Fairhead, 1994). The repeated mounding and organic-matter incorporation during the
'gardening' of peanuts and root crops 'opens' and 'ripens' the soil, making it 'oily',
and creating conditions in which trees can establish more easily once gardening
ceases. Such patches of long-occupied and worked soil with improved water relations are a characteristic of old habitation sites where there used to be gardens.
Where farmers ripen soils on purpose elsewhere, metaphorically, they liken the
resulting land to the land of such old sites.

The concentration of woody vegetation in lived in, socialized spaces is mir-
rored for villagers in its concentration on termite mounds. The spatial association between termite 'settlements' (mounds) and forest patches in many ways
parallels the association in the human world, providing Kissia and Kuranko with
a powerful metaphor for their own impact on vegetation (Figure 1). Villagers
have a profound understanding of termite social organization, and recognize in it
a social world parallel to their own: one of male and female chiefs, and of
different categories of worker. Recognizing the concentration of fertility and
water-availability in and around termite-worked soil, farmers take advantage of
certain types of termite mound as 'gardens' for vegetable planting. But, if left
uncultivated, soil improved by termites tends to develop dense, woody growth.
In this sense they parallel gardens which develop a distinctive woody vegetation
when abandoned, and similar pioneer tree species are typical of both cases: for
example, *Allophylus spicatus*; *Bridelia ferruginea*; *Nauclea latifolia*; and *Newbouldia laevis*. Villagers' understanding of the effects of termites on vegetation
as a metaphor for their effect on soil and vegetation is missed by ecologists of the
region. While they now appreciate the ability of termites to promote forest
establishment in savannah (Hopkins, 1992), they consider this only as a 'natural'
phenomenon, rather than a 'settlement-social' one analogous to human activity.

The landscape also accommodates another parallel 'social' world, of djinn
spirits (*nyina*). Villagers describe *nyina* of many types and characters – as many
as there are human beings – and too many to know, although many have names.
They consider them to have a 'social' existence which parallels their own lives
but which also inverts social norms; they live in towns and houses and make
farms, for example, but eat their rice cold. Individuals with special vision and
gifts can strike up alliances with particular *nyina*, and exceptional abilities in
farming, hunting, or wealth-acquisition are often explained in terms of *nyina*
'help'. Because they can also make unexpected physical attacks or outrageous
demands, however, villagers generally consider the proper and safe relationship
between human and *nyina* society as one of separation and respectful distance,
which they sometimes ensure by making offerings (Jackson, 1977: 37).

While diverse landscape forms such as large rocks and pools are favourite
resting places for *nyina*, there are also *nyina* villages (*nyina so* in Kuranko) and
habitual *nyina* settlements which, like human settlements, are usually associated
with forest patches. Kuranko often refer to forest patches on rocky outcrops or
groundwater-fed gallery forests as *nyina's* places. Equally, some individual trees
(often *Ceiba pentandra*, *Afzelia africana* or *Bombax buonopozense*) are also
considered as the homes of particular *nyina*. Felling any such patches or trees
without *nyina* consent and appropriate sacrifices can prompt retribution. Indeed,
many of the inhabitants of our study village, Sandaya, suggested that the death of

10m

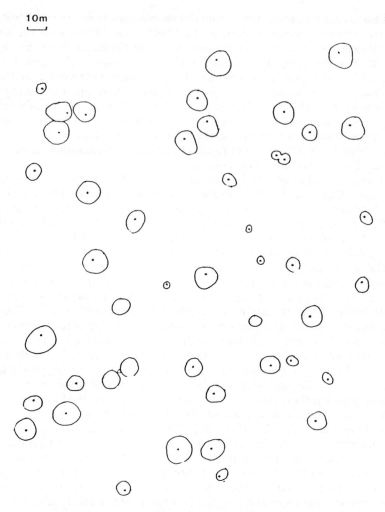

Figure 1: *Termite islands of woody vegetation in savannah.*
          Map showing the distribution of old Macrotermes *mounds in open*
          shrub savannah at Lamto Côte d'Ivoire.
          Adapted from Abbadie, L. M. LePage and X. Le Roux in Furley *et al.*,
          (eds.) 1992, p.476.

the chief hunter in 1993 was revenge for his ill-considered tree cutting in farm-
site preparation.

Certain chiefly lineages ascribe their power partly to an alliance established
with a particularly powerful *nyina* when the village was founded (Jackson, 1977).
Offerings to this *nyina* are important to upholding the authority of chiefs and
ruling families, and in securing general prosperity. In Sandaya, such offerings are
made at a particular *Afzelia africana* tree on the edge of a *Carapa procera* forest,
widely regarded as the principal *nyina* village.

Central to the prosperity of many villages is the *nyina* of crops and the land;
the '*sene*' (farm) *nyina*. Commonly this spirit is incarnated as a rainbow

(*ninkinanka*) in the sky and as a python on land, which provides conceptual links between water movements, termites, and forest. Thus, as a rainbow, its path in the sky influences cloud directions and the path of rain. A rainbow commonly emerges from one termite mound and arcs over to another, or to a stream. In the earth, and as a snake, the same *nyina* inhabits termite mounds and moves along the underground pathways dug between them. It is in this incarnation, and its association with termites, that the *nyina* influences groundwater movement. Within broader Mande conceptions, termite society is under the authority of the *ninkinanka*. This relationship is represented in tales (Houis, 1958) and, indeed, its documentation goes back to the first Portuguese description of West Africa from the fifteenth century:

> It is said that these great [snakes] are found in swarms in some parts of the country, where there are also enormous quantities of white ants [termites] which, by instinct, make houses for these snakes with earth which they carry in their mouths. Of these houses they make a hundred or a hundred and fifty in one spot, like fine towns.
> (Cadamosto, in Crone (ed.), 1937)

Some Kuranko explain how the underground movement of the python and the arc of the rainbow join in a circle, and find in this an explanation for the movement of water underground, using it to describe the paths of water flow to feed particular field sites and enable their productivity, or the development of forest as opposed to savannah patches.

Representations of forest-island creation and enrichment

For both Kissia and Kuranko, forest islands around villages play important roles in protecting the settlement from dry-season bush fires, high winds, and excessive heat. They also provide convenient sources of forest products, and shelter for tree crops and social activities. In the past, they were central to settlement fortification.

Today, villagers encourage forest-island development, occasionally by tree planting, but principally by creating the fire and soil conditions which favour forest regeneration in savannah. Fire-breaks – which prevent annual savannah fires destroying their thatched houses and garden fences – are created largely through everyday activities which reduce the quantity of flammable grasses on the village margins. Men collect thatch and fencing grass there and, during the farming season families frequently tether their cattle that graze and trample the grass. Early in the dry season, young men and elders alike set and monitor a controlled burn to eliminate the fuel for more threatening late season fires. Thus protected, village-edge areas develop dense, semi-deciduous, moist-forest vegetation and, as the island of forest expands, grass collection and grazing are gradually moved further out. The fertilization of village-edge soils by human and animal faeces, ash, and household waste further encourages forest development. Villagers sometimes garden for a limited period around an inhabited settlement specifically to encourage forest establishment by removing grasses and ripening the soils. But the link between gardening and forest-patch formation is more commonly manifested when once-gardened village and farm hamlet sites are abandoned, or when a new settlement is established on an old garden site.

While forest-promoting activities can be deliberately targeted, the individual activities which contribute to forest establishment are frequently undertaken without this outcome in mind. Forest-island development in this sense depends on the diverse activities of a community, and not on deliberate management by community institutions. For most village men and women, the origins of forest islands are, therefore, the logical extension into the past of processes experienced in the present. It is unremarkable to them that the gradual, cumulative effect of diverse activities on savannah village margins should be the establishment and expansion of a belt of woodland. Not every resident will know a forest island's particular history, especially if he or she has come from another area as a male immigrant or as a new wife. They may suppose that the forest has 'always' existed, while remaining very aware that everyday activities cause the gradual extension of forest-island area. Within this perspective, the rings of large silk-cotton trees (*Ceiba pentandra*) and *Bombax buonopozense* – a distinctive feature of many forest islands – tend to be interpreted as the overgrown relics of living fence poles of past garden sites. People are highly aware of how effectively fence poles 'take' in fertile garden soils, and these tree species are among those used to make garden enclosures today.

In many villages, certain elderly men and women – usually from landowning families – represent forest-patch formation in a more punctuated, intentional way. Leaders of descendants who claim founder status in a territory, and the political authority that goes with it, often emphasize how their ancestors arrived in empty, relatively inhospitable savannah and initiated the beginnings of a forest island and a settlement there by planting 'starter' trees. As one Kissia elder said of his village, Yiffo: 'The firstcomers planted cotton trees. There is still one which carries the name of the planter'.[3] Specific trees are attributed origins emphasizing the founders' extraordinary capabilities (for example, at Fondambadou, an *Erythrophleum guineensis* tree grew from the founder's powerful staff placed in the ground). But, more commonly, founding trees are remembered more prosaically as individuals of fast-growing species which were transplanted from wild saplings to suppress fire and accelerate rapid forest succession within their protection (using, for example *Triplochiton scleroxyllon* and *Ceiba pentandra*).

Frequently, one of these founding trees becomes a marker of the establishment of the 'contract' with the land spirits; the contract which ensures a place for human settlement and reproduction and for farming, hunting, and fishing to sustain it. In Kuranko, it is usually the founding family which manages this contract and makes the sacrifices necessary to maintain it, often with the assistance of trained chief-hunters. In Kissi villages, the land contract enshrined in foundational trees is usually managed by a family reputed to have been the first to bury a member in the new settlement; a role distinguished from political chieftaincy, assumed by other possible village founders. As an elder in Ningbeda succinctly put it: 'You have founded a village, you go, you build, he whose child dies first, it is he who is the land chief; even if you are the first in the village, you are not the land chief'. The representation of forest-island origins in terms of the planting of initial trees is significant in upholding relations between families. For ruling families, the trees remain markers invoking historical planting events which legitimize their current social and political status.

'Punctuated' views of forest-island origin also draw on the planting of trees and the establishment of forest islands as fortresses. From this perspective, the rings of cotton trees are represented as having grown from the stakes of the stockades which were used in combination with ditches and closely-interplanted thorn bushes and lianas in pre-twentieth century fortification strategies. As the rings of closely staked cotton trees grew, trees were often trained for particular purposes. Some would have their apical meristem cut to promote a dense spreading and interlocking crown for maximum concealment, grass suppression, and fire control. A few would be fertilized and trimmed of their lateral branches to encourage rapid upward growth into look-out trees and gate posts. The training of trees to take on different forms – whether the spreading form known by the Kuranko as *bolonani* (four arms/branches) or tall straight forms suitable for timber – is a common practice in the region. Foresters, by contrast, tend to attribute tree form only to natural conditions, assuming heavily branched specimens to have grown up in savannah or forest clearings, and tall, straight ones – the 'forest form' – in forest. Thus, they infer wrongly that all forest-form trees on more open land are relics of deforestation.

In addition to fortification, villagers have enriched and altered the species composition of forest islands for a wide range of purposes. As people of different gender, age, and social position use and value island resources in different ways, the species composition in forest islands comes to reflect the patterning of socially varied priorities, albeit mediated by people's differential ability to realize them. Use-priorities also change over time, so forest islands acquire a layering of changing enrichment legacies.

From the beginning, forest islands were enriched with kola trees (*Cola nitida*), earning the Kissidougou region the name *Worodu* (Kola-land) within Mande-speaking West Africa. The nuts produced in this area are highly valued, not only in local health and cultural practice, but also as an important trading commodity in long-established forest-savannah commerce. Women are prohibited from planting and harvesting (though not trading) kola, but men frequently transplant wildlings, acquiring individual control over the resulting tree wherever it may be in the forest island. Both Kissia and Kuranko plant kola with the buried umbilical cord of a newborn baby, to 'grow up with the child'. From the 1930s, men planted coffee in forest islands; labour and tenure arrangements excluding almost all women. When necessary, forest islands were extended to house more coffee, and were adapted by removing undergrowth and selectively thinning the canopy, leaving some trees for shade and valued timber, fruit, and oilseed resources. More recently, coffee profitability has declined, and bananas have come into favour as forest-island tree crops, along with fruit trees which are planted by women and children as well as by men. All these tree crops are owned by their planters as heritable property. While some village forest islands are divided into plots, complicated inheritance patterns and spontaneous transplanting mean that people often have individual tenure over trees scattered throughout the island.

Valued gathering species also become concentrated in forest islands through their selective preservation. Medicinal and craft specialists often preserve supplies of their favoured species, and elderly women, in particular, keep transplanted supplies of common herbal remedies at the edge of the forest, near their houses. Oil palms self-seed from women's palm oil processing activities on the village edge, and are subsequently protected within the island. Women especially value the forest island as a convenient source of the edible nuts and fruits they use in sauces and sell. They also collect dead branches for fuelwood during the dry season, when obtaining preferred species from open land and farm-sites is less convenient. Cotton trees and thorny bushes from past fortification, together with ancient but no longer productive kola trees and oilseed species, remain in the forest island alongside useful species. Forest islands are, therefore, not only represented differently according to people's interpretations of resource value, but they are also, in effect, a living archive – a repository of layered social memories – albeit one open to different interpretations.

'Sacred' institutions in forest islands

The memories evoked by the forest island are made explicit in the shrines devoted to ancestors and cult figures. The silk-cotton and *Triplochiton scleroxyllon* trees planted by founders often become sites where descendents seek their ancestors' help, often through sacrifices. In many forest islands, hunters maintain an altar to the area's most renowned hunters, who trace back their skills and success to Mandenbori, the legendary father-figure of all hunters. In Kissia forest islands, a place is reserved for the burial of the first-dead children of each family who, unlike other people, are buried 'with the land' rather than among the living in the village, and whose death is neither recognized nor mourned. The first-dead are called *cuei pieeo*, literally 'child (buried in) the leaves' (Paulme, 1950); the leaves of *Newbouldia laevis*, a pioneer forest species which eventually dominates the burial site. Within most Kissia forest islands, there is an additional shrine to the chief land spirit (*Luande*), managed by the family of the land-chief, access to which is strictly limited to initiated members of the men's society.

The men's society (*tɔɔma vanpiandua* in southern Kissi areas) is a secret society which trains young men, over at least two initiation stages, in the skills and knowledge central to male social roles, as well as to manage important aspects of community and inter-village life and political relations. Schooling and society business take place in a delimited part of the forest island, hidden away from women and non-initiates. The boundaries are made clear to potential trespassers by the planting of distinctive *Dracaena arborea* trees. The installation of this specialized arena for *tɔɔma vanpiandua* activities, and of the 'medicines' (*koan*), special plants and expertise needed to run the society, is an important sign of a well-established, politically influential settlement, as distinct from a subordinate hamlet or farm camp. Women have a parallel initiation society (*tɔɔma vanlandua*) which educates young initiates, transacts women's business, and holds gender-specific knowledge, on fertility and reproduction in particular. Women's society affairs are conducted at streamside locations, where shrines to female ancestors are maintained. The place is usually concealed from men and non-initiates by a forest patch, often a part of the village forest island.

Thus, most forest islands contain male and female 'sacred' places. Yet their quality derives from the setting up of the institutions, rather than the inherent sacredness of 'forest' in Kissia thought. Equally, this institutional quality applies to specific areas, not to the forest as a whole. These points have often been overlooked by foresters, who have attributed the preservation of forest relics around villages to their sacred character: in effect seeing them as islands of pristine nature in an otherwise profane and degraded landscape. The French term for the institutions, *forêt sacrée*, only serves to emphasize this vision. This perception, held by botanists in Guinea since the 1930s (for example, Chevalier, 1933), and persisting today among conservationists in Guinea and wider Africa, erroneously attributes forest preservation to cultural beliefs about the forest and nature. As a misperception, it is made possible only by considering local thought within Western notions of nature and culture.

In Kuranko regions, men and women also maintain particular forest spaces for initiation activities, often in the village forest island, while certain areas of the forest carry ancestral significance, and others are reserved for men's society activities. Several more northerly Kissia areas have these institutions rather than the *tɔɔma* type found further south. Indeed, the secret societies vary widely, and throughout history have been acquired and discarded in different areas as they have gained and lost popularity. MacCormack (1980) for example, describes how Sherbro people nearer the coast 'bought' the joint male-female form of *tɔɔma* from specialists invited from Kissia regions. Exclusively male societies teaching particular warfare skills, such as talking drums, which have spread during the last two centuries originate, many Kissia believe, in Loma country. In this respect, and as D'Azevedo (1962) has emphasized, secret society organizations – and their particular forms of vegetation manipulation – should be understood as a regional, rather than as an ethnic, phenomenon.

Forest representation in ethnic identity and political discourse

Foresters' and botanists' perceptions of the ethnic basis of *forêt sacrée* institutions have contributed to the stereotyping of the Kissia as a 'forest people' like other groups further south (Loma, Guerze), with cultural proclivities towards forest conservation. Since the early colonial period, they have been contrasted ethnically with the more northerly 'savannah people' of Mandinka origin – including Kissidougou's Kuranko populations. In the context of past and present southwards Mandinka migration, their fire-setting in savannah farming, honey collecting, and hunting was considered responsible for southwards savannization (Adam, 1948). Where Kuranko lived within forest islands, this was perceived as a habit acquired from the Kissia, as it is by modern foresters and environmental policymakers. This ethnic stereotyping of forest-related behaviour overlooks Kuranko practical knowledge and experience of forest-island formation, as well as the fluid character of ethnic affiliation in a region of longstanding migration and political turbulence. Where Kuranko immigrants have moved into Kissia villages, they have often been incorporated into Kissia society and land management. Indeed, many supposedly 'forest' Kissia families can trace descent from a Mandinka family of savannah origin.

Nevertheless, as local politics have articulated with wider political structures, certain Kissia have come to draw on such stereotypes in their own assertions of identity. Islamic Mandinka groups have long played key roles in forest-savannah commerce and, as powerful traders, have at times represented a threat to Kissia community cohesion and politico-economic interests. This was the emphasis of a man's description of his southern Kissia village in modern times: 'We do not have strangers here; the Mandinka came but the youth chased them away because they were enriching themselves on one hand, and distracting the young girls on the other'. In such circumstances, attributions of forest-related behaviour can provide a powerful way of emphasizing difference: 'When the Mandinka lived here, this was an open clearing. Wherever Mandinka sit down, you will not see forest'.

During Guinea's First Republic, between 1958 and 1984, the regime of President Sekou Touré pursued a 'demystification' policy, encouraging villages to move out of the obscurity of their forest islands and into 'the open': the enlightened clarity and modernity upheld by the regime's cultural values, and the roadside world more accessible to the state's demands (Rivière, 1969). This policy drew on and reinforced both ethnic stereotypes and their forest reference. It upheld the ideals of social clarity, and of openness and simplicity in language and expression: of clear 'savannah language' (*kan gbe*) and lifestyles. These were already part of Mandinka (and Kuranko) self-representations, in contrast with the secrecy and obscurity of the forest culture and languages which they find difficult to learn, but they now became significant in maintaining a favourable relationship with the State. Many Kissia perceived Sekou Touré's regime as Mandinka-biased, and its attempts to evict Kissia from their forest islands and suppress *forêt sacrée* schools were interpreted as attempts to disempower the Kissi institution which had hitherto defended Kissia from Mandinka domination, whether cultural or military. The political environment from 1958 to 1984 reinforced, therefore, the significance of forest symbolism in Kissidougou.

In this context, the emphasis on the forest in national and international environmental discussions, and the images of forest loss and of threatened relics projected by the forestry service, have merged to coincide with the broader politico-ethnic interests of Kissia: interests heightened in the run-up to Guinea's multi-party elections of December 1993. Sharing one forest – where the forest islands of neighbouring villages have come to touch each other – is one of the strongest metaphors of Kissia political solidarity, historically linked to alliance in warfare and secret society initiation. The idea that the Kissia region – even recently – could have been united within one forest provides a politically appealing vision of unity, as does the analysis that forest loss was due to Mandinka immigration. The memory of forest islands as literal fortresses strengthens the association between forest and political defence in a modern world in which Kissia men's societies are still training youth in fortification and warfare techniques. Although the interpretation of forest islands as threatened relics is most often voiced within the politically influential urban Kissia community, it can also be heard in villages when rural Kissia use environmental images to make politico-ethnic points.

Felling trees and forests

Kissidougou's inhabitants do not consider forest islands or the trees within them as objects for eternal preservation, neither do they share foresters' reverence for the most voluminous trees. While large, individual specimens are valued for fortification, shade, and certain food and ritual purposes, for many food, medicine and woodworking uses (poles, carving etc.) smaller trees are preferred, either from younger forest-island growth or surrounding fallows and savannahs. Large forest hardwoods are difficult to work with and, as they get old, may pose a danger to people and property. In the past, specialist tree-fellers based further south – Guékédou-Kissi, Loma or Mende – where men's bush schools give training in high forest felling skills and medicines, would be invited to remove troublesome, overgrown trees. When this was impossible, the whole village was forced to relocate.

These days, the same service is performed by one of the numerous private chainsaw operators active in the Kissidougou area. Since the early 1980s, commercial timber-felling has become big business, which, although villagers sometimes profit from it, is generally a source of major tension. Given that the state forestry service claims a monopoly right to grant permits for timber-felling, the villagers have very little control. State control over a list of forest species, part of national forestry policy since the early colonial period, is based on the idea of these trees as endangered 'natural patrimony'. This vision, and its legal institutionalization, competes with customary tenurial claims over trees which villagers know to have developed because of settlement. Despite the high value of their timber resources, villagers have generally been unable to negotiate higher returns than a standard one plank in ten. Loggers cannot begin work in a village without both the chief's and the elders' permission, but permission is hard to refuse given the weight of urban authority which the loggers have or claim to have. Younger urban-based men with powerful village relatives sometimes profit as intermediaries. Once loggers are in the village, it is difficult to control which trees they fell.

Young men and women are often angry about tree-felling as they receive so little of the value. A mature *Afzelia africana* tree would pay a young man's brideprice if he could realize its full cash returns. If timber trees are protected within the apportioned tree-crop plots within forest islands, or near people's personal rice swamps, the owner can claim them as his or her own. But those who fell and saw trees usually operate with pseudo-state consent and under the local authority of the village chief who can claim that the trees are under village, not individual, authority, especially if the plantations are no longer worked. Thus, the plot-holder might receive minimal compensation for damage to tree crops, but no direct timber revenues, losing his tenurial control as well as money. And felling families' special trees is, normally, the prerogative of members of that family, and, only after careful ritual preparation, sacrifices to ancestors, and negotiations with spirits to move elsewhere. Family members fear adverse consequences for their relatives, as well as for the loggers, if they are felled. Women resent the felling of convenient fruit and nut trees for timber, although they gladly make use of the firewood available from plank remnants. It is such diverse concerns that are at stake, not the loss of the large trees *per se*. Nor does the felling of large forest trees compromise the future integrity of the forest island, which continues to be valued and maintained for the diverse reasons for which it originally formed.

In some cases, villagers themselves have felled whole forest islands, but only when abandoned after the inhabitants have moved to a new settlement site. Forest-island uses diminish once they are no longer inhabited and, as villagers shift their attention to the new forest island developing around the new site, they consider it only sensible to convert large parts of the old one to agricultural land to take advantage of the highly fertile soils. Environmentalists have cited this as evidence of the destructive tendencies of local land-use practices towards forest 'nature'. But for Kissia and Kuranko the same practices are simply part of the dynamic character of forest patches which now, as always, come, go, and shift as social settlements do.

Conclusions

The significance of Kissidougou's forest islands varies widely depending on one's identity, and which of the many aspects is being highlighted: the everyday provisioning and village protection, village origins and dynastic political relationships, the power and military structures of men's societies, fertility control in women's societies, the economic value of tree crops and timber, or assertions of ethnic identity and relationships with the state. This is equally true for particular tree species and, indeed, particular trees.

Given that representations of trees and forests are contextual and socially differentiated, the temptation to identify a shared set of 'cultural' meanings – a single indigenous knowledge – is misplaced. Doing so would obscure social difference and detract from more compelling intellectual arguments. It would give the false impression that such knowledge can be examined in isolation from broader economic and global processes. Such a view is clearly untenable in Kissidougou, where people's attitudes towards forest islands have been shaped by war, national and international environmental ideas and institutions, and shifts in regional and international trade.

Diverse as they are, local views on vegetation nevertheless bear little resemblance to Western views of 'nature' in general, and Western representations of these 'relic forest patches' in particular. Indeed, many Kissia and Kuranko representations transcend the basic Western division between nature and culture; ecology can be socialized, so that forest islands or particular trees are thought of in terms of the social processes of which they are a part (Croll and Parkin, 1992). And, in as much as ideas of society (and reproduction) are embodied in settlements, so the changes in soil and vegetation associated with settlement are thought of as an integral part of the settlement process, not as society acting on a conceptually distinct environment. This social/forest patch association has its counterpart in the termite and *nyina* worlds which Western thought would relegate to the natural and supernatural but which, to Kissidougou villagers, reflect their own sociality. Stressing the social character of forest patches in the landscape is not to imply that the spaces between them are in some sense asocial. But they are socialized in different ways, through farming, hunting, gathering, and fishing, in sharp contrast to the islands of settlement and settled reproduction.

Any elision between the West's seemingly de-socialized visions of nature and those of Kissidougou, has tended to occur at the local and national political level. When, for example, Kissi describe Mandinka destruction of an original forest, they are making use of Western environmental categories for political ends within the national and international state arena which spawned them.

Kissia and Kuranko have a detailed understanding of vegetation and the soil, water, fire and animal processes which influence it. Their landscape, with its forest patches, testifies to their skills in working with ecology to enrich and upgrade vegetation to suit their needs. But indigenous knowledge of trees and forests does not relate only to such practical concerns; it is also about people's understanding of themselves and their place in wider social and political struggles.

3 The perceived environment as a system of knowledge and meaning: a study of the Mewahang Rai of eastern Nepal

BARUN GURUNG

IN RECENT YEARS there has been growing interest in the incorporation of indigenous knowledge into agricultural research and development programmes (Brokensha *et al.*, 1980; Richards, 1985; Chambers *et al.*, 1989), with research indicating that communities operating smallholder agricultural and forest production systems possess a great deal of knowledge about their environments and how to manipulate them to best meet their needs. While a lot is known about these knowledge systems in terms of the decision-making rules, there is very little substantial understanding of the epistemologies on which they are based.

There is sufficient literature to suggest that 'deeper knowledge' exists beyond the decision-making rules. While focusing on the distinction between utilitarian/non-utilitarian concepts attached to the natural environment, some suggest that local knowledge is based entirely on what people think is necessary to know (Niamir, 1990), while others suggest that indigenous knowledge is more than a sum of its utility functions – Berlin (1992) and Howes (1980). In a similar vein, Howes and Chambers (1980) state that 'indigenous technical knowledge', like scientific knowledge, should be regarded as an intellectual process of creating order out of disorder, and not simply as a response to subsistence needs. Berlin *et al.* (1973) show that not only are there close similarities between folk and scientific classifications, but that 'there is, at present, a growing body of evidence that suggests that the fundamental taxa recognized in folk systematics correspond fairly closely with the scientifically known species', thus implying a 'universal ordering of the natural world' (see also Berlin, 1992; Brown, 1989).

In the Himalayan region, mountain farmers have developed substantial knowledge systems based on the considerable experience of their adaptation processes. The extent, structure, and content of these systems need to be examined not only in terms of the decision-making rules (e.g. Tamang, 1990; Fisher, 1989; Gilmour, 1989) but, more importantly, through an examination of the epistemologies that determine and give meaning to decisions related to the environment. Given the pressing demographic and ecological challenges facing these communities, it seems ever more pertinent to understand the cultural nature of natural-resource use, and the ways in which indigenous epistemologies promote sustainable strategies for survival. In sum, any discussion of indigenous knowledge systems must include an examination of how people perceive their environment and how they behave in response. An understanding of the content, nature and types of 'information source' that determine the perceived environment is crucial to the analysis of ecological relations.

If the development agenda is to include a search for sustainable strategies within an indigenous paradigm, there must be more research both into how people adapt their behaviour and the cultural meanings through which they perceive and respond to their natural environment. Because the perceived environment is based on the cultural images of the workings of nature, its

19

significance as a complex mechanism for producing the actual physical behaviour that manipulates ecological relations cannot be overestimated.

The Rai of eastern Nepal

Tamku, in the Sankhuwa Sabha district of eastern Nepal, is home to the Mewahang, a sub-tribe of the Rai. The Rai are a distinct ethnic group which, together with the Limbus further east, form the larger association of peoples called the Kirati. Physically, linguistically and, to some extent, culturally, they are said to be related to the large Mongol population of Tibeto-Burman-speaking tribal peoples spread eastward through the sub-Himalayan region and the hills of Assam. Each of the Rai sub-groups has a distinct language and cultural traditions. The other large sub-tribe is formed by the descendants of the Khambu.

Perceptions of the environment in Rai culture

People's knowledge of the natural environment is based on the perceptions which help form a 'cultural approximation' of the real workings of nature. The underlying cognitive structures that are instrumental in producing the actual behaviour within the natural environment form part of the information source that determine how people perceive their environment. Their relationship with the supernatural also helps to define these perceptions. Together, the cognitive structures based on empirical constructions and people's relationships with the supernatural – expressed through ritual – define and give meaning to the broader system of indigenous knowledge.

Environmental knowledge

Among the Mewahang, the level of environmental knowledge ranges from resource classification to extensive usage and management. The farmers can identify over 200 plant species which, in Table 1, are grouped into 20 uses.

Some species have multiple uses; Seeland (1980) has recorded an impressive list of items made from bamboo: 20 household articles; 12 types of agricultural, hunting, and fishing implements; and a further 22 tools, toys, musical instruments, baskets, and miscellaneous items. Existing agroforestry practices reveal extensive knowledge of plant/crop combinations, where tree or shrub-plantation crops such as banana, orange, pear and peach are combined with cereals such as maize and millet. There is also evidence of *taungya*, where a forest crop like nettle is raised in conjunction with an annual agricultural crop. Trees are also effective as wind-breaks, and farmers use 'shelter belts' for bamboo cultivation.

The Rai farmers' management practices indicate that they are also knowledgeable about the biological relationship of crops and other natural resources, and that they implement this effectively.

Erosion control

Inhabiting an ecologically fragile ecosystem prone to significant seasonal losses of valuable soil has forced eastern Himalayan farmers to generate and adapt soil-engineering practices capable of retaining soil throughout monsoonal rains and other erosion processes. Erosion-control practices are evident on both *khet* (rainfed) and *bari* (dry) lands. On the *khet* there are, essentially, two practices:

Table 1:   Plant use among the Mewahang

Use	Preference ranking	No. of species
Fuelwood	1	56
Fodder	2	84
Agri. equipment	3	2
Timber	4	9
Fencing	5	9
Ritual	6	11
Rope	7	2
Household equipment	8	15
Food	9	35
Shade	10	3
Medicine	11	18
Dyes	12	1
Erosion control	13	16
Poison	14	4
Animal feed	15	13
Roof	16	2
Manure	17	12
Animal bedding	18	7
Mulching	19	4
Soap	20	3

○ the preparation of bunds by building up walls which retain soil during the artificial flooding during paddy season, and help to keep the water within its boundary; and
○ the maintenance of long fallow periods with vegetative cover following the harvest of paddy reduces wind erosion, preserves moisture, and maintains soil fertility.

On *bari* land, the control of soil erosion is more extensive:

○ after ploughing the field and before sowing, small drains are constructed around each terrace to prevent the loss of water and soil;
○ ploughing is always practised along the contour of the slope;
○ high concentration of fodder trees have roots which retain soil particles;
○ there is increasing evidence of the propagation of erosion-control species, such as *napier, setaria, amliso* and *desideria*; and
○ 'live' fences are built from species with other purposes, for example, *dab-dabey, khiro*, and *sajeevan*.

Soil-fertility management

In addition to retaining soil particles, farmers must also maintain soil fertility levels to ensure good crop production. With no cheap and reliable source of chemical fertilizers, the mountain farmers of Tamku rely on adding manure, crop residues, and green litter to ameliorate soils continuously to replace lost nutrients. They must be good judges of the soil's capabilities to match conditions to crop requirements. One way in which they do this is by observing 'indicator' plants, such as ferns: edible ferns are found only on fertile soil.

The Tamku farmers maintain soil fertility through effective manuring, and good management:

○ On the *bari* they obtain manure by tethering livestock in the croplands, burning crop residues, adding ash to kitchen gardens, distributing pig and goat waste in the fields, spreading leaf litter and forest soil on gardens, and making compost. In the *khet*, special manuring practices are only extended to the preparation of seed beds for millet and paddy.
○ The Tamku farmers practise good soil management by manipulating existing natural conditions. In the case of paddy, the *khet* land is flooded to create an ephemeral pond ecosystem, where the irrigation system ensures that water exists for short periods of time. Such rice paddies are an excellent example of the ecological principle which stipulates that unchanging nutrient flows tend to be less productive than systems with nutrient cycles or 'pulses' (Odum, 1983). In addition to rice the Tamku community also obtains animal protein from frogs and pests.

Other management practices include the ploughing of existing weeds and residue *in situ*, intercropping cereal crops with leguminous crops, maintaining high seed rate practices in rainfed conditions, and maintaining soil moisture. The common practice of shaving the bunds improves soil fertility levels, because the vegetation often consists of nitrogen-fixing leguminous crops, also valuable for the nutrient residues caught in the last irrigation flow. The burning of *khar* grasses before the rains also enhances fertility levels through the release of nutrients.

Pest management

Indigenous pest-management strategies are heavily relied on by farmers unable to afford or obtain chemical pesticides. Also, farmers are often hesitant to use poisons which can have harsh effects on both plants and humans. Without access to training in their use, the farmers do not know enough about how much to use, or how they should be applied.

Over the generations, farmers in remote areas such as Tamku have devised their own crop protection methods. Common pests like the stem-borer (*chillozonellis*) attack wheat and maize stocks. Farmers spread affected wheat plants with the ground pulp of the *khira* leaf; the scent of the pulp is sufficient to kill the pests. In the case of maize, farmers remove the dried infected stems, and the pulp of *khira* leaf is also added to the channel of the irrigation system to control insects in the paddy field. Specific rice pests, such as the rice moth which creates clusters of rice stalks, can be combed out with sticks. This combing action deposits the moths in the water, and to ensure disintegration, this process is carried out in sunlight.

Weed control

Chemically produced commercial herbicides are not commonly used in Tamku. Instead, farmers have devised their own methods of controlling weeds using locally available materials. They control weeds on agricultural land by ploughing the fields approximately 15 days before planting, in the belief that exposure to the sun will kill them. During the land preparation for seeds, weeding is done manually. Burning is still prevalent and, in the rainfed *khet* lands, flooding through irrigation is an effective method of weed control.

Genetic resource management

Paddy

There are five varieties of paddy in the gene pool; the Mewahang farmers of Tamku manage these genetic resources through a series of selection and maintenance procedures based on phenotype:

○ First, land for the seed-bed is selected on the basis of soil type. There are three types of seed bed: dry, mud, and water.
○ Second, the seed is selected; during the harvest the best paddy is selected on the basis of health (no insects). It should be dark green, with an upright stalk, and a comparatively large stem. Farmers harvest these seeds by cutting them from the top of the stem. A further selection – just before planting in the seed bed – is made by rejecting poor-quality grains.
○ The third process involves the selection of land where seedlings that have been selected as gene pools are to be sown. The soil will have been fertilized through manuring.
○ Once again, plants are selected from among those grown in line with the above criteria, for further regeneration.
○ Lastly, after the harvest, these selected plants are threshed separately by people, rather than cattle, – the usual practice with paddy destined for human consumption.

Millet and maize

There are three varieties of millet and four varieties of maize. Selected millet seed should be insect-free, have large kernels, and come from healthy stock. Maize seeds are chosen after the harvest season but before storage, according to the size of the cob; a further selection is done before planting.

Microclimatic management

The sometimes harsh and varying climatic conditions within the Himalayan agro-ecosystem make human intervention essential to produce food crops, and farmers have developed various ways of manipulating microclimates for crop protection. Mulching is commonly practised to protect vegetable seedlings from frost and intense sunlight; vegetable gardens are covered by improvised roofing structures; and tuber crops such as yams, colocasia, cardamom, and sweet potatoes are cultivated under tree canopies. The kitchen gardens of the Mewahang contain a multitude of species of different shapes, heights, and sizes and are laid out so that large leafy species like tobacco, mustard leaves, cabbage and cauliflower surround smaller vegetables like onions and carrots, protecting the smaller vegetables from the sun and wind, while also maintaining moisture levels. The tobacco leaves have the added benefit of repelling insects.

The water logging practised in paddy cultivation is also a form of microclimate management; the soil moisture levels activating microbial activities beneficial to paddy. Finally, bamboo groves are usually found in areas protected from the wind by trees.

The cognitive structure of the environment

Subsistence behaviour within the environment is closely linked to how people classify natural resources. The principles of classification represent the cognitive domain which determines resource selection, a better understanding of which could lead to more insight into production behaviour.

The utility classification of plant resources among the Rai demonstrates a fairly elaborate process of selection upon which appropriate behaviour is determined. In general, a first distinction is made between the types of plant that exist· in the forest. Trees, bushes, grasses, vines and tubers are then categorized according to rooting structure, height, density, shade potential, location and elevation. Then each species is further classified according to uses and, depending on the selection criteria, each species is given a name.

Table 2 illustrates how the Mewahang farmers select and name fodder trees. In this example, trees are selected from all the other plant species found in the forest. Then, a further selection is made according to the identification of all the uses for the trees. Each use is then organized on the selection criteria of fodder preference and requirement. Finally, each tree species that fits the preference and requirement criteria is named. Implicit in this classification system is the extensive cognitive structure that determines how the Rai perceive their environment.

The ecology of ritual

Rai perceptions of the environment are also influenced significantly by the creation myth, a distinctive part of the *Muddum* or oral tradition. The creation myth itself is divided into four parts, recounting the origin, differentiation, migration, and creative deeds of the Rai ancestors, starting from the very beginning of the world, continuing with the establishment of the traditional order, and concluding with the more immediate roots of the present era.

The origin of the natural world, resulting from the union of the first cosmic couple, also saw the birth of the first human, *Tumno*, who was born equipped with a bow and arrow. His siblings are the wild animals and he is the middle brother, between the bear and the tiger. The 'great divorce' between nature and culture is implicit in the relationship that develops between the first human and his animal siblings. Their relationship deteriorates as they compete for the food that their mother prepares during their hunting sojourns, ending eventually in the death of the animals at the hand of their human brother, *Tumno*.

The migration of the ancestors and their eventual split accounts for the various sub-tribes among the present-day Rai. The significance of the ancestral deeds lie in the *Sakhewalung* or ancestral stone, which symbolizes clan-settlement patterns. The *Sakhewalung* gives meaning to the concept of *Ca:ri* or clan territory, and all ecological behaviour finds expression as well as meaning within this defined boundary.

The ecological significance of Rai ritual must be examined in the light of its function as a set of rules that operationalizes production behaviour as meaningful activity, because the rituals are the medium through which the *Muddum* is made socially significant. Among the Mewahang Rai, there are three types of ritual specialist: the *Purkha*, the *Nokchung*, and the *Bijuwa* or shaman. In their collective role as knowledge holders, they are the source of cultural continuity, while also serving to bridge the gap between the spiritual and secular aspects of

Rules for selecting and naming fodder trees.

Plant

Bushes · Vines · Trees · Grasses · Tubers

Fuelwood · Equipment · Timber and fence · Ritual · Shade · Fodder · Medicine · Equipment · Manure · Erosion control · Bedding · Mulch

Easy to propogate	Harmless to crops	Palatable	Milk-producing	High fodder quantity	Frequently harvestable	Available during dry season	Long-lasting	Multi-purpose	High in nutrients	High moisture content
Bans	Siris	Badahar	Dudhilo	Paphu	Siris	Khaneu	Badahar	Siris	Badahar	Badahar
Daar	Utis	Koiralo	Paphu	Dudhilo		(Rani)	Kutmiro	Kabra	Dudhilo	Dudhilo
Kabro	Paphu	Dudhilo	Nivaro	Nivaro		Khaneu	Khaneu	Sil timbur	Tanki	
Lapsi	Koiralo		Badahar	Gogan		(phusre)	(Rani)			
Khaneu			Kutmiro	Doer		Kabro				
Dudhilo				Koirala		Nivaro				
Kutmir				Khaneu						
Sil timbur										

See annex of scientific names.

the natural environment. It is this very absence of distinction between spiritual and mundane that provides us with the context to examine indigenous knowledge of production as a system that is essentially meaningful, and behaviour within the real environment as meaningful activity.

The *Purkha*, or clan elder, is the overall knowledge holder of the *Muddum*. His source of knowledge need not necessarily be divinely sanctioned in that it is a source of learned knowledge, and not received through supernatural dreams or visions. In some cases, the *Purkha* may have arrived at his knowledge through dreams, but it is not a pre-condition of his status. The *Purkha* is almost always present at occasions in which the other ritual specialists are involved and, in the words of one Rai, serves as 'commander' of all *Muddum*-related knowledge.

The *Nokchung* is a priest who officiates at functions with special significance in relation to production. His status as priest is divinely sanctioned, either through dreams or visions. In the context of his role, there are two production concepts of particular importance: '*Ubhauli*' and '*Udhauli*', which signify the change of season.

Ubhauli refers to the traditional upward migration of cattle and people to the higher pastures during the Nepali month of *Phalgun* – February/March in the Gregorian calendar. Several indicators, both symbolic as well as ecological, mark the onset of spring. The Rai believe that the clan deities also move up into the hills and to commemorate this the *Nokchung* performs the *Ca:ri puja* (clan territory ceremony).

Traditionally, migratory patterns were also based on the ecological factors of seasonal change. The migratory patterns of wildlife provided the cue for the migration of people and livestock: the upstream movement of fish in the rivers; the *Orwo* bird's changing voice, caused by the rush of hormones that comes with increased daylight; the upward movement of wild animals; the sprouting of deciduous plants; and the 'thinning of human blood' – the onset of lethargy as temperatures rise, all serve as natural indicators of spring.

The *Ca:ri puja* to mark the onset of *Ubhauli* is performed by the *Nokchung* on the night of the full moon in *Phalgun* in the presence of all the Tamku within the *Ca:ri* or clan territory. In the morning, the ceremony begins with the symbolic closing-off of the *Ca:ri* from evil forces by the construction of wooden replicas of male and female gentalia. After this, the *Nokchung* and the clan leaders proceed to the community water source and perform a divine act by beheading a chicken. Good fortune will follow if the head falls in the direction of *Sakhewalung*, the ancestor stone that marks the *Ca:ri* territory. Towards the end of the ceremony the whole congregation gathers at the *Sakhewalung*, where water from the community water source has been channelled into a temporary pond, to sacrifice a chicken. This time, the chicken head must end up facing the water source to be auspicious. Then, in an adjoining field, the villagers worship their ancestors whom they appease once again by sacrificing a chicken, and offering up millet beer, rice wine, and cooked rice and chicken. The ancestors are requested to grant their benevolence to the clan, and to protect them from the untoward forces of nature.

To commemorate this ceremony, the community performs a series of *Sili*, or ritual dances, that retell the origin myth of the Rai. The *Nokchung* assumes the role of *Sili Makpa*, one who has received the dance instructions through divine forces. The dance re-enacts the ritual journey made by the messenger bird sent by *Ninamridum*, the mother of mankind, to ascertain her pregnancy with *Paroyenda*, the *Nag* king. As a result of their cosmic union *Ninamridum* gives birth to the plants in the forest, then the animals, and, finally, to *Tumno*, the first human.

The *Udhauli* coincides with the end of the monsoons and the beginning of winter. Now, the Rai believe, the deities move south; and the movement of people and their cattle from the highland pastures once again follow natural patterns. The wild animals begin their movement south; the swallow leaves its nest and its unhatched eggs; and the *Orwo* bird's voice changes.

At home, families perform the '*Nwagi*' festival at their *Khamang* or ancestor shrines. As the grain is harvested they give thanks to their ancestors for their protection.

The *Bijuwa* serves an important function as healer and diviner and, in his role as communicator between the gods and the people he performs the ritual journey that re-enacts the origin myth. Once again, the *sili* are performed. It is to the cosmic realm of *Paroyenda* that the shaman travels when performing divination or transporting the souls of those who have died unnatural deaths.

The ritual journey of the shaman to the land of the divinities has special ecological significance. Throughout his journey, he refers to actual places which signify clan territory. Beginning with the hearth in the household and finishing in the cosmic realm, the references to *Ca:ri* that belong to the clan serve to signify their symbolic and natural relationship to ancestral lands. Equally significantly, the shaman re-enacts, through dance, the various stages of creation; from the creation of forests, to the animals, and then humans, to the final separation of nature and culture that results from humans clearing land for cultivation.

Conclusions

People's perceptions of the environment are based on both their knowledge of the environment as well as their relationship with the supernatural. The first is a function of management know-how and cognitive structures that determine production behaviour. The latter, through a network of ritual and symbolism, transforms the mundane into a set of meaningful actions. Nature is appropriated discursively in that it serves both a practical, as well as a spiritual function and, to this extent, there is no distinction between the sacred and the material. Nature is at once the source of human subsistence and creation.

The indigenous system of knowledge among the Mewahang Rai is, therefore, much more than just technical know-how resulting from their adaptation patterns. Development strategies that incorporate cultural explanations of the human-environment relationship must be examined for their efficacy in empowering groups of people, like the Rai, who are economically and politically marginalized by society. Attempts to ensure their livelihoods should, perhaps, be based on an objective recognition of their cultural fortitude and ability to subsist in the harsh mountain conditions that form their reality.

4 *Tatari:* livelihood and danger in upland Japan

JOHN KNIGHT

HUMAN EXISTENCE DEPENDS on lifetaking. The lives of non-humans – plants and (usually) animals – must be ended in order for human lives to be lived. If this is a universal fact, societies none the less differ in the degree to which they acknowledge it. At one extreme, nature and society – or nature and culture – may be imagined in dichotomous terms. The taking of non-human lives can proceed in a morally unproblematical way insofar as plants and animals are viewed as an economic or livelihood 'resource' available for human appropriation. It is where the social and natural environments are *not* seen to contrast so starkly that moral concerns become more pressing. Social anthropologists have shown how in many (often foraging) societies the non-human parts of the natural world may be represented non-dichotomously in various social idioms – as a nurturing parent, a sibling or other kinsman, or a sexual partner – or otherwise attributed human characteristics, and how, as a result, the taking of non-human life assumes great moral importance for, while posing spiritual danger to, those responsible (see, for example, Bloch, 1992; Descola, 1996).

The concern of this chapter is the livelihood of Japanese mountain villagers, and the way in which the predatory character of certain activities is culturally recognized. This recognition takes the form of a perception of danger from the souls of the animals and plants whose lives are taken, and the ritual measures aimed at limiting this danger.

Danger is something that has long been viewed as an aspect of the Japanese relationship to nature. The basic Japanese disposition to the natural world, it has been argued, was one of fear and distance, with human-nature interactions ruled by the principle that 'distant spirits impose no curse' (*sawaranu kami ni tatari nashi*) and, therefore, marked by a great wariness (Shidei, 1985; Higuchi, 1979; Oyadomari, 1989). When the rules of nature were infringed, *tatari* – a curse or retribution in the form of illness, death, personal misfortune or some other calamity – occurred (Higuchi, 1979). The model for nature in such arguments tends to be the mountains – a remote, separate world which inspires awe in human beings. *Tatari* is associated with a wild, mysterious natural world governed by the fickle, moody, unpredictable and even vindictive character of the mountain spirit, interactions with which are fraught with danger and uncertainty (Chiba, 1975; Yukawa, 1991; see also Yanagita, 1970).

Yet mountain forests have long contributed to the livelihoods of upland villagers. Nature, in the form of the plants and animals of the mountain forest, formed a routine part of human lives. But this familiarity did not remove the danger of nature's *tatari* and, in fact, can be seen as accentuating it. Thus, in the examples of spiritual retribution from hunting and forestry that follow, I shall show that nature's *tatari* has to do with proximity no less than distance, applying to that part of the forest that lies within the sphere of upland livelihoods as much as to the distant mountains. The ideas about *tatari* presented below, therefore, express not the alien character of nature, but the cultural recognition of the predatory relationship of upland dwellers towards it. The ritual response to *tatari*, moreover, shows how the moral dilemma of human livelihood is resolved by means of socializing nature. This chapter draws on enthnographic fieldwork carried out in the upland municipality of Hongū-chō which lies on the Kii

Peninsula in western Japan, and on the documented folklore of upland regions across the country.

Forest livelihoods

The mountain forests of the Kii Peninsula are renowned in Japanese history for their wild, natural qualities, for example as the *yamazato* or mountain retreat where famous monks, such as Saigyō (in Yoshino), practised meditation and wrote poems. But for the mountain villagers themselves, the forests are a source of livelihood. Although Japan is known as a rice-growing culture, for those who live in upland areas, where suitable, flat, rice-growing land is scarce, great economic reliance was placed on the mountain forests.

Local people do not commonly distinguish between forests and mountains. Ecologically, they tend to be synonymous in Japan, as most forests are mountainous and most mountains wooded, and the word *yama* (literally 'mountain') is used for both, effectively fusing the two notions into one. *Yama* traditionally referred to a wild, uncultivated place, as opposed to the village, *sato*, and the ricefields enclosed within it. A distinction is commonly made, however, between the *okuyama*, the distant forest, and the *satoyama*, the forest near the village.

The *satoyama* was a site of slash-and-burn farming where wheat, buckwheat, millet, and tubers were grown. For much of their history, mountain villages have depended on such non-rice cultivation. Yukawa, (1988) even suggests that, for mountain villagers, the forests were the site of production (hunting, gathering, and swidden farming), while the village was the site of consumption. The later introduction of rice farming meant that the village also became a site of production but, given the paucity of suitable rice-farming land, the *yama* continued to be important for cultivation. The fallen leaves of the deciduous parts of the forest were used for farm fertilizer, and forest greenery was used for animal fodder. The *yama* was a direct source of gathered food such as chestnuts, horse chestnuts and acorns, wild mushrooms, and a wide range of *sansai* or edible mountain plants (bracken, silvervine, and bamboo root), while other plants of the forest were the source of remedies for illness. Forest wood was used for fuel (firewood and charcoal), and building, but timber stands were also a 'place of savings' which could be felled and sold in times of need (for example, the wedding of a daughter, or the funeral of a parent).

Forest animals and birds also formed an important part of upland livelihoods. Wild boar, deer, serow, bear, sable, raccoon-dog, badger, and hare were hunted for their meat, pelts or the medicinal qualities of their internal organs. The serow and the bear were particularly highly valued because with them 'nothing is thrown away'. Serow meat was eaten both for its taste and its curative properties, the horns (ground and boiled) were used against beriberi and as an antifebrile, while the hooves were used for neuralgia, and the small intestines for stomachaches. Ue (1983) mentions a local apothecary known as the 'bear shop' (*kuma no mise*) – where the body-parts of bears and other animals were sold – which was run by a 90-year-old former bear hunter. Bear flesh was associated with the potency of the animal, its brain (in charred form) was a cure for headaches or sickness during pregnancy (see Nebuka, 1991), the heart and lungs were used for asthma, the paws for neuralgia and rheumatism, and bear fat provided relief when applied to cuts, burns, and rashes (Ue, 1983). But the most important animal organ by far was the gall bladder or *i*, associated with anger and, therefore, ferocity and power, which was viewed as a general panacea (Hida, 1972).

The bear, wild boar, serow, badger and raccoon-dog were all hunted for their gall bladders, but it was the bear's gall bladder which was most valuable, and which could be sold for a high price to the *kanpōyakuya* (specialists in Chinese-style medicine), or just kept at home and used for family members at times of sickness.

Each animal species has its own distinctive character. This was something which tended to be related to its effect on human livelihoods. Forest animals can be divided into antagonistic and beneficial categories. The raccoon-dog or *tanuki* is a crafty, deceptive animal that plays tricks on hunters and foresters, but is also clumsy, dirty and cowardly (Ue, 1983). Monkeys (*saru*, *Macaca fuscata*) are disliked as 'thieves' – they steal from mountain-huts and farms – but also because they are extravagantly wasteful. The monkey will nibble at a piece of fruit and then throw it aside, and start on the next, and so on, leading to an inordinate amount of damage. The fox, on the other hand, although a farm thief and (according to folk legend) a deceiver of Man, is valued by villagers as a predator of the hare, a major forest pest, and is also associated with bountiful rice harvests. Like the fox, the now extinct wolf was valued in rural Japan as an important predator of other pests. When much shifting cultivation was carried out in the mountains, the wolf was seen as the villager's ally, because it preyed on deer, wild boar and hares when they gathered to ravage these upland plots (Nakamura, 1987).

Forest animals tend to be associated with the spirit world, for example as attendants or messengers of the *kami* spirits. Images of monkeys, wolves, deer, and foxes are to be found at Shinto shrines throughout Japan. In ancient times, the monkey was viewed as a mediator between the *yama no kami* (the mountain spirit) and human beings (see Ohnuki-Tierney, 1987), the wolf, another animal of the remote mountains, was likewise associated with the *yama no kami* (WKMK, 1981), while the serow was a 'cow demon' (*ushioni*), an animal ghost in the mountains (Kaneko *et al*, 1992). The raccoon-dog, fox, and snake assumed human form, and birds such as the crow, pheasant and woodpecker had powers of prophecy (disaster, earthquakes, and rain, respectively).

The *yama* has undergone great change during this century. When some of the older foresters began to work in the mountains, most felling took place in the mixed woodland. By the post-war years much of this forest had been felled and a large-scale re-planting programme was launched. While nationally, the proportion of planted forest is around 40 per cent of the woodland area, in Hongū – 93 per cent of which is mountain forest – 64 per cent is plantations. These plantations comprise two types of (native) conifer: cryptomeria (*sugi*, *Cryptomeria japonica*), and Japanese cypress (*hinoki*, *Chamaecyparis obtusa*). By the late 1980s, the Hongū mountain forests, like much of the rest of the country, had largely become a sea of dark-green coniferous uniformity, occasionally punctuated by pockets of natural growth (often the location of Shinto shrines). Much of the mixed woodland has become an 'industrial forest' of timber plantations and, to a large extent, the earlier wide-ranging livelihood relationship to the forest has been replaced by one of forestry wage-labour.

Hunting and fishing

For hunters on the Kii Peninsula, the wild boar has long been the preferred game. Typically, a single hunter, with his dog and hunting musket, would go into the mountains and track down the wild boar's resting-place. Most mountain villages can boast famous boar hunters. One hunter I knew had killed over 300 wild boars (46 in one year alone), and, now in his mid-70s, still hunts with his son throughout the winter season. Another renowned boar hunter is said to have hunted 134 boar over one winter season at the turn of the century (Yoshigaitō, 1987). Today, boar-hunting tends to be in groups of four to ten men (and their dogs), some of whom flush the boar out from the mountainside while the others wait with their guns along the various escape routes. Bears were also hunted, usually by stalking their hibernation resting-places. The Kii Peninsula has its own famed bear hunters (Ue, 1983).

Hunting is a dangerous activity. Stray bullets, encounters with wild boars (and their tusks), and slipping when in pursuit of prey or in catching up with the dogs, are some of the routine dangers. But the Japanese hunter also faces another kind of danger: from the souls of his prey. There is a rich lore on hunting *tatari* – the sometimes fatal curses that dead animals can impose on those who hunt and kill them.

A Hongū woman claimed that hunting was the cause of a series of family misfortunes. She attributed her mother-in-law's long illness to her father-in-law's hunting. The souls of the dead animals were now exacting revenge for the old man's deeds. But this woman claims to have suffered a number of times herself from spirit-related sickness caused by the hunting of the men of the family. Finally, some years ago, she managed to persuade her nephew to stop hunting. The family members have enjoyed good health ever since.

Ue Toshikatsu tells the story of a lifelong raccoon-dog hunter. Before the Second World War, raccoon-dogs were in great demand; their pelts were used to make overcoats, and their hair was used for toothbrushes and paintbrushes, in addition to the price their gall bladders could fetch as medicine. After the war, however, the market collapsed, and the hunter found he could hardly sell his catch. His livelihood denied him, and forced into idleness, the old hunter lost the will to live. One day, he was found with a rope around his neck hanging from a pine tree in the forest. After his death, a rumour went around the village that he had been a victim of the raccoon-dogs' *tatari* because of the great number he had killed (Ue, 1983).

On the Kii Peninsula, monkeys are a designated farm pest which are caught and traded in at the town hall for money. Totsugawa-mura, north of Hongū, suffers particularly seriously from 'monkey damage' (*engai*), and hires full-time monkey-catchers to control the numbers. Hunters are reluctant, however, to kill monkeys, because of their human-like, and especially child-like features. But some do, and it is said that in one case, some years ago, a 'monkey-like child' (*saru no yō na kodomo*) was born to a monkey-catcher's family (cf Suzuki, 1982)! Chiba tells the story of a monkey-catcher in Miyazaki prefecture. As the only person willing to kill monkeys in the area, this man took a great many monkey lives and became reasonably wealthy as a result. In his old age, however, he fell seriously ill. As he lay ill in bed, he noticed just beyond the veranda a great horde of monkeys watching him. Neatly lined up, they beckoned him to come to them. Frightened, he screamed at the family members nursing him that monkeys were watching him and calling him, but nobody else could see them. The monkey-catcher went on to die a slow and painful death before this audience of monkey victims (Chiba, 1995).

Snakes are commonly encountered in the forest and in the village, and are often beaten to death. But the snake is another animal which may curse its killer (see Matsutani, 1994a). Yukawa (1991) reports that among swidden farmers in Shikoku there was a fear of the *tatari* of the snakes which perish when the land is set on fire. Ue (1987) reports one such local example of a 'snake curse' (*kuchinawa no tatari*). In the mid-1920s, two young men captured two snakes in the mountains which they then took to local festivals to display for money, but the snakes soon died. As a result, the houses of the families of the two men eventually burned down. The origin of the curse may well be ancestral, going back many generations. In 1995, I interviewed the parents of a teenage girl, whose tragic death was believed to have been caused by the *tatari* of a snake killed many generations back. Her parents stressed, however, that it was not the family ancestors who were responsible, but those of the family which previously owned the plot of land on the mountainside where they lived. Unwittingly, by setting up house there, they inherited the curse.

The risk of *tatari* is especially great with those animals associated with particular spirits, such as bears in Yamagata prefecture (Sakuma, 1985) and in Shikoku (Tanigawa, 1980) which are associated with the mountain spirit, or the wolf (Chiba, 1977). Deerhunters too are at risk. A Wakayama hunter, who had killed some 400 animals, shot a stag which turned out to have four antlers, and was associated, therefore, with the Kasuga Myōjin deity; he was dead within the year (Chiba, 1977).

There are certain times when it is particularly dangerous to hunt. One of these is when the hunter's wife is pregnant. In Kōchi prefecture, to kill a wild boar at such a time is to risk one's wife giving birth to a child covered with wild-boar fur (Suzuki, 1982), while on the Kii Peninsula, monkey-killing (as the story above shows) at such a time poses the risk of a deformed child being born (Chiba, 1977). Yet it is no less widely reported, often from the very same regions, that the man with a pregnant wife, who does hunt, may be very successful, as though the animals were attracted to him (Chiba, 1977; Tanigawa, 1980).

Multiple killers are most vulnerable of all. Not to stop hunting when one should entails a risk of *tatari*. In Miyazaki, when a hunter kills his hundredth wild boar, he incurs the *tatari* of the mountain spirit (Suzuki, 1982). This *tatari* may take the form of an encounter with a monster in the mountains, the hunter's dog turning on him (Chiba, 1975; Koyama, 1992), or the death of a family member such as the hunter's daughter (Sutō, 1991). Chiba tells of the legend (from Saga prefecture) of the boar-hunter who, approaching his hundredth kill, found his old mother beseeching him to stop his 'killing' (*sesshō*). Ignoring her pleas, he went on to make his hundredth kill. But the animal felled turned out, on inspection, to be his own mother (wearing a wild-boar skin) (Chiba, 1995)!

Hunters could counter this danger by means of ritual. In many parts of Japan, *kuyōtō* (memorial stones) or *senpikizuka* ('one thousand head mounds') are erected for the souls of the wild boar or deer hunted (Kaneko *et al*, 1992; Chiba, 1975). The reference to a thousand kills is not meant literally, but tends to stand for the idea of *many*; hunters establish such memorials when they feel that they have killed enough animals, and this limit may well be placed at 100 kills or 80 kills (Sutō, 1991); these figures are for animals in general (including birds) or for specific classes of animal. Some memorial stones are for wild boars only, others for wild boar and deer, and yet others for wild boar, deer, and bears. In one part of Kyūshū, a memorial stone is erected for *each* bear killed, indicating that a single bear's life is equivalent to a 100 or even 1000 other animals (Chiba, 1975). On the Kii Peninsula (one of the areas where a hunter would stop hunting after a thousand kills), on killing his third bear the hunter should carry out a *kuyō*, although even then his luck may turn bad (Chiba, 1977).

In practice, not all prolific hunters established memorial stones. It has been suggested that the distribution of such stones and sites – concentrated in some areas and scarce in others – indicates that special factors might have been at work, such as an influential religious figure exhorting the hunters of the area to observe the custom (Sutō, 1991). In other words, the successful hunter did not automatically erect such a stone; rather, the act would probably have been triggered by some misfortune – injury to the hunter himself, or sudden serious illness in the family – which was interpreted as an expression of retribution (ibid.). This would also explain the inconsistency of the animal head-count engraved on the stones.

In 1979, the Hongū-chō Hunters' Association (*ryōyūkai*) erected a memorial stone (*chōjū ireihi*) for the souls of the birds and animals killed in the hunting season. The memorial is an impressive natural stone of an irregular oblong shape which stands around 1.5m high. The monument is actually located on the edge of the forest (a mature cryptomeria plantation), looking out over the school base-ball ground. Here, at the end of the hunting season in the early spring, the members of the Hunters' Association gather to hold a *kuyō* or requiem for the souls of the hunted game animals. A Shinto priest (himself an enthusiastic hunter and Association member) in white robes recites a prayer to console the animals' souls. A variety of offerings are laid before the stone, including un-cooked rice, rice-wine, salt, saltwater fish (mackerel), freshwater fish (sweetfish), vegetables and seaweed, and each hunter in turn lays a sprig of *sakaki* (*Cleyera ochnacca*) before the stone, clapping his hands and bowing solemnly.

On enquiring about the origin of the memorial stone and the requiem, I was told by the head of the Hunters' Association that there was a general feeling among local hunters that 'it was not right just to go on taking life', and that some sort of memorial event should be held. I soon discovered, however, that actual participation in the requiem has always been poor and in recent years has dimin-ished even further. Initially, a twice-yearly ritual timetable was instituted – at the beginning and end of the hunting season – but this soon contracted into a single annual event, and now it is held only every other year. The 1991 requiem was attended by just one in five members of the Hunters' Association (18 out of a total membership of around 80).

A common expression applied to hunters (by non-hunters) is that 'their final days will be bad' (*shinigiwa ga warui*). As a result of their hunting, 'misfortune' (*fukō*) is likely to befall them and their families. It follows on from this percep-tion that even where the hunter himself expresses indifference, other members of his family may be greatly concerned about the possible negative consequences of his hunting. For example, a Hongū hunter in his 50s told me that, while he himself does not believe in things like *tatari*, each time he has hunting success his wife goes to the local temple to pray for the soul of the animal.

Fishing too is recognized as a life-taking activity which is morally problematic. One expression of this is the 'life-releasing ceremony' (*hōjōe*) dating back to the seventh century, in which fish – which would otherwise be killed and eaten – would be released back into the river (and birds into the mountains) (see de Wisser, 1935; Nishitsunoi, 1958). In medieval Japan, the fisherman was seen as committing a bad act and, therefore, as susceptible to negative karmic con-sequences (Chiba, 1995).

Fish (especially larger ones) can curse those who catch them (Naumann, 1974). Even in present-day Japan, a *kuyō* should be carried out for the souls of the fish. This applies first and foremost to the whale, for Japanese the biggest fish of all. In Japanese whaling villages, 'it is not uncommon to find whalers offering daily prayers to the killed whales', while one whaling village (Taiji) on the south-east coast of the Kii Peninsula holds an annual *kuyō* for the whales caught during the year (Kalland and Moeran, 1992). (In Taiji, there was also the custom of erecting a memorial stone on killing 35 or more whales [Naumann, 1974].) Similarly, in nearby Katsu'ura, an annual *kuyō* is held for the tuna fish (*maguro no kuyō*).

Freshwater fishermen in the mountainous interior of the peninsula also hold a *kuyō*. In one village in Hongū, a *kuyō* is held at the beginning of the fishing season, the first day of June, to 'console' (*nagusameru*) the 'souls of the sweet-fish' (*ayu no tamashii*). Until the mid-1980s, a Buddhist priest recited a *sutra* in a short ceremony involving the offering of incense at the riverside in the late afternoon, after which a lively drinking-party ensued that continued until late in the evening. Today, the Buddhist ceremony has been dropped, and the event officially renamed *kawabiraki* or 'the river opening'. The local priest still attends and lights incense sticks on the riverside, although he stresses that he goes there as a resident rather than as a priest.

Despite the formal change in the name of the event, local people continue to refer to it as 'the sweetfish requiem' (*ayu no kuyō*) and, in the course of an interview, the local priest stressed the spiritual importance of the *kuyō* as follows.

> When you take the lives of living things day after day, as with fishermen who do it as an occupation, somewhere in your heart you will think that something might happen. This is an invisible threat. *Kuyō* can help to alleviate such fears. That is why there are sweetfish *kuyō*.

The priest is referring to the meaning that the ritual should have. But among local people it is seen rather differently. For example, one forest landowner from a neighbouring village criticized this annual event as 'mistaken'. The *kuyō* for animal souls should take place at the *end* of the (hunting or fishing) season, not (as in this case) at the beginning (when I put it to him, the priest concurred with this point). He went on to point out that a central part of the event should be the symbolic release of sweetfish back into the river. The implication of this criticism was that the event was really just a pretext for an open-air summer drinking-party. To a certain extent, participants themselves concur with this assessment. Indeed, one local villager warned me not to take this particular *kuyō* too ser-iously, adding that it ought rather to be called a *kuō*, a 'let's eat'!

Forestry

The human consumption or use of plants also raises moral questions in Japan. In Japanese (and Chinese) Buddhism the issue of whether 'plants and trees' (*sōmoku*) could attain Buddhahood has been much discussed; the idea exists that 'each rice-grain has a soul, and that rice is alive in its hull' (Ohnuki-Tierney, 1993); and there are *kuyō* dedicated to the souls of grass burned in a forest fire (Kimura and Tsutsui, 1990). But of all plants, it is trees which tend to be at-tributed *tamashii* or souls in Japan. This confers on forestry an element of risk in addition to the danger of losing one's footing, of being hit by falling rocks or branches or, in the case of tree-felling, of being injured by falling trees. For like hunting, tree-felling is recognized as a life-taking activity that makes those engaged in it vulnerable to spiritual retribution.

The felling of old, sacred trees by misguided officials or greedy merchants, and the dire consequences of such acts, is a common theme in Japanese folktales. Throughout Japan, there are tales of *tatari no ki* or 'curse trees' which, in reaction to being cut down or to having a part (branch or root) cut off, inflict suffering on those responsible. The famous tree doctor, Yamano Tadahiko, gives a number of examples of 'the sufferings of old trees which have been bullied by waves of development' – and their vengeful reactions (Yamano, 1989).

Makino gives the example of a giant tree in a Yamagata village. During a fire in the late nineteenth century, a *kami* appeared (in the form of an old man) to stop the fire and save the tree. If the tree were destroyed, not only would it cease to protect, but those responsible would suffer its *tatari*. Indeed, the tree is believed to have the power to cause misfortune to anyone who even so much as brings a bladed object near it (Makino, 1986)!

Guthrie has a similar example of a village tree from a mountain village in the Kantō region. The large pine 'is said to have been planted when the hamlet was founded' and is believed to 'live as long as the hamlet does'. It must never be felled.

> The tree is said to produce hallucinations in anyone who climbs it with malicious intent. Some sixty years ago, a villager climbed it to cut off branches interfering with his adjacent fields. Beginning to cut, he found himself and the tree surrounded by a sea. Frightened and confused, he quit and began to descend, and the sea disappeared. The tree is also said to be protected by an unusual number of adders in its vicinity. It is further protected by hamlet residents. In 1971, for example, the Yamanaka Old People's Association . . . put up a fence protecting its roots from visitors . . . (Guthrie, 1988)

Because the longevity of the tree stands for the continuity of the village, it is in the interests of the village as a whole that it be protected from particular villagers.

Given that trees have tree spirits, all trees can be said to be inhabited. But some trees pose an extra danger because they are also the home of another sort of spirit or demon. Animal spirits may colonize certain trees. De Wisser points out that there are many eighteenth century tales which tell of the danger of cutting down sacred trees associated with the fox spirit: 'Madness, suicide and death by lightning fell upon the unhappy culprit and his family' (De Wisser, 1908).

Other trees dangerous to fell are those in which the various mountain demons live. 'Tengu pines' (*tengu matsu*) and 'demon pines' (*oni matsu*) can be found throughout Japan (Naumann, 1994). The *tengu* is a half-bird, half-human figure that resides in the mountains at the top of trees. The presence of *tengu* in the mountains is dangerous enough, but a number of Hongū myths suggest that the felling of such a tree – destroying the *tengu*'s home – is certain to incur its wrath. In 1959, when a transport cable for timber was being set up, a large tree had to be felled. Afterwards, it was rumoured that the tree was a 'tengu-rest tree' (*tengu yasumi ki*), and one of the men involved in the felling became ill, eventually asking a Shinto priest to help. The priest is said to have duly performed a rite in which the *tengu* was asked for forgiveness (WKMK, 1981).

Hayashi (1980) mentions a dangerous forest road in Yoshino (on the northern part of the Kii Peninsula). Local people attribute the frequency of accidents there to the fact that a large *sakaki* tree was felled to make way for the road. The problem created by the felling was resolved by means of a compensatory replanting. A ceremony was held at which a Buddhist priest planted a cypress sapling by the roadside, thereby providing a new abode for the displaced tree spirit. In other parts of Japan, accidents are attributed to the legacy of the felling and pruning of trees involved in road extensions (Matsutani, 1994a).

Many of the sacred shrine tress on the Kii Peninsula were felled at the beginning of the century as part of the Government's shrine-merger policy. Wakayama Prefecture, in which Hongū lies, was particularly seriously affected, with around 80 per cent of its shrines eliminated (Irokawa, 1985). Formally, the abolition of a shrine meant that the trees associated with it no longer had a sacred character, and could be felled by foresters at a time of great national demand for wood. In practice, however, this policy aroused opposition, and many attempts to save old sacred trees. Some of those who actually carried out the merger policy died.[1] Even today in Wakayama, there is a wariness towards cutting down older trees, for fear of the (possibly fatal) consequences (cf Umeda, 1992, Hayashi, 1980).

In the mid-1980s, villagers in Hongū agreed that a large maidenhair (*ichō*) tree in the shrine courtyard should be cut down, because its roots were damaging the stone wall of the courtyard, which, because of the adjacent downhill footpath, made the place dangerous to passers-by. A villager, himself a forest labourer, agreed to fell the unsightly tree which, in any case, had recently lost a large trunk in a storm. Before he got around to it, however, the forester was stopped by his wife. To fell a shrine tree, she warned him, was very dangerous and could cause serious misfortune for the family later on. I heard from other villagers that what ought to be done is to call a priest to conduct a 'spirit-removing' (*shōne nuki*) ceremony; only then could the tree be safely felled. But villagers could not agree on such a measure especially given the money it would cost, and the tree still stands today.

There is a tall cryptomeria tree across the road from the house of the K family. It has a *hokora* (stone alcove) at its base, indicating its sacred status. Offerings are regularly made to the tree which, the family claims, protects its members. The origins of the worship of this tree lie in the felling of an old evergreen oak (*kashi no ki, Quercus spp.*) on the same site by a member of the family. Soon afterwards, a family member gave birth to an abnormal child, something widely attributed to the felling of the old tree. The 'K' family planted a cryptomeria sapling on the site of the old tree, and worshipped the tree thereafter in an attempt to replicate or offset the loss of an earlier tree and, thereby, lift the curse. Although a different tree, it is planted in the same spot, growing in the same soil, and is, in a sense, a continuation of the earlier tree cut down. In this case, the replacement planting attempts to mitigate – or symbolically negate – the felling of the earlier tree. Perhaps this was why the fast-growing cryptomeria was chosen – because it would more quickly assume the size of the felled tree.

Matsutani gives an example from Gifu prefecture of a family which decided to cut down and sell a large horse-chestnut tree which had stood for many hundreds of years in the family-owned mountains around the house. Soon afterwards, a strong typhoon blew, causing a mountain landslide which devastated the family home (Matsutani, 1994a). Instead of contributing to family prosperity, the felling of the old tree brought (self-inflicted) disaster to the family. The story illustrates powerfully the intimate connection between the fate of trees in the mountains and the fate of people in the village and, more specifically, how the irresponsible felling of trees can bring about human catastrophe. Matsutani's example is from the mid-1920s, but the moral of the story has an obvious resonance in the aftermath of the war, 20 years later, when many upland villages were subjected to recurrent landslides due to reckless wartime tree-felling.

Other tales recount the misfortune which befalls those who cut down old trees to make space for dwellings. A rich man built an annexe to his house, but fell sick afterwards. A fortune-teller discovered that a camphor tree had been cut down five or six years before to make way for the annexe, and a root of the tree had remained trapped beneath the building. The rich man's sickness was cured by digging up the tree root and then worshipping it in his house (Yanagita, 1970; Yen, 1974).[2]

Those people most likely to cut down sacred trees are, of course, the lumberjacks. Some years ago, the career of M, a Hongū forest labourer, was ended by a serious accident in the mountains. While chainsawing his way through a plantation, he inadvertently cut down a tree with a nearby stone Jizō (a *boddhisattva*).

That day, early in the morning, I was cutting bamboo nearby and got a black eye when I was caught by a bamboo branch. At that time I thought that this was not going to be my day and that I should stop work that day then and there.

But that day was pay-day and M could hardly go home, so he continued to work.

After I cut down a cryptomeria, I then started cutting down a pasania tree [*Castanopsis spp.*]. But the wind was blowing hard, and as it was falling the tree swayed around and came towards me, but I was caught between two rocks [and could not escape]. There was a stone [close by] covered with moss. This was a Jizō but I hadn't realized it. That place in the valley was bad.

Owing to the wind, the tree fell in the opposite direction, and M found himself trapped. Overlooking the spot was the small Jizō, the (normally) compassionate *boddhisattva*. Lumberjacks are used to stepping nimbly out of the path of a falling tree but, on this occasion, the sacred tree associated with the Jizō seemed to follow M in its fall, with the result that he broke his leg in nine different places and had to have 30 pins inserted. His leg was then a good 2cm shorter.

Lumberjacks are traditionally protected from such calamities by a short ritual held before felling begins on a new mountain. *Yama'iri* (or 'mountain entry', directed to the mountain spirit (*yama no kami*), is carried out with the workforce assembled and the *oyakata* or forest landowner presiding (see Ue, 1980; Ue, 1987; Nakazawa, 1992). An outstanding tree – the tallest, or one with a strange shape – is selected, at the foot of which offerings of sake, rice, salt, *sakaki* and, sometimes, even fish are made. A Shinto priest might even be called to recite a *norito* prayer. Taking turns, the forest workers make offerings and ask the mountain spirit for protection from injury or worse during the felling. At a time when serious, even disabling forestry injuries were common, the rite had an important function in reassuring the workforce. Sometimes, where an unusual number of injuries occurred, a further ceremony would be carried out in an attempt to mitigate the misfortune. In addition, there was often a *kamidana* in the workers' mountain-hut where the men could petition the mountain spirit each morning for safety at work.

Felling mountain trees is dangerous because it risks offending the mountain spirit. This danger is offset by ritually removing or relocating the mountain spirit from the trees to be felled to a safe tree. There is the sense in the *yama'iri* above that the selected tree becomes the exclusive abode of the mountain spirit, thereby liberating the other trees on the mountain for felling and human appropriation. The selected tree remains standing, and once the felling is completed a 'mountain closing' (*yamajimai*) ritual takes place at which further offerings are made to the tree before the workforce leaves the mountain (Ue, 1980).

A similar logic is at work in the custom of warning the mountain spirit in advance by knocking three times with the back of the axe on the trunk of the tree to be felled (Matsutani, 1994a). In some cases, a simple preliminary knocking on the tree would elicit a sign – the sudden escape of a bird or a squirrel – indicating that the tree was not ready, and that the felling should take place on another day (Ichikawa, 1989). Knocking might be coupled with the planting of a sapling nearby, to which the mountain spirit was invited to move, allowing the felling to proceed without the risk of offending him (Matsutani, *ibid*). Naumann similarly reports the custom of planting a sapling where the felled tree stood, or placing some greenery of the felled tree on to its stump (Naumann, 1963). The same practice – of leaving one tree standing – was observed by swidden farmers when clearing forest land for cultivation (Yukawa, 1991).

Plate 2: *A tree requiem.*

In the nearby timber-market town of Shingu on the coast (where much Hongū wood is sold), an annual *mokurei kuyō* or 'tree-spirit requiem' is held at which the souls of the trees felled over the past year are remembered.[3] At 10 o'clock on the morning of the 15 October 1994, the 69-year-old head of the Hongū Foresters' Cooperative unveiled a 4.5m-long Japanese cryptomeria timber, erected on a dais in the courtyard of the Shingū Wood-Growers Association (see Plate 2). As the 'Tree Offerer' (*kenbokusha*) for the 35th annual ceremony, this man supplied the 100-year old timber from his own mountains, and was called on to make the key address to the timber merchants, forest landowners and assorted regional dignitaries. On the timber was written the three characters *moku-rei-tō*, 'tree spirit tower', while in front of it was a tablet – resembling the ancestral tablets in domestic altars, only much larger – bearing the two characters for 'tree' and 'spirit'. Immediately before the tablet and the timber a range of offerings had been placed, including fruit, vegetables, fish, rice-cakes and rice-wine. A Buddhist priest recited a *sutra* to comfort and console the souls of the felled trees.

In his address, the Tree Offerer expressed deep gratitude to the tree souls for their 'blessing' (*ki no megumi*). He felt honoured at being selected as this year's Tree Offerer, and wanted to express his appreciation to other Association members. He then recalled how, at the end of the war, he returned from New Guinea 'physically and mentally broken', the warm welcome he received back in his village, the half a century he had spent working in forestry, and 'the blessings I have received from thousands, even tens of thousands of trees'. This year's low rainfall and exceptionally severe summer, and the resulting water-shortage, he suggested, should teach us not to take for granted the importance of our forests and the efforts of our forebears who passed them down to us. Afterwards, those assembled offered incense before the timber, just as at a funeral or memorial service for human beings.

This rite has a post-war origin. A forest landowner, on visiting a felling site, noticed the creaking sound made by the tree just as it was about to fall, and declared this to be the sound of the tree 'crying' (*ki ga naitoru*), even its 'dying scream' (*danmatsuma no himei*). 'As we make our living by taking the life of the tree, we should conduct a *Kuyō* for its spirit' (Ue, 1987). I heard a similar sentiment from a recent Tree Offerer. He stressed that Man cannot but be moved by the death of an old tree for 'it is something older than yourself' (*jibun yori furui dakara*), and that the tree *kuyō* was 'the same as a funeral' (*ososhiki to onaji*).

Livelihood and danger?

Tatari tales are characterized by the motif of what LaFleur has called 'poetic justice' (LaFleur, 1983). In Japan, there are many other possible sources of *tatari*, apart from game animals, fish, and trees. Chickens, cows, horses, dogs and cats each exact retribution on those who cause their deaths,[4] while *kuyō* (or *ireisai*[5]) are held for the souls of a range of different categories of animals, including livestock, pets, police-dogs, guide-dogs for the blind, stray dogs and cats (destroyed by the public health office), laboratory animals, insects, and even (what are otherwise considered) inanimate objects such as needles, dolls, and printing blocks.[6]

Hunters are especially vulnerable to the logic of *tatari* because they kill deliberately and recurrently. In the past, the word used for hunters was *sesshōnin*, literally 'a person who takes life'. It has strong negative religious connotations because *sesshō*, or lifetaking, is expressly forbidden by Buddhism. Applied to hunting, the term *sesshō* emphasizes the fact of killing. I have only heard the word *sesshōnin* used in reference to present-day hunters (or *sesshō* for hunting) by a local Buddhist priest, who was expressing his disapproval of the activity. Hunters themselves use the terms when talking about hunting in their father's, or more likely their grandfather's generation. For example, a hunter pointed out that when his grandfather hunted, it was forbidden for *sesshōnin* to bring the meat of the kill into the house – it would be eaten outside (cf Chiba, 1977; Sakuma, 1985). The word *sesshōnin* evokes an earlier world in which hunting was surrounded by all manner of interdictions and a good deal of moral concern.

Japanese Buddhism defines life-taking negatively, as a precept-breaking activity. *Fusesshokai*, 'the precept of no life-taking' is a central Buddhist precept. The good hunter cannot be a good Buddhist for, in terms of Japanese Buddhist ideas about posthumous salvation or well-being, the act of killing condemns that which is killed to a prolonged suffering. In inflicting this misery on another sentient being, the hunter exactly inverts the good Buddhist's normative behaviour. In essence, deliberate life-taking is bad because it blocks the posthumous progress of the animal's soul towards a Buddhistic repose (*jōbutsu*).

Many *Mahayana* Buddhist texts condemn meat-eating and hunting, warning of the karmic consequences of such action. The *sutra bonmōkyō*, for example, proclaims that all sentient creatures are the reincarnated forms of the mothers and fathers of living people and, therefore, should not be killed and eaten. Chiba (1977) suggests that, in medieval Japan, livestock animals were considered to be reincarnated people, and that this was why the killing of livestock was stigmatized. By contrast, wild animals could be killed without such a sense of stigma because they were viewed as from the 'other world' (*ikai*) of the *yama* and, therefore, outside the 'six paths' (six different forms of existence) of the universe across which reincarnation took place. It was medieval Buddhism's stress on the imperative of respecting the lives of all animals – indeed, all sentient beings – that led to wild animals being assimilated to the same general category as domestic animals, and to hunting becoming likened to livestock killing as an immoral activity.

Hunters do not necessarily accept this representation of what they do. Chiba gives the example of a seventeenth-century hunter who found himself being condemned by a Buddhist priest. The priest warned him that hunting lots of wild boar was bad and that he should recite the *nenbutsu* ('Praise to Amida Buddha') often to atone, otherwise he would go to hell in his afterlife. But the hunter responds by claiming that the wild boars he catches are the reincarnated form assumed by 'people who do not attain enlightenment' (*satori o hirakanu mono*). As wild boars, these people now live lives of great suffering. To hunt these wretched boar-people is to end their suffering and is, therefore, a form of kindness. What he, the hunter, does is to send their (human) souls to the Buddhist paradise. Hunting is, in short, an act of compassion. Naturally enough, the priest is deeply angered by such a claim – a hunter claiming a priest-like role! – and repeats his warning that hunting is 'the conduct of an evil person' (*akunin no gyō*) (Chiba, 1995).

In another tale, from the late thirteenth century, a priest, watching a fisherman catch fish, advises him to stop taking the lives of living creatures. The priest buys the fish from him and releases them into the sea. That night, the priest is visited by the released fish in a dream, but rather than thank him for saving them, the fish proceed to rebuke him for what he has done.

Small creatures like us can only expect to be reborn [in another lowly form] and cannot hope to go to the western paradise and live in heaven. But if we are eaten by people, we become part of their bodies and form a part of a human-being who can go to heaven. When we were caught in the fisherman's net yesterday, our chance of salvation (*jōbutsu*) had arrived. But then you came along and gave us your uncalled-for help and we ended up being released into water to live a life full of suffering once more. Chiba 1995

An identical logic applied to hunting is found in the fourteenth century work, *Shintōshū*. Again, a Buddhist priest sees a practice he disapproves of, this time the common people's joyful offering of the meat of wild animals, birds and fish to a shrine. He warns them that they should not feel happy about taking such lives, especially in front of the spirit. But that night, in a dream, he is visited by the shrine *kami* spirit which received the offered meat, and is told that the lowly status of such creatures means that they cannot attain buddhahood (*jōbutsu*), but that by being offered to the spirit, then eaten by those present, they become a part of human beings and are able to go to heaven. In this way, the priest learns, the spirit extends its compassion to the animals concerned (Chiba, 1995). Chiba finds this self-understanding reflected in the ritual words uttered by present-day hunters when making a kill (Chiba, 1995; Sutō, 1991).

Rather than live their lives burdened by a Buddhist guilt for the suffering they cause, hunters could counter with a different, even opposed Buddhistic inter-pretation of their actions. Instead of being the source of suffering, hunting is a means of ending it. By killing and then consuming lowly animals, human beings incorporate them, elevate their status, and improve their prospects for salvation. Human concern for animals is not inconsistent with livelihood activities, but realized through them. For life-taking, as the foreshortening of lives of endemic suffering, accelerates the spiritual progress of animal souls towards Buddhist salvation, and precludes the alternative course of an incremental (but uncertain) progress by means of transmigration across the different status levels of the universe.

While the mainstream Buddhist interpretation of hunting would assign the hunters themselves to the lowest moral status and, therefore, the worst prospects for salvation, this counter-interpretation inverts such a judgement. Indeed, the successful hunter might even be said to epitomize the Mahayana ideal of the *boddhisattva*: one who makes possible the salvation of a great many others.

Chiba sees Japanese hunters as responding skillfully to the Buddhist orthodoxy which would censure them. Rather than passively accept the immoral, stigmatized status of the life-taker, they redefine the religious significance of life-taking. (The idea that the hunter sends the soul of the prey to heaven recalls the pattern of exchange associated with the Ainu bear ceremony which, Umehara Takeshi [1988] and others have argued, represents the original, indigenous logic of Japanese religion.)

Arguably this anxiety about life-taking is expressed in the tendency of Jap-anese hunters to characterize their activity as *mabiki*, or 'thinning'. *Mabiki* ori-ginally referred to the removal of inferior rice-stalks from the paddyfield, but the term was also a euphemism for infanticide (LaFleur, 1992). In upland Japan, the term is commonly applied to the thinning of timber plantations. The implication is that animal populations in the forests, like past human populations in the village and the trees in the plantation, need to be thinned. The hunter is a source of security to the village because he kills farm pests, such as the wild boar and the deer, and each hunting success brings some relief to anxious villages.

Whether it is the forester cutting down trees, or the hunter killing animals, the idiom of *mabiki* makes the focus of the activity the larger population (that continues), rather than individual members of it (that are eliminated). In his own terms, then, the hunter is not a taker of life, but one who ensures continuity of life *overall*. Cartmill (1993) has pointed out that this population-centred attitude is widespread among hunters, though condemned by animal-rights protesters as 'environmental fascism'.

While foresters of the region may carry out a *kuyō* for the souls of the trees felled, this does not necessarily mean that they fully and explicitly identify themselves as life-takers, akin to hunters. One way in which the life-taking character of tree-felling is denied, is by stressing the importance of tree-planting. Instead of the life-taking discontinuity of tree-felling, the emphasis is on the longer-term continuity of the *yama* achieved by immediate reforestation. Another means of denying the life-taking character of logging is by claiming that the tree continues to live as building timber. The wooden beams of the house represent the 'second life' of the tree, in contrast to its first life in the forest. While this is especially the case with timber from family forests used to build or rebuild the family house, it extends to the logs that are sold.

Whether it is hunters, fishermen or foresters, the negative Buddhist representation of their livelihood activity is not passively accepted, but challenged by means of invoking various counter-representations. Yet it would be wrong to conclude that *kuyō* is no more than an élite sensibility. Hunters and other life-takers, as well as the wider communities in which they live, *are* sensitive to the spiritual danger of their activities; after all, tales of *tatari* continue to arise and *kuyō* continues to be carried out. Often the life-takers themselves reject belief in *tatari* pointing to *mawari no hito* – the people around them – who 'tie things together' (*musubitsuke*), so that any misfortunes affecting the life-takers or their families are linked to the life-taking. But this wider concern none the less disposes them to respond through appropriate ritual activity.

Conclusion

One ambiguity running through these various examples of *tatari* has to do with their source. On the one hand, the danger of *tatari* appears to emanate from the mountain spirit where the principle of reciprocity is breached. Man takes too much from the mountains, risking spiritual punishment. In return for what is taken, an offering should be made, as appeasement, to the mountain spirit. According to this interpretation, *tatari* is a function of excess.

On the other hand, the effect of the Buddhist stress on avoiding life-taking is to make the danger of *tatari* apply to livelihood activities as such. Making a living through the taking of life is culturally marked in Japan as morally problematic. According to official Buddhist teachings, both humans and animals undergo transmigration and rebirth, making for 'a fluid demarcation line [in which] the essential distinction between them is denied' (Ohnuki-Tierney, 1990). Livelihood activities take on a transgressive character because of the cultural recognition of commonality between social and natural realms, an institutionalized sense that the different lives involved – human, animal, plant – are *not* radically different in kind. The *kuyō* rite seems to grant the souls of animals and plants a sort of spiritual parity with human beings. What is differentiated in one respect – food, fuel, building materials, on the one hand, and their human consumers, on the other – is undifferentiated in this other, spiritual respect. The consumption of plants and animals becomes the consumption of something *similar in kind* and, therefore, something deeply problematic.[7]

Under the impact of Buddhism, ideas of *tatari* become much more ethicized, and associated with animal and plant *souls* rather than an overarching mountain spirit. *Tatari* is not just a matter of the amount of lives taken, but also of the spiritual attitude of the life-taker towards the life taken. *Tatari* is a punishment for ingratitude. All life-taking, therefore, is potentially dangerous to its practitioners, and this danger is assuaged by the life-taker taking on responsibility for the souls of those killed. Therefore, *tatari* can serve a rehabilitative, and not just punitive, purpose.

There is a clear correlation with ancestor worship. The *tatari* of human souls too is recognized in Japan. Neglected ancestors, as well as human beings who die prematurely or painfully (including aborted foetuses), present a potentially mortal danger to those most closely related to them (or, in the case of abandoned souls, those who happen to encounter them). Although not predicated on the life-taking relationship present in the hunting or forestry *kuyō*, *kuyō* for ancestral or other dead family members may have a similar purpose in pacifying irate souls. Whether it is the *tatari* of animals, plants, or people, it is overcome only by establishing a relationship of ritual care and attention (or, in those cases where *tatari* is fatal, that the victim's family do so). The *kuyō* rituals outlined above illustrate how social morality is extended to the forest.

Most Japanese today, however, have little direct economic connection with the forests. Does it follow from this that the sensibility of the *kuyō* is of no more than historical interest, unrelated to the lives and livelihoods of present-day Japanese? Two points should be made. First, there is ample evidence to suggest that the *kuyō* are not so many ritual leftovers or 'survivals' from another era, but that they are *contemporary* social phenomena. Both the tree and the hunting *kuyō* rites described are post-war creations, and elsewhere on the Kii Peninsula there are a number of examples of *new kuyō* for animal souls. Secondly, participation in the *kuyō* may come to extend beyond those directly involved in life-taking. This trend is evident in the Shingū tree-soul *kuyō*. While originally confined to loggers, it now includes saw-millers, and the Wood-Growers Association official believes that, in the future, consumers of wood – construction companies, housebuilders, and even house-dwellers – should also take part because the trees are, after all, being cut down for them. In other words, what are basically producer rituals should incorporate consumers within them.

In the mass production of industrialized societies, the scale of life-taking rises, but because of the advanced division of labour, the increased danger is more narrowly distributed. Producers find themselves spiritually liable for all that is consumed by other people. Hence it is quite common for larger livestock farmers to establish *kuyōtō* on their own farms, recalling the thousand-head memorial stones of the (over-)successful hunter. But it is against this background that, as with the wood-growers, those not engaged in occupational life-taking should be brought into the ritual ambit, and made to assume their share of responsibility for the non-human suffering on which human livelihoods depend.[8]

5 Forests and trees in the cultural landscape of Lawa swidden farmers in northern Thailand

DIETRICH SCHMIDT-VOGT

CONCERN ABOUT TROPICAL forests is, at present, focused primarily on the rain-forests of the humid Inner Tropics, which are seen as endangered by forest clearance for the extension of agricultural land, and by logging of timber for export. Rain forests are virgin forests, and our preoccupation with their fate may be due to the awareness that, once these intricate and delicate ecosystems are destroyed they are irretrievably lost.

Forests of the semi-humid Outer Tropics, for example the monsoon forests of south-east Asia, have not received the same attention, despite the fact that they have been subject to a greater degree of human pressure and for longer than the wet Tropics rainforests. They have been altered to such an extent that 'it is doubtful, if any of the original monsoon forest cover now remains' (Whitmore, 1984). Pressure on the monsoon forests of south-east Asia is mainly the result of swidden farming, an agricultural practice, also known as 'shifting cultivation' or 'slash-and-burn agriculture'. The elementary components of swidden farming comprise the clearance of a patch of forest near the end of the dry season, and the fertilization of the ground by burning the felled trees before the onset of the wet season in order to release nutrients stored in the forest biomass. The cleared patches are then cultivated for periods of varying length, and subsequently re-vert to natural regrowth through several stages of secondary succession. The process of secondary succession is strongly influenced by the manner in which swidden farming is carried out. In northern Thailand, swidden farming has been practised for such a long time, and in so many places, that it must be regarded, along with climate and soil conditions, as one of the chief determinants of vegetation composition and development (Santisuk, 1988). Swidden farming is carried out mostly by ethnic groups who live in the uplands and are, therefore, referred to as 'hilltribes'.

The various tribes practise different forms of swidden farming, commonly grouped into two categories which we shall term 'primary forest swiddening' and 'secondary forest swiddening' corresponding closely with the two basic types of 'pioneer' and 'established' swiddening identified by Conklin in the 1950s.

Primary forest swiddening is carried out by ethnic groups who arrived in northern Thailand relatively recently – from about 1850 until today. These are the Hmong, Yao, Akha, Lahu, and Lisu, all of whom belong to the Tibeto-Burman language family. This form of swidden farming is characterized by the clearance of primary forest and the cultivation of swiddens for an unspecified time – usually between 4 and 5 years, but sometimes up to 10 or even 15 years – until either soil depletion, or weed infestation render farming no longer profit-able. Secondary succession after such treatment consists of a long period in which weed and grass associations dominate, only gradually superseded by woody plants. When most of the primary forest in an area has been transformed in this way, and as long as primary forests are still available and accessible elsewhere, farmers will abandon their fields and their settlements and move on. The growing scarcity of primary forests in northern Thailand, as well as the Forest Department's increasingly restrictive attitude, impede to the inherent mobility of primary swiddeners, forcing them to remain sedentary and to make their fields in the early stages of secondary succession.

Secondary forest swiddening, on the other hand, is practised by ethnic groups who have lived and farmed in northern Thailand for several centuries. They include the Karen, a Sino-Tibetan group numbering about 300000, who represent the largest tribal group in the North, as well as Mon-Khmer groups like the Lawa, Khmu, and T'in, who are the oldests residents of northern Thailand. Secondary forest swiddening systems are characterized by a rotational sequence of short cultivation periods of 1 to 2 years, and long fallow periods of more than 10 years, during which a secondary forest can develop and mature. Secondary forest swiddeners, in contrast to primary forest swiddeners, are basically sedentary, occasionally moving their villages, and periodically rotating their fields within fixed boundaries.

The Lawa of northern Thailand

The Lawa represent the oldest stratum of settlers in mountainous northern Thailand. They ruled over kingdoms at the site of present-day Chiang Mai and further to the west, prior to the thirteenth century creation of the kingdom of Lanna by Thai immigrants, which eventually absorbed those principalities, pushing the Lawa into the mountains.

The Lawa is now one of the smallest ethnic groups in the region, with a population of 1845 in 1988 – just 1.42 per cent of the total tribal population in the North (McKinnon and Vienne, 1989).

The pattern of Lawa settlements is fragmented, the most conspicuous cluster of villages being located near the town of Mae Sariang in Mae Hong Son Province. The villages are situated at an average altitude of 1000m.

Since the middle of the nineteenth century, Sgaw Karen from Burma have infiltrated the Lawa domain of Mae Hong Son Province, filling in the space between Lawa settlements with their own villages. The Karen today vastly outnumber the original occupants of this territory (Kauffmann, 1972). The first Hmong (Meo) households were established in the early 1860s, since when the Hmong population has grown rapidly (Kunstadter, 1983). Because of the encroachment of the Karen, the influence of missionaries – who first appeared in the 1930s, and the long exposure to the Thai culture of the lowlands, the Lawa culture is undergoing a rapid process of disintegration and reorientation towards Thai norms.

The farming economy

The Lawa are credited with the creation of the most sustainable and conservationist form of swidden farming in northern Thailand. Their farming economy has been studied and documented by Kunstadter and his research associates (Kunstadter *et al.*, 1978) at the village of Ban Pa Pae, which is located east of Mae Sariang at an altitude of 720m – the lowest of all the Lawa villages in the area. This chapter is based both on the work of Kunstadter, and on my own research in the Lawa village of Ban Tun, about 15km north-east of Ban Pa Pae, at an altitude of 1000m.[1]

At Ban Tun, a fallow period of between 15 and 17 years was still being maintained at the time of my field work (March 1990 to December 1992). This was a unique phenomenon in an area where otherwise swidden farming was either practised with shorter fallow periods due to a growing shortage of land, or had been replaced by permanent farming systems. In this respect, Ban Tun represented a relic of the original Lawa swidden farming system.

The relic situation at Ban Tun can be explained by the demographic development of the village. Ban Tun was totally destroyed in around 1963, when 34 houses burned down (Kauffmann, 1972). The village was then relocated from its previous site on a ridge to a new location near a watercourse; about half of the village population split off in the process, and joined other communities. Today, Ban Tun is made up of 27 households numbering 177 people. Population increase by births is, to some extent, compensated for by migration to the lowlands, especially to the suburbs of Mae Sariang.

For these reasons Ban Tun has been able to retain a favourable ratio of population to cultivated land and, thus, to preserve the traditional swiddening system.

But change was imminent when I last visited Ban Tan in December 1992. The village had been relocated once again, now to a site close to the main road, and the villagers were just about to finish a feeder road, which would provide access to lowland markets and thus induce the transformation of swiddens to permanent farmland, with cabbage as the main cash crop.

The farming economy of Ban Tun is based both on the cultivation of rice in swiddens, and on irrigated fields. Each household has access to, on average, 1ha irrigated land and 2ha swiddens. Irrigated land is owned by individuals and may be transferred by sale or by inheritance. Only one crop of irrigated rice is planted each year. Rice seedlings are raised in irrigated nurseries around May, after the beginning of the rains, and are transplanted into the flooded fields by July. After the harvest, which begins in September and ends in November, cows and water buffaloes are allowed on to the fields to browse on the stubble. Swidden fields are cultivated for one year only, and each year a solid block of land is cleared in a communal effort.

Plots are allocated to each household and normally households will return to the same plot already used in the previous cycle of swidden farming. Any disputes over the allocation of land are settled by the village priests.

The swiddening cycle

In 1991, the annual swiddening cycle at Ban Tun was initiated on 28 January with a ceremony in a sacred grove on an adjacent ridge-top, which included the sacrifice of a pig. Trees and the forest play an important role in the ritual life of the Lawa, as is manifested in the worship of ancestor spirits with holy trees, which are erected in the house, outside the wooden wall of the inner room (Kauffmann, 1977), and in the protection of sacred groves as places of worship and sacrifice for animistic spirits. The January ceremony was carried out to obtain permission from the forest spirits to encroach once more on their domain for the purpose of clearing swiddens in accordance with the belief that swidden land actually belongs to the spirit world, and that its use is only possible on the basis of a temporary contract, which involves payment to the spirits (Kunstadter, 1983).

Clearing of the new swiddens at Ban Tun started on 6 February. The village community co-operated in this effort, women cutting the brush and small trees with a diameter generally less than 12cm, leaving 0.5 to 1m high stumps, the men climbing into the larger trees – which are not cut down on account of their size – to trim their crowns to prevent shading of the future crop. Sometimes, the entire foliage is removed by lopping but, more often, a few branches are left at the top to ensure the tree's survival. This procedure creates the most characteristic component of the Lawa cultural landscape: swidden fields, dotted with trees, closely resembling open woodland scenery when looked at from a distance. Trees on swiddens are often referred to as seed-trees in the literature. They certainly fulfill this function, but I refrain from the use of this term, which suggests that villagers preserve trees consciously in order to assist the regrowth of forest.

My enquiries in Ban Tun have not yielded sufficient evidence to support such a supposition. The standard answer to my question, 'why are trees were left on swiddens?' pointed to the thickness of trees or the toughness of their wood as the reason for not cutting them. This information was corroborated by tree and stump measurements: the diameter of trees left standing exceeded 12cm, while the diameter of stumps was generally less than that. Trees on ridge-tops and along streams were also preserved in an effort to ensure water-supply (Kunstadter, 1978a). Clearing was completed after 15 days; trees, branches and foliage were left on the ground to dry in the scalding sun of the hot pre-monsoon season until ready for burning.

Burning is normally carried out between the beginning and the middle of April – just before the onset of the monsoon rains. In Ban Tun in 1991, burning was started earlier, on 25 March, because of the danger of early thunderstorms. The burning process is divided into two stages. The first and most spectacular burn is organized as a communal activity. It produces a huge wall of flames, which rapidly moves up-slope, consuming the brittle mass of dry foliage and branches, leaving behind the charred logs. This first burn is crucial for the fertilization of swiddens because foliage and branches contain 80 per cent of the nutrients stored in a tree. That the Lawa farmers are well aware of this fact is indicated by their practice of leaving swiddens uncultivated after an unsatisfactory first burn. In the second stage of the burning process, the charred logs are collected into piles and burned in the afternoon, when up-slope winds fan the fires. This takes about two weeks and is carried out by each household on the assigned plot. Not all logs are disposed of in this manner: some are used to demarcate field boundaries and to stabilize footpaths, while others are carried into the villages as firewood. Kunstadter (1978a) reports that poles are arranged along the contour of a hillside, held by stumps, in order to prevent soil erosion. When all the plots have been cleared, shelters are constructed, and the fields are ready for planting.

The 1991 rice-planting season on swiddens at Ban Tun started on 21 April, after the first monsoon rains. Prior to planting, a ceremony, including the sacrifice of a pig, several young chickens, and a dog, was held on the plot of each household to elicit the support of the spirits. Planting is again a communal effort, the young men punching holes into the ground with their long planting-sticks, the girls following behind and throwing several grains of rice into each hole. The main crop on swiddens is rice. Other crops include sorghum, which is planted in long rows to demarcate field boundaries, chilli peppers, several varieties of bean, maize, and cucumber.

Secondary succession on fallow swiddens

Secondary succession on swiddens is setting in even before the first tips of the young rice make their appearance, with the emergence of weeds and the development of woody regrowth from stumps. Weeds grow so plentifully that weeding has to be carried out at least three times during a cropping season. The last weeding takes place about one month before the autumn's rice harvest. When the rice stalks have been cut, the ground is, therefore, already covered with a relatively dense carpet of weeds, which provides protection against evaporation. Exotic weeds from tropical America, which are spreading rapidly over south and south-east Asia, prevail in this carpet. The most notorious representatives are *Eupatorium odoratum* and *Eupatorium adenophorum*. Their appearance on fallow swiddens in northern Thailand was first reported by Credner in 1935. Other important exotics are *Ageratum conyzoidis* and *Crassocephalum crepidioides*. One year after harvest, the weed cover has increased in height, as well as in density, and is now dominated by two species: *Eupatorium odoratum* and *Blumea balsamifera* which, in some places, form an almost impenetrable jungle up to 2m high. Various species of fern are also common.

The weed stage persists for three to four years, and is then gradually replaced by a bush stage, which develops out of the growth of coppice shoots and root suckers from the stumps left in the ground after clearing. Initially overwhelmed by the dense tangle of weeds, they outgrow this cover after about three years and, by the fourth and fifth years, close their canopy and suppress the herbaceous undergrowth by shading.

During the fifth and sixth years the succession passes on from the bush stage to the secondary-forest stage. The trees have now reached a height of 5m and more, and canopy closure is so effective that only scattered remnants of the former weed and herb cover are left on the forest floor. Seedling establishment is setting in at this stage. At an age of about twelve the forest has reached maturity – in the context of a swidden-farming system – and is now ready for clearing. Secondary forests at Ban Tun are allowed to grow for 12, sometimes even 15 or 17 years, before they are cut. A casual observer would not hesitate to describe such a forest as 'natural'. A thorough analysis of 'mature' secondary forests reveals a remarkable complexity, not only in terms of species composition, but also in terms of stand structure. Secondary forests in the Lawa cultural landscape are often composed of three different layers:

o a top layer of scattered emergents with a height of 12 to 14m or more, and a stem diameter exceeding 12cm. These are the trees which have been spared in the clearing process;
o an upper storey of trees, which have developed from coppice shoots and root suckers, their height ranging from 6 to 10m, their diameter from 8 to 10cm;
o a lower storey of saplings, grown from seeds; and
o a herb layer, which is generally sparse, except in places where gaps have opened in the canopy; it consists of herbs, grasses, and tree seedlings.

These forests are also rich in species. In sample plots measuring 10m by 50m, I distinguished 25 to 30 different tree species in the upper storey alone. Some of the more common species are *Lithocarpus elegans*, *Castanopsis armata*, *Aporusa villosa*, *Schima wallichii*, *Glochidion sphaerogynum*, *Engelhardia spicata*, *Phyllanthus emblica*, *Dalbergia fusca*, *Eleocarpus floribundus*, *Anneslea fragrans* and *Wendlandia tinctoria*. It is difficult to specify the differences between these secondary stands and the original forest cover.

Stands of mature forest, which have been preserved by villagers for religious or conservation purposes, cannot serve as indicators of natural conditions, because they are usually located on ridges or hill-tops and are, therefore, unrepresentative of the forests on slopes, which have been transformed by swidden farming. Preservation, moreover, does not mean total protection. Stands are utilized for certain purposes, most importantly for forest grazing, and are, therefore, no longer natural forests, in the strict sense of the word.

The role of trees and forests in the Lawa cultural landscape

Through swiddening, the Lawa have achieved a thorough transformation of the environment within their realm. Nevertheless, the Lawa cultural landscape is remarkable for its close resemblance to a 'natural landscape', which is chiefly due to the fact that forests and trees constitute its most important elements. With the exception of irrigated land, the Lawa cultural landscape is a mosaic composed of woodlands in different stages of development: freshly cleared or cultivated swiddens with an open cover of scattered 'seed-trees', weed and scrub formations, secondary forests, and remnant stands of preserved and, presumably, primary forest.

The most important function of forests is to restore the fertility of the soil on swiddens after cultivation. Zinke *et al.* (1978) have demonstrated that nutrient levels can be restored after a fallow period of at least 10 years duration, during which a secondary forest is able to develop. The swidden-farming system of the Lawa is designed to keep the impact of cultivation on the soil at a minimum and to promote the rapid and unimpeded regeneration of the forest cover. Rapid forest regrowth is made feasible, chiefly, by a biological process of weed control

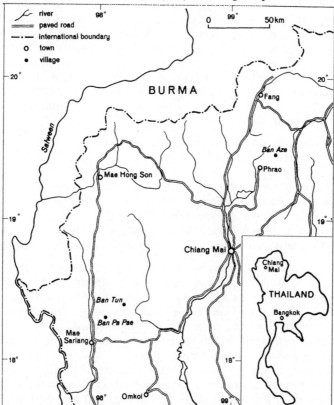

Lawa settlements in northern Thailand

in which the continuity of succession beyond the weed stage is broken by the emergence of coppice shoots and root suckers, which clear the ground for the establishment of seeds from trees on swiddens, or from adjacent forest fringes (*see* also Nakano, 1978).

Vegetation formations on fallow swiddens also provide a large number of plants, which are used for food, medicine, textile-making, ritual purposes, and fuel. Kunstadter counted a total of 204 uncultivated species of useful plants, which are collected on swiddens. He also argues that the complexity of the forest fallow environment as a whole, which consists of a number of diverse micro-environments, provides a greater variety of plants than would be available to the Lawa from an unaltered environment.

The Lawa cultural landscape retains trees and forests as an inherent component of the swidden-farming system. While the composition and structure of forests has been altered in the recurrent cycle of forest clearance and forest fallow, the same process initiates a series of different successional stages. The dynamics of Lawa swidden farming preserve, therefore, the physiognomy of a wooded landscape, altering the original forest cover but, at the same time, increasing the diversity of this landscape, both in terms of available plant species, as well as in terms of environments.[2]

6   Tree marriage in India

ROBERT PARKIN

THE MARRIAGE OF women to inanimate objects, or to men who immediately disappear from their lives, is well attested in South Asia, though it is a marginal practice and has not really been discussed in a comparative way. This is an attempt to set one particular example of this phenomenon, tree marriage, into its most probable cultural and historical contexts. The focus will be on possible linkages between ideas, and there will be no attempt to be exhaustive in uncovering ethnographic examples.

In *Homo Hierarchicus*, Dumont takes the view that 'marriages' to an inanimate object or some other symbolic husband stand for a woman's first marriage, which is ordinarily her most important in any group which has pretensions to status in India. Such 'marriages' give her the status of a married person, allowing her to conduct other unions which would otherwise be degrading. Thus in Nepal, Newar women may marry the fruit of a *bel* tree (*Aegle marmelos*), 'probably', says Dumont, 'to have unions with men of inferior status' (1972:161; also 1964:92ff.), although Greenwold reports (1981:97f.) that they can also be joined to men of higher status under certain conditions. Greenwold also points out that the practice enables the woman to avoid the normally inauspicious status of widowhood: any subsequent, 'real' husbands may predecease her, but her symbolic, first marriage ends only with her own death. Dumont mentions other examples, mostly from south India (1983:128–32). Before puberty, Devadesi girls marry a god, represented by his image or a sword, in order to be able to act as temple prostitutes later on. The term 'Basavi' is applied to girls of any caste who are married to a god in order to provide a son for their otherwise sonless fathers. In adopting the social role of a son, a girl inherits from her father and ensures the continuity of his line through her unions with other men.

The most famous example of a substitute marriage of this sort was provided by the Nayar of Kerala.[1] Before puberty, a woman in this low but not untouchable caste of Shudras would 'marry' a high-status Nambudiri Brahman in a *tali*-tying rite that he himself did not regard as a marriage.[2] He then disappeared from her life, though his eventual death would pollute her and her children, even though the latter were biologically all by other men. The purpose from the women's point of view was to be able to have unions subsequently, either with Nayar men, the paternity of the children being of no consequence in this extremely matrilineal society, or with other Nambudiri men who, unless eldest sons, could not marry in their own caste.[3] The women with whom Nambudiri men entered such unions were for them merely concubines, and their death did not pollute them. In entering such relationships they did not risk loss of status, as would have been the case had they married these women. One problem for the Nayar was to retain their children within the matrilineal *taravad* or extended family, despite giving their women, for reasons of status, to higher-status castes which were patrilineal. While they regarded unions at which the *tali* was tied as marriages and any issue from them as legitimate, the Nambudiri took the opposite view of both, being content to leave any issue with the Nayar rather than claim them as their own.

The device of marrying something symbolic is not limited to women in India: 'A Brahman may avoid the inauspiciousness of a third marriage by marrying the *arka* plant (*Calatropis* or *Ascelpis gigantea*), so that his real marriage will be the fourth' (Dumont, 1983, after Thurston). Similarly, O'Malley reports (1932:93): 'In Orissa, a widower may marry a widow in most castes; if a bachelor intends to do so, he is first married to a tree, which is cut down so as to make him symbolically a widower.' Bailey gives examples from 'clean' castes in highland Orissa, where the reason is to obviate the danger of disgrace should a pre-pubertal girl begin to menstruate while she is still living in her father's house (1957:68). The nature of the substitute 'husband' varies with the caste: among herdsmen, it is a sword, among warriors an old man (who receives a present but no rights over the girl), among Brahmans a prayer (*mantra*) – thus assumes Bailey), in this case, there is actually no symbolic husband, but simply the ritual. In Gujarat, the Kunbi marry a young girl to a bunch of flowers, which is then thrown in a well, or else to a man who immediately divorces her. In either case, she may marry later in the less regular form (Crooke 1906:317).[4]

The same rationale reappears in similar examples from Chhattisgarh and Orissa among both tribes and castes (Dube, 1953). Here, the general term for such marriages seems to be *kanda bara*, 'arrow marriage', although an arrow is not the only object used. A girl who began menstruating or who obtained sexual experience before this rite took place would be defiled: she would be debarred from taking part in most rituals and, subsequently, could not marry with full marriage rites, but only by elopement or so-called intrusion (forced entry into the home of a man she desires). To prevent these situations arising, she is married at the age of nine or ten to a token object, an arrow in the Chinda and Chaukhutia Bhunjia tribes, a branch of the *mohua* tree (*Bassia latifolia*) among the Raj Gond, or a wooden pestle used for paddy among Hindu castes (all non-Brahmin, Oriya-speaking). The ceremony is an abridged form of an ordinary wedding, without the normal engagement ceremony or gifts, but with all the other ceremonies, including walking around the wedding post; its status as the girl's primary marriage is indicated by its alternative name, 'first marriage'. A real or classificatory sister's husband acts for the groom and receives a gift of money or cloth at the girl's subsequent wedding, but it is the object that she marries. Both castes and tribes justify the holding of the ritual by referring to prescriptions laid down for them in a mythical past, by Hindu gods in the former case and by tribal culture heroes in the latter. Dube sees the rite as an alternative to child marriage, which none of these groups practise. More recently Good (1991) has discussed in detail south Indian examples of girls puberty rites which involve their 'marriage' to a female cross cousin or other relative – the 'female bridegroom' of his title.[5]

What unites these examples, apart from their nominal status as 'marriages', is their occurrence in social milieus that are sensitive to Hindu ideas of status through, and involving, marriage. Although not all of high status, these groups see marriage as important for both personhood and status and, like so many Hindu groups, marriage is one way in which they try to increase or at any rate maintain the latter. Marriage to inanimate objects, and even to men as substitute husbands, allows women to enjoy the full personhood that only a primary marriage can provide, while either devoting their procreative powers to other purposes than the interests of ordinary, mortal husbands (*see* again Dumont 1964:80ff.; 1972:Ch. 5, especially pp.156ff.), or simply avoiding possible inauspiciousness and permanent loss of status. Besides the danger to the girl herself, her father is disgraced if she becomes sexually mature without being married or at least betrothed, because he then becomes responsible for the monthly destruction of an egg, a potential life.

But these are not the only reasons for such 'marriages' in India. Lower down the hierarchy, among so-called 'tribal' groups, the practice may be linked instead either to increasing fertility, or to reincarnation in the form of the re-entry of soul substance into new members of the society (the latter might, of course, be seen as a special instance of the former). Reincarnation in India is usually associated with the Hindu doctrine of *karma*, in which it is regarded as an undesirable aspect of one's fate brought about by the sins one has committed in this and all previous existences. The very fact of reincarnation is inauspicious, since it indicates a failure to achieve *moksha* or liberation from the endless and painful cycle of rebirths and, therefore, to attain *nirvana*, the blessed state of nothingness. But tribal groups, even in the heart of India, have a different set of ideas which are to be seen not as a debased adoption of the Hindu version but as a self-sufficient ideology. In most such groups, there is a distinction between the personalized soul, which eventually joins the undifferentiated mass of ancestors, and soul substance, which is usually 'de-personalized' but which is reincarnated back into society. Here, reincarnation exists largely in a moral vacuum and, if anything, is to be desired, not avoided. Its absence threatens only those whose deaths were inauspicious (infants, tiger kills, suicides etc.), not those who have led bad lives. Of course, the karmic doctrine is capable of influencing tribals, so that morality may come to be a part of their version, but this is not essential, simply a historically contingent phenomenon.

This version of reincarnation can be connected with the kinship system. One normally derives one's soul substance from a recent ancestor, preferably a same-sex ancestor of the +2 generation in the direct line.[6] This is normally the case for the first-born child of each sex: other children may be the reincarnations of collateral kin of the +2 or +1 generations, but never of their parents, *i.e.* immediate ascendants. This is often associated with naming, which is divined at, or shortly after, birth, the name identifying the relative who has been reincarnated. Other aspects of the association of alternating generations, that this preference implies, are the contrast in stereotyped behaviour between sets of generations (formality or avoidance with members of adjacent generations, but familiarity and joking with members of one's own generation and of alternating generations); kinship terminology, in which the same terms are often repeated in alternating generations; and marriage options and preferences, which often specify a kin category, uniting referents in +2 and -2 as well as in ego's generation while banning relatives of all adjacent generations as marriage partners.[7] Among the Santal, this alternation is also evident in the mound of earth which is erected as a temporary altar as part of the final rite of purification in relation to the dead. Sal leaves (*Shorea robusta*) are planted in a row upon the altar, representing the Creator, followed by the mythical ancestral couple and the household god, then by three human beings, one from each of ego's set of alternate generations, grandmother, brother and grandson (Bouez, 1985:130–1).

In other words, reincarnation here is an aspect of a structure which unites and even identifies sets of alternating generations: +2, ego's and -2 form one set, which is opposed to that of +1 and -1 (and +3, -3 etc.). In a sense, there are only two generations, each being re-created continually. In its fullest form, this opposition is, perhaps, especially to be associated with systems of regular, symmetric, affinal alliance (or restricted exchange, bilateral cross-cousin marriage), as expressed especially by those two-line symmetric prescriptive terminologies that equate members of alternating generations. It is a pattern that can be identified world-wide, not only in Middle India, but also in the Amazon Basin, Australia, and parts of the Pacific (*see* Parkin, 1988 and 1992: Chs. 9–11).

This distribution is the basic reason for arguing for the independence of this ideological structure from the karmic doctrine in India. Being the local version of a global, though not universal, phenomenon, the idea of reincarnation among middle Indian tribes is not dependent on high-status ideology, even though it may borrow ideas from it. One can argue further, however, that historically the tribal version might actually have been an important source for the doctrine of *karma* when this was developed by speculative religious thinkers in post-Vedic times. Ideas of reincarnation appear to be absent from the Vedas, as well as (apart from the ancient Greek doctrine of the transmigration of souls) from beliefs in the Indo-European field, with which those of Vedic India have frequently been considered comparable (*cf.* Parkin, 1992:Ch. 11).

I shall be arguing later that there is a similar continuity between tree marriage and the practices of the caste society mentioned earlier. First, however, we must discuss the role of the former among tribal groups and see how it relates to the 'tribal' view of reincarnation. *Inter alia*, we shall see that the reincarnated soul substance does not necessarily enter its new human body directly on reincarnation.

The association of the dead with trees, through tree burial, symbolism and metaphors is reported from many parts of the world, such as Australia and Indonesia. Similar associations can also be found in central India, for example among the Juang (McDougal, 1963, p. 333) and Santal (Hodson, 1921b, pp. 212–13). Among the latter, the souls of the auspicious dead pass into mango or *mahua* trees (Hodson, 1921a:1–2). The connection with reincarnation is sometimes explicit, sometimes implied by the ethnography. For Hodson, reincarnation and marriage are bound up together in an interdependent spiral; marriages cannot take place while secondary mortuary rituals still have to be performed. But also, reincarnation originates with tree marriage, which Hodson calls 'a definite specific fertility rite to enable the wedded pair to produce a deceased ancestor whose spirit is associated with the trees. [. . .] The deceased ancestor comes to them from the storehouse where the discarnate spirits of the departed ancestors are lodged' (1921a, p. 2; b, p. 205). In other words, 'marriage rites are the positive means by which this succession of reincarnations is brought about' (ibid.:13) and they are 'meant to ensure the success of the marriage as a whole, that is, to secure the reincarnation of a deceased ancestor' (1921b, p. 208).[8] Among the related Munda, tree marriage is known as *uli sakhi*, literally 'mango namesake (or witness)' (Hodson, 1921a, p. 3), an expression which links the name of the tree with the practice of naming after the deceased and, through it, with reincarnation, a connection the Munda also make (*cf.* Parkin, 1992, p. 206). A Toda myth, collected in the Nilgiri Hills in Tamil Nadu by Zvelebil (1988, p. 157), is also relevant:

> There was once a man belonging to the Melgas clan who married a woman of Konos and took her to Melgas. When she became pregnant, he took her to Konos and, on their way back to Melgas, they passed the place where the funeral ceremonies of Melgas took place. They were standing in front of the funeral hut when the man found a twary tree, cut a few sticks from it, and brought them to his wife, who stripped the bark from them. While she was thus engaged, the pains of labour came on, and soon after she gave birth to a gourd. . . .

Out of shame, the couple cremated the gourd, which disintegrated; one of the pieces turned into a little boy.

Presler (1970, pp. 155–6), writing of north-east India, suggests that the soul of the deceased actually enters the tree, since the corpse is laid against its trunk or in its branches, a ritual specialist effecting its transfer into the tree. Here it remains until the wedding of the deceased's son, whereupon the son's bride is married to the tree, which gives up the soul within it to the bride. Thus, the father becomes the child of the son – the grandfather turns into his own grandson. Presler regards the bride's marriage to the groom as secondary in importance as well as in time. It is also antagonistic to pre-marital pregnancy, 'not from the standpoint of adultery, but because the offspring would contain an unidentified soul, an interloper, perhaps a demon'. Here we see again the avoidance of uncontrolled sexual activity by the girl, though the rationale is different. Presler concludes: 'Thus, the funeral ceremony, the marriage to the tree, the marriage to the human, and the birth of the offspring, are points on a circuit routing a departed soul back to the same family.' Although he does not distinguish between soul substance and personalized soul here, he mentions the latter in a further example, the Raj Gond of central India. They regard the *sal* tree as the permanent abode of ancestral souls, which the personalized souls of the deceased join. This is less often the case further east in middle India, where the personalized soul returns frequently, indeed, is led back to, the hearth of its old home (eg the Munda and Kharia, Parkin, 1992: 206, 210).

Marriage is used to ensure the effectiveness of many things in central Indian societies. Among the Ho, for example, not only people but also the gods, the sun and the moon – and even fishing nets and hunting weapons — are ritually 'married', otherwise they will be of no use. This is possible because many other natural objects, including all plant species, are thought to have gender. Before ploughing can begin, the sun is ritually married to the earth, whose coming of age is marked by the blossoming of *sal* trees each year. In this rite, the village priest takes the place of the sun, his wife that of the earth; only after it has taken place can humans marry (Majumdar, 1950:123).

Majumdar does not make it clear whether these non-human marriage partners have souls. This is the case among the Santal, where rice transplants are 'married' by the wives of the village to ensure the reincarnation of the *roa* or souls of the rice from season to season (Bouez, 1985:72–3). Finally, marriage, if not childbirth, is a vital step in achieving personhood, and is essential for full adult, indeed tribal and even human status, with the right to take part in *panchayat* discussions (Parkin, 1992:Ch. 2). In some cases, this seems to be connected with the ability to achieve the reincarnation of souls that are presently in limbo. Hodson reports (1921a:8): 'The Khonds hold that the power to re-enter the family at some future time is acquired only when the child has become an adult and has been married.' Another indication of this is the rule, among the War Khasi of north-east India, that a male ego must not marry his mother's brother's daughter while his maternal uncle is still alive, lest he die (Das Gupta, 1984:148). This may indicate reincarnation: his daughter's marriage would then be a preparation for his own rebirth, which necessitates his prior death. Although the War Khasi have a bilateral descent system, not matrilineal like other Khasi, this would still facilitate reincarnation in the direct line between ego and his daughter's son (not son's son, as among the patrilineally ordered societies of central India).

Acceptance of the Hindu karmic doctrine and its ethical component introduces a degree of uncertainty in the matter of the fate of one's soul substance. This uncertainty is not absent from the tribal version, where divination is regularly required to determine which ancestor has been reincarnated in a newborn child. But the options are, relatively, more limited than in higher-status groups, where the course of one's reincarnations depends on one's behaviour in all

Nature is Culture

previous lives, and has numerous possibilities in the range of creatures and plants that are potential destinations for one's soul.

Yet, as we have seen, the idea of tree marriage does not necessarily disappear with Hinduism, even though an analogue may be substituted for the tree itself. Hodson's statement (1921b:220 n.22), that in Hindu areas 'we do not get tree marriage, which is practised . . . where a deceased ancestor is to be reincarnated', is thus only partly true. Presler contends (1970:156 n.15) that the bride and groom's circulation of the 'marriage post' seven times in some high-status marriages is a continuation of the practice in another form. Hodson himself mentions (1921b:210f.) a case from Karnataka where, among some groups believing in the reincarnation of ancestors, with naming to suit, the bride and groom merely 'worship' the 'milk post'.

Actually, the co-occurrence of this practice with marriage to a symbolic groom in one of the rites mentioned by Dube indicates that the two are distinct. But, here too there is variation. Sanskritic law books prescribe circumambulation of the sacred fire by the bridal pair, a usage that has Vedic authority. This is not to say it is followed everywhere, however, nor that where it does exist it is an ancient practice. Kolenda (1984:106–7) calls many such examples 'Vedicizations,' which appear to draw on wedding manuals and films rather than directly on tradition for inspiration. The use of a 'milk post', rather than a fire, in many groups allows a little more confidence in suggesting a transition from the tribal to the caste version in the use of such symbols, one in which tree marriage becomes circumambulation of the 'milk post' or something similar. Only when special needs arise does the idea of a substitute groom enter the picture, supplementing – though not necessarily replacing – the other form.

It might be argued, therefore, that a certain structure is retained, if Presler is right that, in 'tribal marriages' as in Hindu caste marriages, it is the marriage to the tree that is primary in both chronology and status. Other common factors might be cited, such as the ritual construction of the person and ensuring the continuity of the group through the birth of new members, but these are common justifications for marriage generally. It is the specific purpose of such marriages that is altered with the acceptance of Hinduism, where it is retained at all. From being a standard event in the traverse of the soul from one, often alternate generation to another, it becomes an element of worship in an ordinary Hindu wedding and, in some cases, a special device for handling succession and/or sexuality where these are seen as being at least potentially problematic, ensuring that the personhood and status of the woman and her family in providing issue are not diminished.

As with reincarnation, therefore, it may be that upper-status groups have adopted and adapted an idea from lower down the hierarchy and applied it in accordance with their own values. And, as with reincarnation, this suggestion helps modify that school of thought which sees Hinduism as the only source of values throughout Indian society in the direction of allowing lower-status groups some independent values. Far from being debased versions of Hinduism, the values concerned most probably predate it by many centuries. The fact that the associations involved, between trees, the dead and reincarnation, can be found in other continents is again evidence that many ideas are not culture-specific but replicated in parts of the world immune, until very recently, from mutual influences by the wide distances that separate them. To put it bluntly, Hinduism can explain nothing among tribal groups outside India. Can it always, therefore, explain ideas and complexes of ideas among similar groups within India itself? Or is it not sometimes the heir to them?

7 The influence of religious beliefs and rituals on forest conservation in Nepal

ANDREW W. INGLES[1]

'It is a truism worth reiterating that the world-view of a society is what moulds its attitude toward, and its actions upon, its surroundings.'

(Gyawali, 1989a)

FORESTS IN NEPAL are affected directly by the collection of a wide range of forest products used in the performance of religious rituals, and by harvesting for material inputs to community development and charitable activities undertaken to obtain religious merit. Forests are also affected by activities such as tree worship, the establishment and maintenance of sacred sites in forests, religious festivals and rituals conducted within forests, and the management of forests as productive assets by religious organizations.

In this chapter, the influence of religious beliefs and practices on forest conservation is judged by considering in detail the management and condition of religious forests. The influence of such beliefs and practices should be at a maximum within forests dedicated for religious purposes, hence the results achieved in religious forests are pertinent to judging the utility of religious beliefs on nature conservation in general.

For our purposes, religious forests – *dharmic ban* – are defined as shrublands or forests, larger than 0.1ha, where management is associated with the performance of religious rituals at a sacred site. This includes forests that contain a sacred site, such as the abode of a supernatural being, and forests that do not contain a sacred site but are predominantly managed to provide the resources required for the performance of religious rituals at a sacred site located elsewhere. An example of this second group is a forest managed specifically for the provision of fuelwood for funeral pyres.

Religion in Nepal

In the 1981 census, about 90 per cent of the population stated they were adherents of the Hindu religion. The next largest group said they were Buddhists (5 per cent), followed by Muslims (2 per cent) and other groups such as Jains, Christians and animists (Gyawali 1989a; citing Central Bureau of Statistics 1986). However, it should be noted that the statistics on religion may not be a true representation of the situation. Hinduism is the state religion and Hindus dominate national politics and state administration. These factors may encourage the Nepalese to describe their religious beliefs to officialdom as Hinduism. In addition, a major feature of religion in Nepal is the relative lack of dogma and specific definitions about the supernatural world within Hinduism and Buddhism, compared with religions such as Islam and Christianity (*see* Rieffel, 1987). The adoption of popular Hindu cults by Buddhists may lead to the inclusion of many socio-religious groups within Hinduism, whilst not Hindu in a strict sense (Pant, 1993). Such factors result in a blurring of the boundaries between the practice of both Hinduism and Buddhism.

Perceptions of the environment and conservation ethics

Both Hinduism and Buddhism depict a world inhabited by countless supernatural beings who play various roles of destruction, protection, and creation
and, therefore, wield, or are a part of, the forces of nature. Societies holding
these religious views relate to the environment by focusing on supernatural
explanations of natural processes and events and by directly associating particular elements of the environment with the spiritual world (*see* for example Berreman, 1972; Shepherd, 1982; Bjønness, 1986; Seeland, 1986; Majupuria and Joshi,
1988; Gyawali, 1989a; Cox, 1989).

Gyawali (1989a) classified the traditional Nepali world-view as 'oriental', to
distinguish it from the more pragmatic 'occidental', or western, world-view. He
suggested that the major difference between the two is that the first places a
higher value on mastering the spiritual world, whereas the second promotes
modification of the environment to suit human-needs.

Those with an oriental view of the world may hold, at the same time, another
view which is more observant, experienced, and practical. In a study of the
Nepalese Sherpas, the existence of a dualistic world-view meant that the Sherpas
were prepared to discuss, and attempt to minimize, certain environmental hazards in both a religious and practical sense (Bjønness, 1986). Gyawali, (1989a)
also noted that two types of world-view exist in Nepal, although traditionally, the
'oriental' type has played a dominant role in determining the way Nepalese
people relate to the environment.

S. Singh (1986) attributed the origin of a conservation ethic in the Indian sub-
continent to the teachings of Hinduism and Buddhism. He drew attention to the
fact that India both enacted the world's first recorded conservation measures
during the third century BC, and is one of the few countries in the world whose
constitution makes special reference to protecting the natural environment.

Majupuria and Joshi, (1988), Bahl, (1979) and Bahuguna, (1988) have all
provided explanations of why nature is revered in Nepal and India. The natural
environment sustains life; plants provide food and medicines for humans; trees
and forests provide settings conducive to making sound judgements, contemplat-
ing the universe, or achieving enlightenment (as they did for Buddha); certain
flowers and trees provide supernatural beings with abodes, resting places, and
food; and the vegetation protects the land. These attributes are referred to in
Hindu and Buddhist teachings and give rise to sacred plants and animals and
rituals concerned with the worship of nature (*see* Majupuria and Joshi, 1988).

Whether religious teachings about the environment, the existence of sacred
species, or the rhetoric of the constitution of India, prove that a conservation
ethic is prevalent in the Indian region is debatable. India's environment has been
altered substantially by its tremendous human and livestock populations, and its
national programmes for nature conservation have been deficient in both scale
and coverage, and have been characterized by inadequate planning and slow
progress in implementation (S. Singh, 1986). The same can be said of Nepal.

Stracey (1979) believed that the alleged presence of a conservation ethic among
the forest dwellers, urban dwellers and forest contractors of modern India is a myth.
He dismissed as wishful thinking the contribution of sacred groves and nature
worship to nature conservation. S.K. Jain (1979) postulated that conservation of
nature, on religious grounds, has dwindled greatly in recent history and
Chandrakanth *et al.* (1990) agreed, by suggesting that taboos on cutting religious

trees became less effective after the early 1960s when shortages in tree products became common.

On the other hand, a number of authors have documented cases where local people have claimed to have been moved by a conservation ethic, based on religious principles, to protest against environmental exploitation by the state. A widely-cited example concerns the Bishnoi sect of west-central India. Although there is some confusion regarding the year of the event, (probably 1731), it is reported that 363 members of this Hindu sect died while attempting to stop the troops of a local Maharaja from cutting down a grove of trees near Jodhpur in Rajasthan, because it conflicted with their religious beliefs (S. Singh, 1986; Bahuguna, 1988). Fisher (1988b) argued there is evidence the sect may have used conservation issues as a focus for their political resistance to the Rajput rulers. He also argued that the caste cohesion of the Bishnois, useful politically, is largely a result of their religious identity, and this is heavily grounded in a conservation ethic.

Another example of environmental protest is documented by Guha (1988 and 1989). About 100 years ago, the local inhabitants of Kumaun in the central Himalayas waged a long campaign of civil disobedience because of the exploitation of both human and forest resources by the British. In this case, the political objectives are more obvious than the environmental objectives.

More recently, the *Chipko* movement in northern India has received world-wide attention as a significant factor in the protection of India's forests (Jirn, 1984, Bahuguna 1986 and 1988). The roots of this movement, which derives its name from the act of hugging trees to prevent tree-felling by contractors, are attributed to the world-views and values of both the followers of Mahatma Gandhi's disciple, Vinoba Bhave, and the villagers in Uttar Pradesh who were directly affected by government forest policy of the 1970s (Jain, 1984). Again, the *Chipko* protests achieved political goals, but it is interesting to note that the movement has spread during the last two decades through the use of religious teachings concerning the environment.

It appears that India's traditional, socially shared world-views have had some role in promoting a conservation ethic, even if it has not been shown that such an ethic has been adopted widely and maintained. Several authors have written about the decline in traditional values resulting from the increasing influence of culture on the populations of south Asian countries (Singh, 1983, Harrison 1984, HMG Nepal 1988, Singh, 1989, Dixit, 1989); while the National Conservation Strategy for Nepal (HMG Nepal, 1988) identifies the introduction of western culture and lifestyles, through the media and tourism, as a constraint to conserving Nepal's cultural heritage, which includes sacred sites and religious forests. Unfortunately, the magnitude of the impact of western culture on Nepalese society, including the rate at which traditional values are declining, is unknown.

Despite the erosion of these traditional perceptions, it is still possible to explore the conservation significance of socially shared world-views and values by looking at how the religious rituals performed today influence forest use and management in Nepal.

Dharma, and the Hindu and Buddhist pantheons

To understand why people perform religious rituals, one must define the concept of *dharma*, which is the basic value system of traditional Nepalese society.

Dharma is often mis-translated as 'religion'. Instead, it implies a correct life-style, or living in harmony with one's nature in a world of perpetual change,

'. . . a lifestyle in harmony in the three spheres: the philosophical, the social and the environmental' (Gyawali, 1987).

Nepalese society places a high value on *dharma*. People can observe their *dharma* by performing and participating in religious rituals, and by undertaking social activities to gain religious merit (*see* Berreman, 1972; MacFarlane, 1976; N.N. Singh, 1983). The majority of religious rituals are recurrent ceremonies which occur either daily; periodically, according to an annual programme of festivals; or occasionally, when a change in the status of an individual must be observed. During such ceremonies, one or more deities are worshipped using actions and products prescribed by religious texts, religious specialists, and local tradition.

The Hindu and Buddhist pantheons include a huge number of different deities. There are tens of thousands of different gods and goddesses worshipped at the household, family, village, regional, and national level. Many of the major deities have a number of different forms, each requiring ritual worship at different times and in different ways (*see* Deep, 1982). Some deities have influence in particular spheres, such as education, the acquisition of wealth, agriculture, the occurrence of earthquakes and landslides, rainfall, forest growth, famine and disease. Others can cause a range of problems for villages, families or individuals if they are offended in any way.

Tree worship and religious forests

In Hindu theology, specific plant and tree species are deemed to be incarnations, or symbols, of deities and other supernatural forces, and must be worshipped. Majupuria and Joshi, (1988), and Chandrakanth *et al.*, (1990) list those species that are worshipped in Nepal and India as representations of deities, stars, planets, and the zodiac. Some such as *Ficus religiosa*, are widespread, well-known and widely worshipped, whereas other species are not. It has been argued that the reverence towards these species is strengthened by the fact that most feature in the great Hindu legends; their flowers, fruits, and foliage are used in a number of religious rituals; and various parts of the trees are believed to have great medicinal value (Majupuria and Joshi, 1988).

In India, the most common forms of tree worship involve *Ficus religiosa*, *Acacia ferruginea*, *Aegle marmelos*, and *Ficus glomerata* (Chandrakanth *et al.*, 1990). In Nepal, the following tree species are worshipped: *Ficus religiosa*, *Ficus bengalensis*, *Aegle marmelos*, *Mangifera indica*, *Phyllanthus emblica*, *Elaeocarpus spp.*, *Saraca indica*, *Butea monosperma*, *Shorea robusta*, and *Anthocephalus cadamba* (Majupuria and Joshi, 1988). Some of these are worshipped by specific groups of people. For example, *Elaeocarpus spp.* is worshipped by many mystics (Majupuria and Joshi 1988), and *Anthocephalus cadamba* is worshipped by the Dhangar people (Bista, 1987). The first five species listed above, however, are worshipped widely. *Ficus religiosa* has widespread popularity as a sacred tree, and is worshipped by Buddhists as well as Hindus. Because Buddha's enlightenment is believed to have occurred under one of these trees, it has been adopted by Buddhism as the specific symbol of that event (Mansberger, 1988).

How trees are worshipped depends on the age and sex of the worshipper, and the form of the ritual is prescribed by magico-religious specialists (*see* Chandrakanth *et al.* 1990). The act of planting a sacred tree species is also a form of worship, and a method of attaining religious merit. Religious merit can be attained also by building a temple (N.N.Singh, 1983), a rest-house for pilgrims (*see*, for example, Gyawali, 1989b), or some other public facility such as a water tap, resting place, or footpath (*see* Fürer-Haimendorf, 1981; D.K. Gurung, 1987); erecting memorials for dead relatives (*see* Bista, 1987; Fürer-Haimendorf, 1975); donating land to a religious institution (*see* Regmi, 1978); donating land for public grazing (Dhungel, 1987); planting a tree at a water source (*see* Acharya, 1984; D.K. Gurung, 1987); establishing a religious forest (Chandrakanth *et al.*, 1990); making donations of food or money to holy men (MacFarlane, 1976); undertaking a pilgrimage to an important sacred site (Messerschmidt, 1989b); or renouncing physical possessions and living the life of a mystic (*see* for example Berreman, 1972; Shepherd, 1982).

In some places, tree marriage is practised. This involves the symbolic marriage of one tree to another. A common tree-marriage ceremony involves the marriage of a *Ficus religiosa* tree to a nearby *Ocimum sanctum* plant (Majupuria and Joshi, 1988), or to a *Azadirachta indica* tree (Chandrakanth *et al.*, 1990). Tree worship has resulted in the spread of sacred tree species across the landscape, as people have planted and protected them for the performance of religious rituals. A detailed description of the spread of *Ficus religiosa* is given by Mansberger, (1988). The other result of tree worship has been the establishment and management of religious forests, also known as sacred groves and temple forests.

'Many religious performances and rituals are locally conducted in the forests. Particularly, the lineage god, the forest god, and certain evil spirits are worshipped in the forests throughout the hill regions of Nepal' (Acharya, 1984).

Many rituals take place within forests, giving rise to the establishment of religious trees and forests, and the institutions and organizations concerned with their protection and management. Religious trees and forests are identifiable entities in Nepal's rural landscape, and range from several trees to an extensive area of forested land (*see* Ingles, 1990).

In addition to the establishment of religious forests, tree worship and the performance of other recurrent rituals create demands for forest products.

Consumption of forest products

Most of the caste and ethnic groups of Nepal cremate their dead in a prescribed manner (*see* Bista, 1987), consuming a great deal of fuelwood each year. In some parts of the country, communities have attempted to reduce the quantity of fuelwood consumed by constructing fuel-efficient fireplaces. Many of the important lifecycle rituals and religious festivals involve feasting and, for many ethnic groups, consuming large quantities of alcohol. Fuelwood is used to cook food for participants, and to make alcoholic drinks. Fox, (1984) reported that Newars used more fuelwood than other castes, because of the need to make alcohol for festivals and it is known that Newars observe a greater number of festivals than any other group (Bista, 1987).

The performance of religious rituals and the attainment of religious merit also involves the construction of temples, monasteries, rest-houses for pilgrims, schools, and houses for people in desperate need of charity. The construction and maintenance of such buildings is likely to consume significant quantities of construction timber, although estimates of annual consumption for these purposes are unavailable.

A number of other forest products are used in the performance of religious rituals. Majupuria and Joshi, (1988) provided a detailed list of the types of bark, flowers, leaves, and fruit used in worship and folk medicine; the number of species involved is substantial. At high altitudes, some timber poles are required, usually of *Abies spectabilis*, to affix prayer flags, and *Juniperus recurva* wood is used to make incense (Schmidt-Vogt, 1988).

Nepalese religious beliefs and practices have created extra demands on natural resources such as fuelwood and fodder, therefore, which, in turn, influence land-use decisions. Bajracharya (1983) pointed out that the caste and ethnic groups in his study area believed that family deities reside in household hearths and, as a result, are less inclined to install fuel-efficient stoves. With regard to fodder, there was a widely held view that the livestock population in the Indian sub-continent had reached an alarming size because the cow is sacred and the herd is not managed rationally. Recently, studies have shown that this is no longer a valid argument (*see*, for example, Blaikie, 1985; Ives and Messerli 1989). But a high-caste Hindu must have access to cows' milk, urine, and dung in order to perform many of the prescribed rituals (Uprety, 1986).

Throughout Nepal, organizations exist for the purposes of funding and organizing either an important religious festival in a particular area, or a lifecycle ceremony for one of its members. Many of these are modeled on the *guthi* system. A *guthi* is a common trust, consisting of assets and an organization charged with managing the resources of the *guthi* to provide the goods and services required for supporting a particular ritual (*see* Bista, 1987). There are religious *guthis* for worshipping a particular deity during festivals; functional *guthis* for conducting funerals and maintaining public places; and social *guthis* for organizing parties and other forms of entertainment (Uprety, 1986).

The performance of religious rituals gives rise, therefore, to institutions and practices with the potential to create both positive and negative impacts on forests. On the one hand, tree worship, tree planting, the protection of forests containing sacred sites, and the social structures created to manage religious forests, can contribute to forest conservation, and yet the use of a wide range of forest products for religious purposes adds to the harvesting pressure.

The management and condition of religious forests

A primary objective of managing religious forests is to provide a sacred landscape dedicated to the worship of a supernatural being. To facilitate worship, a number of developments, such as temples, rest-houses and paths, may be established inside or adjacent to the forest. Establishing and maintaining these facilities involves, among other things, raising funds and locating building materials such as timber. In addition, a number of the activities conducted in these forests consume forest products, such as cooking food during religious festivals. As a result, a secondary management objective for many religious forests is to provide resources for religious rituals and developments at the sacred site. The primary and secondary objectives are related, and they arise because of the presence of a sacred site and the traditional performance of religious rituals at that site (Ingles, 1990).

On the other hand, there are religious forests that do not have a sacred site. The allocation of management objectives to these forests occurs through a decision-making process which is not influenced by the traditions associated with the presence of a sacred site. Instead, they are influenced by the need to supply particular forest products, which are used directly, or sold to raise funds. The first type of forest gains its management objectives and religious status, therefore, from the presence of a sacred site, while the second gains them from the fact that a decision has been made to sponsor religious rituals and sacred sites using the forest as an asset.

Several other forest-management objectives are shared by both types of religious forests. Providing timber to charitable causes and to schools is one example; as far as it is compatible with other objectives, the forests are treated as reserves of products for assisting in the provision of social services, such as building an orphanage.

Institutionalized rules and organizations

Institutionalized rules governing resource-use are believed to be fundamental to the existence of a local system of managing a forest as common property (Fisher, 1989). Case studies show that each of the religious forests studied in detail operated a set of institutionalized rules, and many also had some form of organization supporting forest management (*see* Acharya, 1984; Messerschmidt, 1986 and 1987; Jackson, 1987; Anon, 1987; Ingles, 1988 and 1990; Gilmour, 1988; Fisher *et. al.*, 1989; Gyawali, 1989b; H. Singh, 1989a and 1989b).

It is necessary to explain the terms institution and organization. They are often used interchangeably, creating ambiguity and confusion. Uphoff, (1986) described institutions as 'complexes of norms and behaviours that persist over time by serving collectively valued purposes', whereas organizations are 'structures of recognized and accepted roles'. This is a useful distinction for discussing local systems of forest management, as it separates the locally agreed rules about forest access and use (institutions), from the roles that may be established from time to time to achieve specific objectives (organizations).

Rules prohibiting the harvesting of products from the overstorey of religious forests are more common than rules prohibiting the harvest of products from the understorey. In a survey of 26 forests, felling and pruning trees was prohibited in 81 per cent and 73 per cent, respectively (Ingles, 1990). In contrast, collecting dry firewood, cutting fodder, and collecting dead leaf-material was prohibited in only 4 per cent, 23 per cent and 12 per cent, respectively. In addition, the results showed that, even when the harvest of products from the understorey was prohibited, these rules were not complied with to the same extent as rules about protecting the overstorey.

There are two possible explanations for this, and both may apply. As discussed above, trees of particular species are worshipped, deities are believed to reside in trees and forests, forests are revered in Hindu and Buddhist theologies, and forests are good environments for making sound judgements and for enjoying religious festivals. All of these factors focus attention on the trees. An understorey may not be a necessary element of a sacred landscape. If this is correct, and a fodder and fuelwood shortage exists, trees will be protected and the understorey will be harvested. Fodder availability has became a major problem for farmers in many districts in Nepal (*see* MacFarlane, 1976; Uprety, 1986; Robinson, 1987; Mahat *et al.*, 1987; Dhungel, 1987; Upreti *et al.*, 1989; Riley *et al.*, 1989; Schreir *et al.*, 1989). It may be possible therefore, for farmers to forgo the timber and wood products tied up in the overstorey of religious forests, but it may be difficult for them to forgo the fodder produced in the understoreys.

The existence of a forest watcher, who is paid in grain contributed by each household to enforce the agreed rules, represents a recognized and accepted role in forest management. There are also roles for making and implementing decisions about sanctions, product distribution, finances and developing facilities.

These are carried out by one or more of the following: a priest, a community leader, or a committee.

These examples show that the social arrangements for managing religious forests conform to Fisher's description of the characteristics of local systems for managing forests as common property. The existence of a set of institutionalized rules is the basic element of the management system and, in some cases, organizational structures are built upon the institutionalized rules. Differences between the systems for managing religious forests, as compared to other forests managed as common property, occur in the specific management objectives adopted by the user group; in the involvement of a priest in many of the organizational roles; in the establishment of temples and recreational facilities in the forest; and in the practice of including the forest in a *guthi* (common trust).

Size and condition of religious forests

Most of the religious forests described are small (*see*, for example, Acharya, 1984; Mahat *et al.*, 1986; Anon., 1987; Jackson, 1987; Ingles, 1988 and 1990; Fisher *et al.*, 1989; H. Singh, 1989a and 1989b; Messerschmidt, 1989a). In the 26-forest survey 65 per cent were found to be 1ha or smaller, with only 8 per cent larger than 4ha (Ingles, 1990). In Nepal, it is possible that the expansion of the agricultural land-base has occurred at the expense of forested land at the periphery of a sacred site. Where the ratio of forested land to agricultural land is critically low, it is possible that only the core area (surrounding the sacred site) of a larger forest can be allocated as a religious forest, because the remainder is required for domestic use. At a famous and popular site containing a deity of major significance, however, a larger area may be required to cater for the demands of visitors and the desires of a powerful god or goddess. One such example is Dakshinkali, south of Kathmandu, where the religious forest covers 30ha. The size of a religious forest might depend on the popularity of the site, the significance or status of the deity, the number and size of sacred sites contained in the forest, and the local ratio of forested land to agricultural land.

Many of Nepal's religious forests are open in structure, both in the overstorey and understorey, without a well-established pool of regeneration (*see* for example V.S. Shrestha, 1984; A.M. Shrestha and R.B. Shrestha, 1988; Ingles, 1988 and 1990; Fisher *et. al.*, 1989). Other religious forests are known once to have been degraded shrublands, and have since regenerated to closed forests after either strong protection measures, or reforestation (*see* for example Jackson, 1987; Ingles, 1988 and 1990; H. Singh, 1989b). Religious forests may go through cycles of decline and regrowth because the emphasis on protecting trees rather than protecting the understorey prevents the development of an uneven-age class structure that could provide for the maintenance of a dense overstorey (*see* Fisher *et al.*, 1989; Ingles, 1990). Aiming to maintain a sacred landscape of trees may ensure that, at some stage, the decline is halted by a change in the institutionalized aiming at restocking the area with trees.

Religious forests have a spiritual value, by making a connection through trees and forests between worshippers and the supernatural world. Religious forests also have recreational and aesthetic value because people go to them to observe and enjoy religious festivals. They have an educational value because their presence can reinforce the messages about conservation and respect for nature provided by the teachings of Hinduism and Buddhism. The 1988 National Conservation Strategy for Nepal identifies the archaeological and historical values of religious forests, especially those located at long-established sacred sites of international significance, such as at Pashupatinath near Kathmandu.

Clearly, religious forests are part of the cultural heritage of Nepal and provide important sites for spiritual and recreational enjoyment. The cultural value of particular religious forests can be significant at one or more of the following levels; local, regional, national, and international. It is likely, therefore, that religious forests are important to forest conservation in a symbolic sense. Religious forests are necessary for observing a traditional lifestyle. Much of the social life of village Nepal occurs in and around religious forests. Even urban Nepalese visit religious forests. Generally speaking, this means that religious forests are encountered by Nepalese youth and play some role in their education. The presence of religious forests in the landscape provides a reminder of the conservation messages in Hinduism and Buddhism and of the beauty and environmental benefits of forests. However, the effectiveness of this symbolism in promoting conservation ethics is under threat from the increasing influence of Western culture on the Nepalese population.

Some authors have written about the positive value of religious forests in conservation and environmental protection (*see* Gadgil, 1987; Guha, 1989; Chandrakanth *et al.*, 1990). But is the protection and management of religious forests important to forest conservation in Nepal? This question can be addressed by considering two separate questions:

○ How do religious forests contribute to the conservation of biological resources and the protection of forest soils?
○ How can the local systems of managing religious forests be utilized in rural development programmes that further the conservation of forests?

It has been shown that religious forests are part of the forest resource that underpins the subsistence-oriented farming systems of Nepal (Ingles, 1990). Religious forests provide a wide range of forest products for both domestic and ritual purposes. As a result, religious forests are not sacrosanct. Some religious forests do not have a sacred site, and such forests are often managed primarily to provide forest products for religious rituals, the development of sacred sites, community development, and to support the disadvantaged. Religious forests are exploited for forest products and many have suffered significant modification, especially in the understorey. In addition, most religious forests in Nepal are small, and are not established or managed for the purposes of conserving biodiversity or preventing soil erosion. It appears that forest protection is focused mainly on mature trees and on the core areas surrounding sacred sites. Understorey and ground-cover species seem to gain little benefit from being located in a religious forest. The poor condition of the understoreys in many of the forests described in the literature, also suggests that soils could be subject to accelerated surface erosion.

If a religious forest covers a relatively large area and has been established for a long time in a region that has been modified greatly by people and livestock, it could constitute an important reserve of the natural vegetation, and could play a role in the conservation of species (*see* for example Gadgil, 1987; Dove and Rao, 1986). In this case, the benefit is probably unintentional, and such situations seem to be rare. For the handful of plant species that are worshipped as sacred species, there is no doubt that their conservation has been assisted by the deliberate proliferation and protection in the landscape for religious purposes.

However, it appears that the direct contribution of religious forests to biological conservation and the protection of forest soils is insignificant in Nepal. On the other hand, the local systems for managing religious forests contribute to forest conservation because they represent the social capacity for managing resources as common property. Current strategies for promoting forest conservation and development in Nepal involve providing external assistance to groups of local people for establishing new forests or managing existing forests as common property. The key elements in making this strategy work are finding the right people and providing the right assistance. The programme must find a workable user group, the benefits of the programme must suit the needs of this group, and its operation must match the individuals' institutional and organizational capacity (*see* Fisher, 1988a and 1989; Jackson and Maharjan, 1988; Fisher *et al.*, 1989).

The existing institutions and organizations for managing both the performance of religious rituals and religious forests provide entry points for implementing community forestry. For example, local people may be interested in creating or improving a religious forest, or they may wish to expand a religious forest under the provisions of a community forestry programme. The user group of a religious forest may wish to establish a new forest as an asset to fund the maintenance or development of a sacred site, or to provide products for the performance of religious rituals. In this case, the needs, and the institutional and organizational capacity of the group can be determined by looking at what social arrangements exist already for managing the religious forest.

The use of religious organizations and forests as entry points for community forestry may have a number of distinct advantages. Compared to the management of other forests, religious forests may be relatively free of conflict. The model of a religious forest that supplies funeral-wood, timber for schools and charities, and fuelwood for festivals and life-cycle rituals could be promoted to great effect. It could have widespread appeal because of the notions of religious merit, and maintaining harmony with the supernatural world, and because it could take the pressure off private resources. Clearly, the benefits of such a forest contribute to the social and spiritual well-being of the village, rather than to the material wealth of an individual. For this reason, it may provide a starting point for community action in an area where user groups have little confidence, and where there is little consensus and co-operation in other resource-management activities.

8 The Huaorani and their trees: managing and imagining the Ecuadorian rainforest

LAURA RIVAL

THE HUAORANI INDIANS of Amazonian Ecuador are, first and foremost, forest people. Their social life, knowledge of the world, and cultural understanding are all, in one form or another, inspired by plant-life which, to them, represents the life-force and energy by which organisms, including humans, are born, grow, mature, and go on living. Because they grow much higher and live much longer than humans, trees are considered the epitome of plant-life. Most of the Huaorani's food (fruit and game) and material culture (houses, weapons, baby slings, and cooking-ware) derive from trees. The Huaorani are, therefore, acutely aware of their unique identity as forest dwellers, especially today when their land is being invaded by oil companies, white settlers, and riverine Indians, who are not only transforming the forest through their economic activities and cultural values, but are also using the environment in ways which appear alien.

The Huaorani in their forested environment

Although their ethnohistory is little known, the Huaorani can fairly confidently be said to have lived in the hinterland area lying between the Napo, the Arajuno, and the Curaray rivers for many centuries (*see* Rival, 1992).

Their homeland is characteristic of much of western Amazonia where, given the relatively high rainfall averages (around 3000mm a year), seasons are almost non-existent. Their tribal territory, criss-crossed by hundreds of small tributaries, and covered with hills ranging from 400m above sea level (in the western part) to 200m above sea level (in the eastern part, near the border with Peru), constitutes a rugged landscape where the diversity of native palms (Balslev and Barford, 1987), and the density of bird pollinators (Prance, personal communication) are higher than in other parts of the Amazon. Attempts to protect this unique regional biodiversity led to the creation, in 1979, of the Yasuní National Park forest reserve. Located in the north-eastern part of the Huaorani's traditional territory, the Yasuní National Park was declared a biosphere reserve for humanity by UNESCO in 1987, and soon after, was made a world centre for plant diversity and endemism under the Joint IUCN-WWF Plant-Conservation Programme and the IUCN Threatened Plants Unit.

Like the rest of the 'Oriente' (the local name for the Amazon region of Ecuador which represents half of the national territory), the Huaorani territory, rich in petrol, is economically integrated in the vast industrial complex that produces 90 per cent of the country's oil, and generates over 60 per cent of Ecuador's wealth. Although less than 25 years old, this large-scale industrial development has led to the irreversible transformation of the northern part of the Oriente. Large areas are now colonized by white and indigenous settlers who work in the oil industry and have established cattle ranches, coffee plantations, and numerous garden plots to feed the Oriente's growing population. This wave of colonization has led to the deforestation of large tracts of land right at the heart of the traditional Huaorani land, around the Tiputini river (see map).

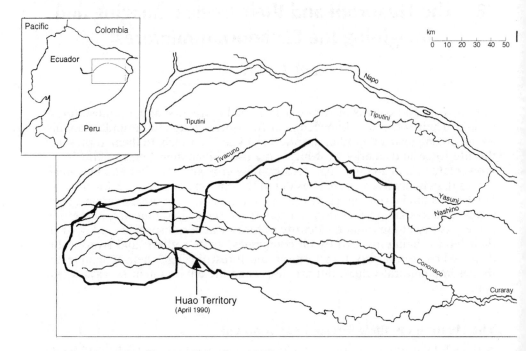

Map 1: *Huao Territory in Ecuador, 1990.*

Fierce isolationists, until recently the Huaorani have avoided contact with outsiders, killing, or fleeing, from trespassers. Although it is difficult to establish whether their autarchic behaviour pre-dates the horrors of the rubber boom, their decision to live away from main rivers and avoid all forms of social contact with non-Huaorani is undoubtedly an ancient one. Today, one (possibly two) sub-groups are still protecting their complete isolation by hiding, moving constantly, and killing those who attempt to pacify them. This extreme limitation of social contacts has led to the formation of a particularly closed and endogamous society.

The extended family-group (*nanicabo*), which forms the basic social unit, usually occupies a longhouse, made of a thatched palm roof extended to the ground. There are usually between 10 and 35 residents – typically an older polygynous couple, their married daughters, husbands and children, and any unmarried children. Ideally, marriage should take place between the children of a sister and her real or classificatory brother. These residential units, although autonomous and dispersed over a relatively big area, are not fully independent of each other. In fact, the Huaorani territory can be imagined as a polarized field in which cohesive nexi formed by two or three allied longhouses maintaining close relations through marriage, form antagonistic poles. In other words, these inter-marrying longhouses are organized in regional groups, the 'we-people' (*huaomoni*) groups. The *huaomoni* groups strive to preserve their endogamous independence through sustained and controlled hostility towards all other groups, considered enemies, and called 'others' (*huarani*). This system of polarized regional groups, separated by large stretches of unoccupied forest, has allowed a fairly small number of Huaorani to control and defend a relatively large territory (22 000km²) with efficacy. In fact, it was not until the late 1950s, when North American missionary pilots flew slowly at low altitude over the area, that the reduced size of the Huaorani population (there were only about 500 in the early 1960s) and the degree of dispersion were recognized.

The Huaorani are, to this day, greatly stigmatized and discriminated against. They are still looked down upon as 'savage killers', 'fierce and ignorant', and 'pagans and uncivilized'. What is seen as their 'backwardness' is often considered a national embarrassment, even though a minority of Ecuadorians regard these 'last stone-age people' with Rousseauian romanticism (Rival, 1994). Even for Christianized Indians such as the Shuar or the Quechua, the Huaorani are still 'savages'. They consider the Huaorani immoral and wild for living deep in the forest and prefering hunting and gathering to gardening (Rival, 1993). Although the Quechua and Shuar Indians live in the forest (albeit usually along river-banks and/or roads leading to jungle towns), they do not consider themselves silvan populations. For them, people of the forest are necessarily sub-human, for *they do not grow garden crops, but feed on forest produce.* There is, in their view, a direct connection between the Huaorani's foraging activities, their lack of horticulture, and their rejection of inter-ethnic contact and social exchange.[1]

The Huaorani have always cultivated manioc incipiently for their marriage ceremonies. Now living, for the most part, in sedentarized villages, they grow manioc on a larger scale and eat it every day; but they are not, by any standards, horticulturists. Incipient horticulture, nomadism, and dispersed habitat are not, however, signs of underdevelopment; on the contrary, they point to an elaborate form of forest management in which trees are more valued than short-lived crops such as manioc. Huaorani reliance on slow-growing, perennial plants – trees – corresponds to a social life in which sharing, not exchange, is the rule, and to a world view that considers the continuity of life – both organic and social – to be embodied in trees.

At the beginning of time, the world was a giant tree

The centrality of trees to Huaorani social life and mythology is well-illustrated by the myth of origin, which develops around the giant ceibo tree, *bobehuè* (*Ceiba pentandra*). The giant ceibo tree is said to have contained all forms of life:

In the beginnings of time, the earth was flat, there were no forests, no hills. The earth was like a dried, barren, and endless beach, stranded at the foot of a giant ceibo tree. This tree, attached to heaven by a strong vine, was the only source of shade against the strong sun. Only seedlings under its direct protec-tive shade could escape from the merciless heat of the sun; this is why there were no hills and no forests. There was no moon, and no night either. All that was alive dwelled in the giant tree. In those times of beginning, most living beings, neither animals nor humans, formed one group. Only birds were dif-ferent and lived apart: the doves which were the only game available to hunters, and two dangerous individuals, Eagle (eater of raw meat) and Condor (eater of rotten flesh),[2] who preyed on people and doves alike. Life in those times would have been good, if it had not been for these two preying birds. Every time someone left home, Eagle or Condor would descend on their victim, kill him, and take him back to its nest on the highest branch of the giant tree. Eagle would be heard eating, undisturbed by the grief of the victim's relatives watching the bones of their dear kin fall to the ground, one after the

other. Fortunately, Squirrel and Spider decided to take action and put an end
to this dreadful business. One day, they climbed up to the very top of the tree.
Eagle had fallen in a deep sleep following a large meal. Spider wove a tight
and intricate web all around his body. Eagle did not feel the web until the
following day, when he attempted to swoop down on new prey. He was soon
seen hanging upside down, his head swinging in the air, and his feet still
attached to the branch. Squirrel's plan was to detach him, and let him fall
heavily to the ground, like a dead log, but the manoeuvre went wrong. Instead
of cutting the web off the branch, Squirrel's teeth incised the vine that linked
up the tree to the sky. While the vine sprang up, with Squirrel still biting on its
end, the giant tree crashed on to the ground, westward.

   To this day, Squirrel's tail can be seen in the sky, especially on the bright
nights that precede heavy rains, where it glows like a fluffy trail of golden
dust. The Amazon basin was born from the fallen giant tree, and the many
species of fish from its leaves. The roots became the Amazon headwaters.
Before the dramatic fall, there was hardly any water, except for scarce rainwater carefully collected in clay pots. But in his fall, the giant tree exposed
the plug which blocked the underground waters. Incapable of resisting the
pressure without the support of the roots, the plug loosened, and the whole
country was soon submerged by the enormous flooding which killed almost
everything in its wake. A few people survived by taking refuge in a hollow
branch, in which they made their way up river. They all died of exhaustion,
except for a brother and a sister, who became husband and wife. The world
was turned into an immense muddy flood plain, until Woodpecker, the
cultural hero, managed to lift the hills out of the mud. The hills were soon
covered with the forests in which the first Huaorani, our ancestors, found
refuge and dwelled. In these forests they multiplied and grew numerous
again.

Although the correlation between mythology and society is far from being direct
or straightforward, cosmologies often provide cues to cultural understandings of
nature and society, and Huaorani mythology is no exception.

   There are grounds for arguing that the myth expresses the fundamental characteristics of the Amazon ecosystem, such as, for example, the fact that its
fertility is not located in the soil, which is arid and devoid of nutrients, but in the
intricate and luxurious vegetation for which the soil acts as a mere support.[3]
There would be no life on earth without the existence of trees (at least one is
needed) for they provide shade, food and shelter, and prompt the formation of
rain. The primordial tree is a small ecosystem in itself, and the world expands
when this perfectly self-contained microcosm collapses. The organic expansion,
cannot occur, however, without the simultaneous creation of hills, forests and
rivers, which all originate with the fall of the great canopy tree. The new ecosystem, the outgrown successor of the primordial tree, is as integrated and self-
generative as the original one. If sky and earth are no longer connected by a vine,
they are still interacting through cycles of rain, flood, evaporation and growth.
At the beginning of the story, the soil is scorched by the heat of the sun, and the
earth water runs beneath the surface, as if in hiding. The fall of the giant tree
suddenly reverses the situation, and the once overheated earth is now flooded.
The myth thus makes clear that neither of these two situations is propitious to
vegetal growth and life. The tropical vegetation engendered by this extraordinary energy requires a *balance* between heat and humidity, shade and light. It is

only with the twin creation of the Amazon tributaries and forested hills that an equilibrium is finally achieved.

This myth of origin unambiguously belongs to the Cosmic Tree religious complex. Like a number of ancient religions founded on the belief in a sacred tree whose existence on earth preceded that of humans, the Huaorani cosmic tree represents the central axis around which the universe is ordered. It is quite remarkable that almost all the Cosmic Tree myths – and the Huaorani myth of origin is no exception – develop around a few recurring themes (Brosse, 1989).

The Cosmic Tree is attached to heaven, its roots reaching the centre of the earth. The roots plunge into the primordial underground river, the river of life and death. This river, manifested as a spring or well, sprouts out of earth from a stone. In many European beliefs, childless women who bathe in these springs, wells, or rivers will conceive. The Cosmic Tree, which is inhabited by two antagonist forces fighting each other, although 'almighty', is not indestructible. It can be unrooted by tempests, fire or flood. All living beings die, except for a surviving couple, the ancestors of humanity; in some Indo-European versions, the first man and first woman are said to be made of wood. Finally, it is important to stress that the cosmic tree corresponds to religions in which trees have more symbolic power than wood. In this context, temples are groves – that is, live trees. It has been proved that, in Europe, sacred groves were progressively replaced with temples made of wood. It is only subsequently that churches were made of stone. These stone buildings not only reproduced the wood structures, but also, at least for some, such as the Gothic churches, evoked forests.[4]

If the Huaorani Cosmic Tree echoes such themes, it should be seen, beyond religious parallels, as firmly embedded in a cultural matrix which greatly elaborates the practical knowledge and representation of trees. Above all, it should be noted that there is only one Huaorani word, *ahuè*, to translate 'wood' and 'tree'. The root of this word /hu/, found in many words and expressions translating as 'to live', 'to feel', 'to be alive' or 'to have emotions', can confidently be said to mean 'life'. Then there is the fact that humans are associated with leaves: new leaves are shiny as newborn babies, falling leaves lose colour and vitality like elderly people, longhouses with an emergent tree, and endogamous groups with palm groves (Rival, 1993). Plant life is not only identified with life and growth, but also with beauty, vigour and energy. Perhaps relating to this powerful association, one finds a real cultural anxiety concerning the felling of trees, which can be intentional during garden clearing, or may result from natural events such as thunderstorms. Although falling trees can be dangerous, the perception of risk in this case is definitely disproportionate to its reality.

The ceibo tree, like other plants and trees, is a physical expression of life, growth and vigour. But, because of its outstanding size, it is also granted with additional attributes. This tree is primarily praised for its kapok, an essential part of the hunting gear[5], which gives its name to one of the three 'seasons', the 'season of wild cotton' (*bohuèca tèrè*, from August to September) when, blown by the winds, it floats all over the forest and becomes available in great quantities. The ceibo tree, with its impressive height and solitary character, is also used as an irreplaceable landmark. Trekkers climb to its top to orientate themselves when lost, or whenever they wish to embrace in one panoramic view the forested landscape – their homeland.

With a life-span of up to 200 years, the ceibo, arguably the tallest tree of the Amazon forest,[6] reaches maturity – and starts flowering – some time between its 40th and 60th year. In other words, it starts reproducing at the age when people usually die, and lives a life roughly corresponding to four Huaorani generations. And, if its longevity is cause for admiration, so is its intricate appearance. Ceibo trees, hosts to many plants and animals, are enlarged over the years by a mass of lianas and climbers that help them stand still and straight in strong winds. The disproportion between their size and the shallowness of their roots, however, renders them vulnerable, and they eventually fall, leaving large gaps in the canopy.

These natural clearings, used by households as gardens or dwelling sites, are not without metaphorical significance. Leaders are called *ahuene*, that is, 'the person of the tree' or 'the master of the tree'. This term refers, in particular, to situations when powerful men invite members of hostile bands to manioc feasts in their attempt to forge or renew politico-marital alliances. According to oral tradition, the longhouses of *ahuene* leaders are like big ceibo trees; they do not divide but grow bigger by 'accumulating' relatives and allies in the same way that ceibo trees amass epiphytes. But, in addition, trust in *ahuene* leaders may be short lived, and violence may befall them just as thunder strikes the large, emergent trees which then crash, dragging in their wake numerous trees and plants, leaving large gaps in the forest canopy. This is why, the tales recount, times of peace and growth are necessarily followed by times of destruction and near-extinction. The moral of these tales is that *ahuene* leaders may give generously and organize lavish feasts, but their proffered abundance is neither as reliable nor as secure as the grandparental seasonal yields of palm fruit.

The *Bactris gasipaes* palm: forest bounty, ancestors' gift, and domestication

The peach-palm (*Bactris gasipaes, daguencat*) fruiting season, which generally lasts from January to April, is expected with great excitement by the Huaorani people who move each year to their palm groves as soon as the fruit starts to ripen. These groves are neither cultivated nor planted, but maintained through what is best described as 'consumption activities'.

Peach-palm groves would probably die out without human intervention, given that the forest is too dense and cool for palm seeds to germinate without some modification of prevailing conditions (Clement, 1992:75). By establishing seasonal forest camps, Huaorani people modify the natural environment in two ways. First, they create gaps by clearing the underbush and felling trees for firewood. Second, they cook great quantities of fruit (the peach-palm is inedible raw), and leave the hips of heated seeds lying around their temporary hearths, where they can germinate easily. Furthermore, they cut down old, unproductive palms, which are highly prized for the quality of their hard wood. Peach-palm wood, *tehuë*[7], is used to make household implements, blowguns, spears, and a wide range of smaller piercing or cutting tools.

The peach-palm is very common throughout Western Amazonia, but we know very little about the range of practices which has led to its present distribution. A quick comparison between Huaorani palm-grove management and Shuar or Quechua cultivation practices suffices to show the range of variation. Riverine Indians and other horticulturists tend to replant basal suckers, which are much easier to grow than germinated seeds. When they use germinated seeds, they plant them in the burned and weeded soil of new manioc plantations. The seed, superficially buried, is thus naturally heated by sunlight, and when the young palm seedling surfaces, the manioc is already tall enough to provide adequate shading. Such differences, which are consequential in terms of biodiversity and evolutionary ecology, are not the mere products of adaptation to environmental conditions, but the result of particular ideas and beliefs about the nature of society.

In the Huaorani case, peach-palm groves are conceptualized as a kind of ancestral gift, representing continuity, and delayed sharing between generations. Groves develop on the ancient dwelling sites, where *huaomoni* forebears lived and died. The fruiting season is spent remembering the dead, celebrating marriages, and rejoicing in the company of friends and relatives rarely seen during the rest of the year. As there is no hunting during the fruiting season, it also becomes a time of celebration shared with monkeys – the favoured game – which are left to fatten and reproduce. Like other egalitarian hunter-gatherers (Turnbull, 1961, Woodburn, 1982, Bird-David, 1990, 1992), the Huaorani obtain their food from the wild, value sharing, and regard the environment as giving and bountiful. The Huaorani's decision to subsist on the natural abundance of peach-palm groves and other forest products is cultural and deliberate.

Today, in Huaorani villages, as in many other Amazonian communities, the people plant peach-palm seeds in swiddens and backyards. But these planted palms have not replaced the ancestral groves to which people continue to go every year. This process of change and continuity is of great interest to the anthropologist. It shows that the term 'cultivation' covers a wide range of practices. And because what constitutes cultivation and domestication is so poorly understood, these practices get ignored or overlooked.

There are clear indications that the peach-palm is economically, if not culturally and socially, important for many native Amazonians – foragers and horticulturists alike. Moore (1973:64), for example, has argued that, given the number of objects made from wood products, or palm-leaves in the tropics, many cultures would simply not survive in these ecosystems without palm forests, even today. His contention is supported by many others who also believe that palms are cultural essentials (Balick 1979; Bodley and Benson, 1979; Balslev and Barford, 1987; Balée, 1988; Hecht *et al.*, 1988). Furthermore, they note that if all palms are useful either as a source of food, or materials for making shelters, tools and ritual objects, the peach palm is particularly valuable because of its multi-uses.

Irvine (1989:236) states that the peach-palm is 'by far the most cultivated tree crop' among lowland Quechua in Ecuador, for whom it is 'the third most important crop after manioc and plantain'.[8] She adds that the Quechua Indians not only consume its fruit and use its hard wood, but also exploit the tree indirectly by hunting at its base in old fallows. In their pioneer study of the cultural ecology of Amazonian palms, Bodley and Benson (1979) report that the peach-palm is the most widely used species for the manufacturing of wooden artefacts. Finally, in Peru and Brazil, where the populations of large jungle towns such as Iquitos, Manaus and Santarem have to rely on food grown locally, because of prohibitive transport costs, the peach-palm is widely cultivated by Indians and cabodos, who market part of their harvest. In fact, given its high-yield capacity, its excellent food value – even compared to seedcrops – and its potential use for animal feed and industrial products, an increasing number of agronomists consider the peach-palm to be a major tropical crop.

The peach-palm is, indisputably, widely used and cultivated in the Amazon. It should be stressed, however, that if the peach-palm is important economically everywhere, management practices, as well as the social and cultural significance of the palm, vary considerably from culture to culture. We have seen that, whereas the Huaorani grow the peach-palm in the wild, their horticulturist neighbours cultivate it in their swiddens. Furthermore, and despite the paucity of ethnographic information, it seems that horticulturists do not invest the forest trees they plant with any particular social or cultural meaning. Clearly these societies are organized around the cultivation of domestic crops such as manioc, maize or plantain, giving each elaborate cultural treatment, and using them to mark the social boundaries between men and women, or between the seasons of ceremonial congregation and those of dispersal.

The processes of cultivation and domestication are still poorly understood because botanists have ignored – or have not sufficiently documented – the wide range of social practices through which humans start cultivating wild plants and, eventually, domesticate them. The peach-palm is currently undergoing intensive experimentation for improved landraces in several research stations in Brazil and Costa Rica. But this research does not appear to include any social or cultural study, despite the fundamental importance of these dimensions to the process of domestication.

Recent research (Clement, 1988, 1992; Mora Urpi, 1984) has already established that pre-Columbian, native Amazonians hybridized the peach-palm from wild species that still occur in western Amazonia, and subsequently modified it by selecting phenotypes for increased starch content. The peach-palm could have originated in south-western Amazonia – probably on the eastern lower slopes of Peru and Ecuador – from the cross-breeding of *Guilielma insignis* and *Guilielma microcarpa*, or, according to Clement, (1992:70) and Cavalcante, (1977:92), of *Bactris dahlgreniana* and *Guilielma microcarpa*.[9] The hypothesis of a hybrid origin accounts satisfactorily for both the great genetic variability found in *Bactris gasipaes* landraces, and the modifications undergone by the fruit mesocarp. *Guilielma* fruits are much smaller than those of *Bactris gasipaes*, and contain hardly any starch, while exhibiting a high oil content. Clement and Mora Urpi (1987:307) put forward, therefore, the hypothesis that this selection conforms to the indigenous preference for starch foods, used in the preparation of fermented drinks and long-life dried meal.

The peach-palm, which has been found to adapt well to poor soils as long as the drainage is good, can produce high yields – up to 25 tonnes of fruit, or 4 tonnes of palm heart per hectare – even in laterite soils (Mora Urpi, 1984:118). Morphologically, leaves are ordered in such a way as to capture a maximum of light, while thorns on the trunk keep it dry by conducting rainwater away from the heart, hence protecting the tree from attacks by insects, or corruption by fungi. A monoecious palm, with masculine and feminine flowers on the same spadix, it reaches sexual maturity in the sixth or seventh year. Pollination is dependent on insects and on wind, flowering is controlled by the alternating of dry and wet seasons, and propagation can be either by seed germination, or, asexually, by basal sucker replanting. As the palm grows, the initial stem develops into a multiple-stem clump.

Not all experts agree on the peach-palm's level of domestication. For most botanists, the palm is semi-domesticated; if, in general it is found under conditions of cultivation in gardens, plantations and old fallows, it can exist in the wild, albeit at the far lower density of one or two clumps per hectare. The critical factor seems to be, therefore, the maintenance of groves, given that they cannot survive for long without human intervention (Mora Urpi, 1984; CATIE-FAO, 1983).

Clement (1992) takes a more radical position and argues that the *Bactris gasipaes* palm is one of the few palms in the world to have been fully domest-icated during the pre-Columbian era, when it was improved and widely distributed. This ancient human manipulation has resulted in landraces exhibit-ing not only noticeable morphological alterations, but also full dependence on human intervention for their continued genetic survival. His arguments regard-ing landrace improvements are convincing: the trunk has become smaller and thorn-free; the bunch weight, the fruit to bunch ratio and the fruit weight (x5000) have increased dramatically; this is due to an increase in both the pulp to fruit ratio and the levels of starch – which now make up 75 per cent of the total fruit weight.

Clement (1992) thus concludes:

> *Bactris gasipaes* is a completely domesticated palm. Because the modifications mentioned above are so extensive and there are no indications of vegetative propagation [. . .] the time scale for this domestication must be at least as long as that for the date, perhaps longer. I think that it is safe to conclude that [*Bactris gasipaes*] started being managed, perhaps even cultivated, before the end of the last glacial event (12 000+ years ago).

Others, for example, Burley and von Carlowitz (1984), still prefer to classify the peach-palm with the sago palm (*Metroxylon sagu*) as a semi-domesticated spe-cies, for, in their view, 'there does not appear to have been much effort to increase their productivity and quality'. Moreover, if it is true that the peach-palm is unknown in the wild, it nevertheless has close wild relatives, which is not the case for a fully domesticated palm such as the coconut palm, a monotypic palm with no close wild relatives. The disagreement between Clement, Burley and von Carlowitz seems largely to be a matter of definition. In the former's view, it is sufficient to find one landrace fully dependent on human intervention to speak of a domesticated species. For the latter, a species can be described as fully domesticated only if no wild relatives exist. For Burley and von Carlowitz, the peach-palm is managed and cultivated, but not domesticated. For Clement, it is all of these at the same time, for if 'managed and cultivated' refers to human actions, 'improved and domesticated' refers to the plant's response. Moreover, even Burley and von Carlowitz (1984:255) admit that, under a state of incipient domestication, palms 'probably represent selected germplasm from the wild, used as planting material because of direct evidence of high productivity'. In the end, this disagreement simply shows that it is very difficult to classify species which have undergone millennia of manipulation; hence domestication must be understood as a gradual process. Given that the correct assessment of the human impact on the Amazon forest partly depends on resolving this sort of theoretical debate, the concepts of domestication, cultivation and management[10] must be redefined as a matter of urgency.

Similar theoretical progress is under way in archaeology, where the traditional concern with the origins of agriculture (Childe, 1936; Ucko and Dimbleby, 1969) is being replaced by a processual model of people-plant interaction, and a search for the social and environmental factors conditioning plant domestication. New research (Chase, 1989; Yen, 1989) has demonstrated that both the ecological knowledge of early hunting-and-gathering populations and their capacity to modify the ecology of plants in their environment, were extensive. The sugges-tion that prehistoric hunter-gatherers realized the domestication, not of specific species, but of the ecosystem of which a part is a useful one for the study of plant cultivation in Amazonia, where 'There are many intermediate stages between the utilization of plants in their wild state and their true cultivation' (Lévi-Strauss, 1950:465).

Native Amazonians as forest managers and agroforesters

Why are Amazonian anthropologists and archaeologists so eager to understand the difference between encouraging the growth of wild trees in the forest, and replanting and cultivating them in garden plots? To find out whether differences in cultivation techniques correlate with differences in social organization, and to determine – through the study of the process of domestication – the conditions giving rise to cultural variations in plant management. Whereas environmental determinism was once the favoured theoretical frameworks, today's dominant explanatory model is historical.

Meggers' famous 1971 book, *Amazonia: Man and Culture in a Counterfeit Paradise* was the first of a long series of works to argue that low population density, incipient warfare, transient slash-and-burn horticulture, and food taboos are all manifestations of human adaptation to environmental limiting factors, in particular, to the depletion of critical natural resources. For Meggers, the more complex societies of the lower Amazon chronicled by the Spanish were originally formed by Andean settlers unable to maintain their high degree of social and cultural sophistication in an environment too poor to sustain intensive maize cultivation. Her model of cultural and social devolution was the first comprehensive formulation of a thesis which has retained some popularity. Subsequent authors (most notably Gross, 1975; Ross, 1978; Harris, 1984) departed from her narrow focus on soil fertility to look for other limiting factors in the environment. In particular, they interpreted the form of Amazonian indigenous settlements, which are typically small, widely scattered, and often deserted for months by their inhabitants (on long treks and foraging expeditions), as evidence of cultural adaptation to game scarcity. Like Meggers, however, they attributed the lack of complex and hierarchical socio-political systems to a lack of resource potential. Needless to say, these naturalistic arguments have attracted numerous critical reviews and discussions.[11]

New archaeological findings seem to give priority to historical conditions. According to Roosevelt (1989, 1993), Amazonian prehistoric populations, who started as hunters-and-gatherers, settled along the floodplains of eastern Amazonia where they developed elaborate ceramic techniques *much earlier* than in the Andean or coastal areas. These early settlements evolved into complex and extensive chiefdoms comprising villages of a thousand or more inhabitants who cultivated seed crops intensively, and were involved in vast trade networks. Given that such social, cultural, economic, and political developments cannot be sustained without large and dense populations, argues Roosevelt, settlement and labour patterns had to be adjusted to the massive post-Conquest demographic decrease, which resulted in the abandonment of intensive agrosystems, the adoption of starchy root crops (such as manioc which is far less labour-intensive than maize), long-fallow swiddens, tree cultivation, and an increased reliance on hunting. For Roosevelt, who concludes that resource management primarily depends on demography and settlement patterns, Amazonian native populations have developed successive resource-management plans according to fluctuations in population dynamics.

Ethnobotanists have also turned to the past to understand present-day interactions between native Amazonians and the rainforest. Their main contention is that a number of Amazonian forests are cultural artefacts (Sponsel, 1986; Eden, 1990; Posey, 1985; Posey and Balée, 1989; Balée, 1988, 1989, 1992, 1993). Some researchers even argue that many of the soil features underlying these forests are also the outcome of human intervention (Hecht and Posey, 1989). If Roosevelt seems to favour the view that, without the Conquest, native populations would have increased, complexified and continued to develop intensive agriculture, authors who have tried to understand the dynamic history of plants/humans interaction seem to suggest that agroforestry, rather than agriculture, has been – and would have been under any circumstance – the cultural choice made by most native Amazonians.

The hypothesis that since prehistoric times the indigenous people of the Amazon, far from being limited by scarce resources, have in fact created biotic niches, and that, therefore, a number of forests are anthropogenic, rests upon a number of observations of contemporary gardening activities and inductions about the long-lasting effects of past human interference. For example, the ethnobotanist William Balée who has worked with a number of Brazilian nomadic bands, has come to the conclusion that these foragers can survive without cultivated crops thanks to a few essential 'wild' resources (palms, fruit trees and bamboos) which are in fact the product of the activities of ancient populations. For Balée, they do not wander at random in the forest, but move their camps between what he calls 'anthropogenic forests' (palm forests, bamboo forests, Brazil-nut forests). These 'cultural forests' could well be ancient dwelling sites, as the frequent occurrence of charcoal and numerous pot-shards in the soil seems to indicate. Moreover, the greater occurrence and concentration of palms, lianas, fruit trees, and other heavily used resources on archaeological sites, seems also to indicate a strong association between these plant species and humans. Balée suggests, therefore, that species distribution may be a good indicator of human disturbance.

Similarly, Posey (1985) has argued that the Kayapo Indians create 'resource islands' and forest patches (*apêtê*) in the midst of the savannah, hence favouring its reforestation. He has documented in great detail the techniques by which soil is composted and transported to strategic places, then used to deposit the seedlings of plants carefully selected and widely used by the Kayapo during the trekking season. He states that native Amazonians have altered the abundance and distribution of wild foods throughout millennia of careful forest management, while Irvine (1989), mentions that the lowland Quechua manipulate critical resources by planting, selecting, transplanting, protecting, using, and discarding a wide range of wild semi-domesticated and domesticated plants found in their environment. She presents an image of an impressive agrosilviculture complex in which it is impossible to differentiate farming strategies (the selection and breeding of domesticated species in order to enhance their yields), from manipulations which can be very deliberate or almost subconscious. In Posey's words, 'no clear-cut demarcation between field and forest exists. Rather, the more general reforestation process is reflected by a continuum between undisturbed and disturbed forest', while for Irvine, 'Swidden agriculture can now be seen as the first stage of a larger agroforestry system rather than a temporary and insignificant opening of the forest canopy, which is soon abandoned after crop harvest.' What all these experts tell us, therefore, is that indigenous peoples living in rainforest areas exert considerable control over both their environment, and the distribution of forest resources.

Conclusion

Far from being a limiting environment to which humans must adapt, the Amazon forest is partly the result of ancient management practices that have enriched its biodiversity. For millennia, native Amazonians have actively manipulated and managed plant species, hence affecting their distribution. As sophisticated resource managers and agroforesters, they have domesticated a wide range of food crops without developing intensive agrosystems.

Once thought of as a 'green desert', a natural environment so poor in resources and nutrients that humans who took refuge in its midst lost both their complex societies and the cultural arts they had developed along the fertile banks of the lower course of the Amazon river, Amazonia is now seen as a rich and extremely varied ecosystem. Moreover, the life way of native Amazonians, living in small groups subsisting on shifting cultivation and foraging, which were once viewed as cultural adaptations to environmental constraints, is now seen as sustaining sophisticated agroforestry systems that have altered the distribution of innumerable plant and animal species, thus contributing to the biodiversity of today's Amazonia. If we accept that indigenous Amazonians, far from having merely *adjusted* their societies and cultures to an impoverished environment have *actively* manipulated the resources on which they depend for their survival, maintenance and reproduction, then the Amazon forest should no longer be considered the pristine, wild and untouched environment (the greatest wilderness left in the world) often portrayed in Western discourse. Rather, it must be viewed as the result of thousands of years of human intervention. Consequently, indigenous agroforestry techniques should be studied as possible models for forest conservation and restoration plans, as well as for the development of new commercial crops such as the peach-palm.

The example of the Huaorani management of the *Bactris gasipaes* palm species, which illustrates the highly diverse cultivation systems developed by Amazonian peoples, shows that agroforestry plans and commercial developments cannot be entirely successful unless they include careful documentation and thorough analyses of the diverse ways in which different indigenous cultures represent and use forest resources.

9   Where trees do matter for society: the socio-cultural aspects of sal (*Shorea robusta*) and salap (*Caryota urens L.*) in the Similipal hills of Orissa, India

MIHIR KUMAR JENA, KLAUS SEELAND and
KAMALA KUMARI PATNAIK

PHENOMENA RELATED TO forest management centre around two major issues – the use of forest, and its preservation. These can be viewed at two levels; the macro-level, involving a global distribution and use of resources, and the micro-level, involving the dynamics of interaction between forest dwellers and their immediate environment. In the process of civilization, two types of human population developed. The first are those who regard the forest as uninhabitable and whose relationship to forest is essential for their survival. The second type lives within the forest, maintains a close relationship with it, and subsists on the forest produce. In other words, it is the world in which one lives that shapes one's perception of what has meaning.

Tribal people who live in traditional conditions maintain a relationship with the forest in which almost all of the resources used are regenerative. But the commercial use of forest resources by both urban and tribal people has led to large-scale denudation which hampers considerably the regeneration of resources. A higher degree of demographic growth and increased consumption has, for example, resulted in the traditional method of foraging honey becoming an uneconomic option. So, now, the considerable ecological wisdom stored within these traditional cultures is little used to manage these resources effectively.

Trees are an integral part of the social and socio-economic life of rural communities. This is demonstrated in both the culture of the Hill Kharia who benefit from honey collection connected with the sal tree, and in the traditions of the Kuttia Kondh who extract palm wine (*toddy*) from the salap tree.

Sal (*Shorea robusta*)

Sal (*Shorea robusta*) is regarded by local people as the king of timber. These tall, straight trees grow well in fertile loamy soil, and flourish with good rainfall. Sal is found throughout northern India – from Kangra Valley in the Punjab, to the Darrong and Nowgang districts of Assam – along the sub-Himalayan region. In southern India, sal grows between the Coromandel Coast and the Puchamarhi Hills. Throughout Orissa, with the exception of some coastal tracts, sal grows quite extensively.

Similipal – a forest reserve in Orissa

Similipal, in the northern part of Orissa, is well known for the production of honey, but its output has decreased over the last few decades. Honey production reflects the forest structure of Similipal. The tribal people believe that good honey production is an indication of the virginity of a forest. Honey-bees collect nectar from most flowers and a substantial quantity of nectar is produced from the climax plant community of the area where sal is found.

Similipal Tiger Reserve is an oval shaped highland, and the meeting-place of India's northern and southern flora. Sal is among the most dominant of the tree species. In ecological succession sal is a member of the climax plant community and is very precious to the tribal people of Similipal and surrounding areas, as it serves their various material and economic needs. It maintains its important position in the peoples' religious cultures and folk festivals: tribespeople establish their clan gods under sal trees, which they regard as holy.

The forest represents a resource base which has been exploited since time immemorial. Forests contribute much to both the large commercial output of the Government, and the marginal economic output of the local and tribal people; from the collection of major forest produce (timber) to minor forest produce (fruits, seeds, latex, resin, barks, leaves and other plant parts) which are used for both food and medicine. Animals and produce of animal origin are also available from the forests.

Sal is the most popular tree species in Similipal and, because it fulfils most of their commercial needs, the tribal people take great care of it. As individuals and in their social organizations the people of the forest refer closely to the ecology of sal trees in their surroundings. Sal provides timber for building houses, making implements, ploughs, and household utensils. The local economy depends on the sale of plates and cups made of sal leaves, and the collection and sale of dust resin and sal seeds. Their greatest source of income, however, derives from the collection and marketing of honey; and sericulture is also a significant feature.

The traders who market the honey are also relevant; the marketing system has, to some extent, resulted in the tribal honey-collectors changing their indigenous methods. This, in turn, has affected the equilibrium in local ecosystem dynamics. Odum, (1969) points out that 'the natural systems seek to reach stability in terms of equalization of input and output and the human systems tend to maximize outputs and minimize inputs.' Because of the immediate demand of the market, tribal people often collect honey to earn quick money, with little regard for what have been traditional, sustainable practices. They sometimes collect honey when production is still in progress, thus disturbing the bees.

Many tribal groups – the Hill Kharia, Bathudi, Ho, Santhal, Mankirdia, Munda, and Bhumji – dwell in and around the Similipal Tiger Reserve forest. The Hill Kharia, in particular, are well-known for their expertise in honey collection. They consider themselves traditional honey-collectors, which they regard as their most important activity. Of all the groups inhabiting the Similipal forest, it is the Hill Kharia who, for many years, have provided the largest quantity of honey at the markets. They collect honey, using indigenous methods, from tall sal trees and stone crevices. Large beehives are usually found suspended at a great height from sal trees; the honey-bees prefer to make hives at the canopy level of the forest so they can remain undisturbed.

The method of collecting honey

The collection of honey is always a hard and troublesome business and depends, in the main, upon the expertise of the collector. Honey from sal trees is usually collected at night because, it is claimed, the honey-bees will not sting the collector in the darkness. The Hill Kharia make a fire with dry wood and branches under the tree homes of the beehives; the heat and smoke force the honey-bees to fly away, and the honey collector climbs up the tree to collect the deserted honeycombs. Sometimes the tree is felled if it is too difficult to climb or if there are small beehives on different branches of the same tree.

The collection of honey from beehives in stone crevices is a particularly difficult job; the men depend on their wives to help them, although it is not easy to secure willing assistance in this demanding and dangerous task. They set fire under the beehives in the stone crevices and, with the help of a siali rope (made out of the bark of *Bauhinia vahlii*) the collector reaches the beehives; the other end of the rope is held firmly by his wife. When all the honey has been gathered, the woman pulls the rope to help the collector back up the cliff. The amount of honey collected may vary considerably but, in all cases, it is small compared to the labour input.

The honey-bees collect nectar and water from different flowers to produce honey; this happens twice a year, in summer and in winter. The honey-bee consumes nectar as a source of energy, while pollen grains provide the protein essential for reproduction and colony multiplication. Honey-bees know which areas have abundant nectar and pollen, and because of their characteristic propensity for floral fidelity, they forage repeatedly upon a single source of nectar and pollen when it is plentiful.

During the dry months, there is some small-scale honey production. The dry-season honey, *Baghua Mahu*, has a high sugar content. In the deciduous forest of Similipal, many other species besides sal provide nectar to the honey-bees: *Crataega spp.*, *Caesalpinia spp.*, *Terminalia alata*, *Aegle marmelos*, *Feronia elephantum*, *Buchanania lanzan* (*Char*), *Dichrostachys cinerea* (?), *Adina cordifolia* (*Kuruma*), *Sterculia urens* (*Genduli*), *Syzygium cumini* (*Jamun*), *Prosopis julifera*, *Soymida febrifuga* (*Suama*), *Grewia spp.* (*Daman*), and *Bauhinia vahlii*.

In the winter months the honey is less liquid. The plant species contributing nectar to the winter honey are *Carum copticum*, *Guizotia abyssinica* (*Alasi*), *Coriandrum sativum* (*Dhania*), *Prosopis julifera*, *Tritax procumbens* (*Bisaly-akarani*), *Ageratum conyzoides* (*Pokasugna*) and *Mangifera indica* (*Amba*).

Trees usually bear flowers in summer. In the winter, honey-bees collect nectar from cultivated species and weeds in the forest. The important sites for honey production in and outside Similipal Reserve forest are Guruguria, Dudihiani, Kendumundi, Satakosia, Thakurmunda and Bangiriposi. Of these, the Guruguria collection centre produces the most honey. The major honey reservoirs around Guruguria are Khijri, Kabataghai, Atharadeuli and Jenabil.

Honey production in Similipal: the Hill Kharias' view

The Hill Kharias claim that about 40 years ago there was an abundance of honey, while today the quantity is much smaller.

Figure 1 shows clearly the reduction of the average honey yield from sal trees between 1950 and 1990. According to personal accounts, in the 1950s, three to four people could collect a maximum of a tin (about 22kg) of honey per day. The weekly collection came to 35–40kg for an efficient collector. The peak occurred in the 1950s, before the Barua Company, a timber contractor, arrived in the area. In the 1960s when trees were lost due to logging, the honey yields dropped to between 20 and 25kg per person per week. By the 1970s, the Tiger Project had been established, and tribal people were prohibited from entering the forest. Although the production of honey was not affected, the number of collectors

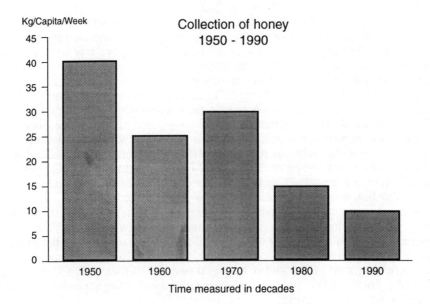

Figure 1: *Collection of honey in Similipal.*
          Source: authors' calculation on the basis of SFDC/OFDC data.

decreased and, towards the end of the decade, honey collection was a healthy
25–30kg per collector per week. In the 1980s, the collection was very poor – only
10–15kg – and, currently, it is down to about 5–10kg per week.
     Figure 2(a) and (b) show the seasonal variation in collection.

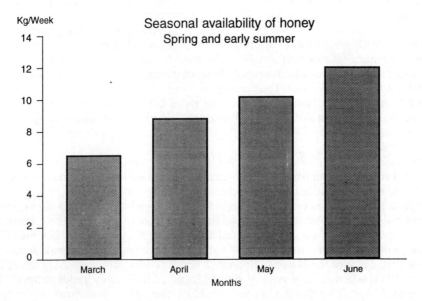

Figure 2(a): *Seasonal availability of honey*
             Source: authors' calculation on the basis of SFDC/OFDC data

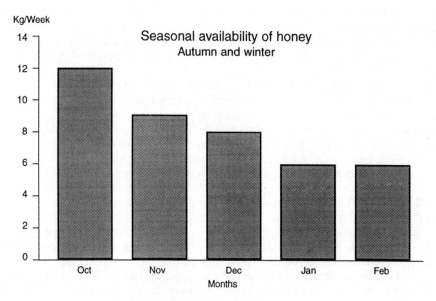

Figure 2(b): *Seasonable availability of honey*
   Source: authors' calculation on the basis of SFDC/OFDC data

Honey production increases between March and June as the major nectar producing species come into flower. The peak season is in June when the sal and the siali are in bloom; then the amount of honey collected per person per week ranges from 6 to 12kg.

After a short break during the rainy season (July to September), collection starts again in October and peaks due to the amount of rainwater in the honey. In November, the collection decreases with the onset of the flowering season. By the end of February the mango trees are in full bloom, providing nectar for the honey to be collected in March. The total output of honey in winter is larger than in summer, because of the humidity in the winter season.

Marketing honey

In Orissa, honey is marketed by government agencies, non-government registered firms, unregistered small procurers, and small businessmen. The purchase and procurement of other minor forest produce is done on both a lease basis as well as on a non-lease basis. The government firms, including nationalized firms, registered private companies and local enterprises, procure on a lease basis. At the collection centres opened by well-to-do businessmen, *rural marketing and illegal trading* are done on a non-lease basis. In the rural markets small businessmen purchase honey on a 'cash-to-crop-barter-basis'. In illegal and black-market trading *Dadan* (paying in advance) is common. Enterprises which procure honey on a lease basis have opened collection centres at different production sites. The entire arrangement is managed according to the rules and regulations of the department concerned at fixed prices. Private firms are run on contracts with the government. Prices rise and fall corresponding to the marketing supply and demand.

There is a canning centre at Jashipur, a small town on the outskirts of Similipal Reserve forest, which was established in 1985–86 by the Similipal Forest Development Corporation (SFDC). The canning centre processes a huge quantity of honey, along with other minor forest produce. It also focuses on food preservation and processing foodstuffs for long-term use. The honey which ends up at the canning centre is refined and sold on by the Orissa Forest Development Corporation (OFDC). Usually, private firms obtain bigger supplies than the government. This is due, in the main, to the poor funding of the government corporations at the time when seasonal, minor forest produce becomes available. As a Jashipur canning centre official said: 'the doctor comes after the patient dies'. The employees of the canning centre sit idle after the opening of the collection centres at the various production sites. The tribal people need to be paid immediately, but the government usually delays providing the money; the honey-collectors prefer, therefore, private firms, who pay at the collection site and obtain the goods at even lower prices than those approved by the government.

Since the merging of SFDC with OFDC in 1989–90, the canning centre has shown a negligible procurement, the funds are released towards the end of the production seasons and sometimes government officials siphon money into their own pockets by allowing private parties to procure honey. The income from government sales of honey goes to the Revenue Department of the State of Orissa. Since the merger, the Forest Department has failed to provide adequate funds, which is why, in 1991, no honey was procured until October.

Tribal honey collectors are victimized by the local procurers as a result of government negligence. The local people prefer the *Dadan* system of payment which ensures that all their collections are sold to businessmen at a very low price. Sometimes rice, flour and other staples are given to the tribal people as an 'advance' for the collection of different types of minor forest produce at different times of the year.

The Hill Kharia have a solution to their exploitation by local businessmen. If the government would provide them with food or funds *when they need them*, or if the money can be released at the collection centres in time for procurement, they would rather deal with the government than with private parties; thus they could provide the government with large quantities of honey. The collection centre procured record levels of honey in 1989–90 (about 10 000kg) when, according to rough estimates, the total production of honey that year was about 30 000kg.

The price the government paid for honey in 1990–1 and 1991–2 was Rs. 15/kg and Rs. 30/kg, respectively, and the selling price after refining was Rs. 30/kg and Rs. 65/kg, respectively. Table 1 lists the prices paid for honey by different purchasers in 1995–6.

Table 1:   Price of unrefined honey in Similipal

Purchaser	Purchasing price (Rs per kg)	
	Dry months	Wet months
Government (collection centre)	25	25
Private farms	22	20
Local traders (directly from honey-collection site of tribal people)	20	15
Dadan	12–15	8–12

Causes of decreasing honey yield

In the past, honey collection was traditionally organized on a family basis. But the population explosion has led to more independent collection; and as a result, less honey was collected as individuals became more concerned about personal economic gain. Family fission has led to poor organization of labour. Some Hill Kharia claim that the government-induced settlement and rehabilitation programmes have accelerated this family fission among their previously semi-nomadic households, and they face competition from the Bathudi tribe.

For short-term economic gain, people began to collect honey from immature beehives. The practice of setting fire under the beehives killed many of the queen bees, leading to a decrease in their numbers. Honey-bee families then disappeared for safety, and the natural apiculture of the forests declined.

Large-scale felling of old sal trees by timber contractors and the Forest Department discourages the honey-bees from making their hives in tree canopies. The decrease in honey production coincides directly with the creation of a secondary environment by replacing naturally growing species with domesticated plants.

Loss of tree cover, particularly of some of the important nectar-producing species such as *Bauhinia vahlii*, *Mangifera indica*, and *Pongamia pinnata*, has a considerable impact on the production of honey.

Social forestry and other types of man-made forests are also interfering with natural vegetation, by the plantating of inappropriate species. The local people should have been consulted by planners to ascertain the suitability of species for the development needs of the particular area.

Salap (*Caryota urens* L.) – the place of the sago-palm in the world of the Kuttia Kondh

The Kuttia Kondh of central Orissa are one of many different sub-sections of the Kondh Tribe. Most live off the beaten track, in the dense forest of the hilly uplands. The Kuttia Kondh are neither fully pastoralists nor farmers. They live almost entirely on forest products such as tubers, fruits, wild herbs, and leafy vegetables. Hunting is also important; meat is an additional luxury. Insufficient agricultural output and the non-availability of food during lean periods have prompted them to seek an alternative source of income in the form of alcohol production.

They collect *toddy* (distilled/fermented alcohol prepared using indigenous methods) from particular plants. This habit is practised regardless of sex and age. Alcohol consumption is approved of both as a custom and as part of religious rites. Country *toddy* is usually collected from the date palm (*Phoenix silvestris*), a tree found throughout the tribal areas. In the southern part of Orissa, however, the sago-palm (*Caryota urens* L.), – in the Oriya language known as *salap* – is an important species for *toddy* production. The salap tree is also known in English as 'kittul palm' (the fish-tail sago-palm) and among the Kuttia Kondh it is popularly known as *Madamara* (*mada* means toddy, *mara* means tree, in Kui).

Description of the sago-palm (*Caryota urens* L.) and its uses

Sago-palm trees are fairly common in certain parts of Orissa (Haines, 1921–25). The seed remains dormant for a prolonged period lasting between two and three

years until it germinates. The tree grows to a height of 15 or 20 feet, with leaves –
similar to those of the maidenhair fern – 10 to 12 feet wide and with very strong
petioles. The tree usually flowers between October and November; these remain
in blossom until March or April. The trunk is erect, branch-free, round, and
smooth. People sometimes plant saplings in kitchen gardens or on the edge of
paths. According to the Kuttia Kondh, the tree grows best on hill slopes and in
the foot-hills. A tree can produce unrefined sago for *toddy* for up to three years,
and becomes fully mature after 15 to 20 years.

Collecting sago

The trunk of the young palm is preferred because the quality of the sago generally contained in its pith is usually good. The pith (*jendi*-KK, *manja*-O)[1] is
collected when a Sago palm dies prematurely and the sago is extracted and sun-
dried. The Kuttia Kondh use sago in different ways: they simply boil and eat it,
prepare bread from the flour, or make various types of cakes. Dried sago is also
stored for use during lean periods.

Yielding 'toddy' from inflorescence (kama-KK) and pith (jendi-KK)

The inflorescences (blossoms) are considered the best part of the plant for
collecting liquid for *toddy*. A fresh transverse cut (about half an inch) from the
hanging terminal end of the inflorescence is made, and an earthen pot is tied to
the neck of a freshly cut end to collect the *toddy* flow. This process is carried out
each morning, again at midday and again in the evening during summer, and
twice a day in winter. A fresh cut is made each time to prevent blocking up the
flow of liquid, which may occur if the terminal end dries up or if there is some
infection. *Toddy* can also be prepared from the pith; and it is sometimes used to
cook meat in the forest, when no water is available.

Indigenous fermentation (Madang Mnipaa-KK)

Toddy is sweet because of its high sugar content; very sweet *toddy* can
sometimes cause diarrhoea. The tribespeople are aware of the varying
degrees of alcohol contained in the fermented *toddy* and drinks of specific
strength are restricted to particular age groups. So the juice is fermented
according to their own indigenous methods of fermentation, passed down
from generation to generation and the drinkers' varying requirements. The
main ingredients used in the fermentation process include: the bark of
Holarrhena antidysenterica (*Kude mara*-KK, *Kuduchi*-O), root bark of *Cas-
sia fistula* (*Pundeni mara*-KK, *Sunari*-O, Indian laburnam/Purging Cassia-
E), root of *Cissampelos pareira* (*Dindidipa tulla*-KK, *Akanbindi*-O, False
Pareira Brava-E), bark of *Mangifera indica* (*Maskamara*-KK, *Amba*-O,
Mango-E) and fruits of *Bauhinia vahlii* (*Paeritulla*-KK, *Siali*-O). The husk-
less grains of *Oryza sativa* (*Kulinga*-KK, *Dhana*-O, Paddy-E) and *Panicum
miliare* (*Kueri*-KK, *Suan*-O, Little millet-E), are also used as fermenting
agents. These are generally deposited into the pitcher used to collect the
sago liquid before it is tied to the cut end of the inflorescences; the amount
put in depends on the required strength of the *toddy*. Fermentation takes
between 8 and 12 hours.

Preparing drums and water pipelines

Different parts of the sago-palm tree have contributed greatly to the culture of the Kuttia Kondh. A drum (*Tapka*-KK), used chiefly at special occasions such as the Meriah festival (*Biakatina*-KK) at which animals are sacrificed, and the New Year festival (*Punikalu*-KK), is made out of the root base. The dome-shaped root base, which is hollow at the top and blunt at the bottom, is cut off the palm once it is dead. The external lateral roots are cut with sharp knives. Each of these pieces is shaped like a big bowl. A tanned skin (preferably a cowskin) is then cut to size and tied over the open end of the bowl-shaped root base. A young, tender, and flexible bamboo stem (*Manisira*-KK) is used as a rope to tie the skin to make it as taut as possible. Gum extracted from a herb called *Jrikeni*-KK is pasted around the bamboo. The result is a perfect musical drum. A further use of the sago-palm is achieved by cutting a matured tree trunk vertically into two equal halves with an axe. The two hollow pieces are used as pipelines to irrigate the fields.

Tree ownership

The tree is considered to be valuable property by the Kuttia Kondh, due to its nutritious *toddy*. In fact, *toddy* plays an important role in ensuring a tribal society remains mentally, physically and socially fit. The sago-palm trees can be owned by individuals or by a family. The person who plants it, owns it. Sometimes, the family-owned trees are divided among its members, although female ownership is rare. The owner reserves the right to tap the inflorescence of the tree for *toddy*. If the owner is no longer able to perform this practice, he chooses a man to do it for him. When the owner dies, the ownership of the tree is transferred to his family, usually his sons. The owner decides who will inherit. He can leave the tree to anyone in his village.

Some tribespeople have recounted that, in ancient times liquor was prepared from other trees such as *Mangifera indica, Madhuka longifolia* (*Puju mara*-KK, *Mahula*-O, Mowra butter tree-E), *Artocarpus heterophyllus* (*Pansi mara*-KK, *Panas*-O, jackfruit-E), *Musa sapientum* (*Tade mara*-KK, *Kadali*-O, Plantain-E), and molasses. But *toddy* from the sago-palm tree is considered to be the best. *Toddy* is sometimes sold at a rate of one rupee for one *dumuni* (big spoon). A high-yielding palm can sometimes make its owner as much as Rs 1000.

The sago-palm tree and social intercourse

The place where the people sit and drink *toddy* is called *Madangbasa*. They gather together to exchange thoughts and ideas, to talk about feelings, and to reach decisions. In a forest, where there is more than one *toddy* tree, people sit under the youngest tree or somewhere convenient to the *toddy* collection points. Many decisions relating to village conflicts or choosing new forest patches for shifting cultivation, for example, are made at *Madangbasa*. The Kuttia Kondh use a big spoon (*dumuni*) made out of a gourd (*Lagenaria piceraria, Anka*-KK, *Lau*-O), to distribute *toddy* equally among those participating in the discussion. Guests are treated to an extra *dumuni* of *toddy*. Women who occasionally visit the *Madangbasa* are served *toddy* separately.

Toddy plays a part in most rituals when it is offered to the gods and goddesses and, more often, to their ancestral spirits (*Dukeli*-KK). When the owner of a tree dies, his successor is required to perform a witch *puja* (veneration of demons) during his first *toddy* collection. On this occasion, the village astrologer (*Kutaka-KK*), or shaman (*Jani-KK*) and headman (*Majhi-KK*) are invited to the spot. The astrologer invokes the owner's spirit and chants 'We are cutting your trees for *toddy*. May your goodwill be with us. May your tree secrete sweet, tasty and plentiful *toddy* for our children (*Miladali-KK*)'. The *toddy* is then distributed among the group according to status and age.

Curiously, when the owner of an immature tree dies, his soul must pass a critical test. If *toddy* collected from the tree (when the tree attains maturity) is plentiful and sweet, it is believed that the departed soul had good and healthy feelings for the village folk. If not, he is regarded as having been a wicked person.

If, for some unknown reason, a palm tree is yielding less *toddy*, the owner has to arrange a ritual. The village astrologer performs a ceremony worship by offering rice, leaves of *Bauhinia vahlii* and *Themda arundinacea* (*Bika-KK*, *Chhona-O*, thatching grass-E) to the tree in order to detect the evil spirit and to satisfy it. Fruits of the *Semecarpus anacardium* (*Ganju-KK*, *Bhalia-O*, marking-nut tree-E) are kept in a packet hidden inside the tree to avoid the evil eye of the spirits.

Tree lore

Certain folk-songs are associated with the sago-palm tree. One reflects the tribe's fondness for *toddy*:

> *There was a sago-palm tree.*
> *Its toddy developed my appetite.*
> *I drank it to my full satisfaction.*
> *It developed my addiction and hunger also,*
> *Which demanded meat.*
> *I went for it and could have it.*
> *Then I slept a sound sleep.*

The preservation of love between lovers is represented in a Kondh folk-song of Koraput: '*Mada mara sinanga dokaritaka rinanga, piopata baisangade . . .*' which translates as: 'Further, the *toddy* replaces pains and agony, sorrows and sufferings, with smiles for the Kuttia Kondh'.

Conservation management

The tree is greatly respected by the Kuttia Kondh for its significance to their social lives, cultural patterns, and aesthetic values. It provides them with food and drink; it has also contributed to their art, crafts, and material culture. *Toddy* plays its role in easing away the pain of the day's hard labour, and is indispensable part of their rituals and festivals. Its importance in their daily lives has motivated them to preserve and conserve the species in their locality. Planting a sago-palm tree and dedicating it to the interest of the local people is the most noble deed a visitor can bestow on the Kuttia Kondh. The tree represents a mother, providing its *toddy* – the *elixir vitae* – on which people of all age groups can survive and enjoy life.

Conclusions

From the socio-economic and socio-cultural point of view, sal and salap are an intrinsic part of the lives of the Hill Kharia and the Kuttia Kondh. Not only are both tribes economically dependent on the trees, but these trees are social and spiritual representations of *what matters*. Their societies, so closely linked to a natural resource base, show that nature and culture amalgamate into each other.

Sal wood is regarded as *Daru*, which means god, because the tribal people say that it may stand alone for years, depending neither on other plants nor animals. Furthermore, sal flowers are used in religious ceremonies and as a cure for diarrhoea and dysentry. Without the nutritious *toddy*, the tribal people would barely survive the lean season.

Life in remote rural areas is almost entirely dependent on the use of locally available regenerative resources. Both tree species have their place in the shared knowledge, religious practices, economic welfare, and customs of tribal people. As long as resources used for economic subsistence also matter socially and spiritually, they will, to some extent, be safeguarded from over-exploitation. The fact that there is no perceived distinction between a plant's economic value, its use to achieve religious merit, and the social obligations concerning its common or private management, characterizes the respective communities as cultures in the sense of holistic resource users.

10   War, forests and the future: the environmental understanding of the young in Sierra Leone

PAUL RICHARDS

IN 1985 IT WAS estimated that in Africa there were 43 million young people aged between 15 and 19. At an annual rate of increase of 3.3 per cent, the fastest in the world, this age group will double in size by the year 2010. Unlike Europe and North America, where the increasing numbers of old people dominate the thoughts of policymakers and politicians, the challenge for African politics is to provide for and harness the talents of the young. The attitude of young people to forests, and their reliance upon forest products, is therefore a matter of outstanding importance to conservation.

Forest products and youth subsistence

Forests once figured in the calculations of economists solely as sources of timber. More recently, various studies have established that a wide range of forest products are of outstanding importance in the lives and survival strategies of the poor in tropical rainforest countries. A 1990 review by Falconer of West Africa emphasizes the importance of a range of non-timber forest products (NTFPs), including medicinal plants, food items and 'bush meat' (game). Foraging provides many of these items, but others are in such high demand that they are regularly traded.

Davies and Richards (1991) report the results of detailed studies of NTFP use around the Gola forest in eastern Sierra Leone, just prior to the onset of the RUF (Revolutionary United Front) rebellion. They make the basic point that the great majority of NTFPs are products not of high forest, but of secondary 'bush' lying within the farm-fallow cycle. The bush is the main source of palm products used for basketry and building materials, of quick-growing light woods used for the carving of masks, drums and kitchen implements (mortars and cooking spoons), and of most of the important gathered foodstuffs (mushrooms, 'bush' yams and leafy vegetables) that figure in the diet of villagers in the Gola forest. Fish is more important than bush meat, and common animals trapped in farm bush figure much more commonly in the diet than large mammals hunted in the forest.

The picture is substantially the same for villages further back from the forest margin and those right on the forest boundary. Even where it is as easy to enter the forest to forage as it is to hunt in farm bush, villagers tend to prefer the latter option. Foraging in the forest is only really at all common for medicinal plants. Davies and Richards conclude that Gola villagers are not so much interested in protecting rainforest, as in ensuring the continued productivity of their farm fallows as sources of NTFPs.

A study of the views of over 400 young Sierra Leoneans in Bo, Kambia, and Freetown attempted to gain some impression of whether they are still substantially dependent on items of forest produce, and what that pattern of dependence might be, as a basis for asking about attitudes to the forest and forest conservation. Questions were asked about items of forest produce used directly by the interviewee, as well as items used in the household-at-large (it was

90

expected that the youngest age group in the sample would not have their own items of kitchen equipment, for example).

The survey secured equal representation of males and females, and the main age classes and educational groupings. Young people with incomplete secondary education are well represented in the sample. This group has the highest unemployment rate in Sierra Leone. If the fabric of society is stretching thin as a result of population pressure on natural resources this is where some of the problems might be expected to be most apparent. Participants in the survey also elaborated their own thoughts about war, forests and environmental conservation, after being presented with six controversial statements to set the conversational ball rolling. The material derives from a comparative study of the political culture of forest conservation in West Africa funded by the Global Environmental Change programme of the UK Economic and Social Research Council. The following paragraphs concentrate on items of forest produce for personal use.

The survey asked whether it was becoming more difficult to obtain these items, and if so why, and how they were acquired (by collection or purchase). The 421 interviewees in Freetown, Kambia and Bo provided information on a total of 1756 items. The single largest category of items (21 per cent) was kitchen implements (mainly mortars, pestles, grinding boards, and cooking spoons). Food items accounted for a further 21 per cent (vegetable products 10 per cent, fruits 6 per cent and bush meat 5 per cent). The last figure confirms that bush meat is of less importance in Sierra Leone, where fish is the main animal protein, than in Ghana and Nigeria. Fuel (mainly firewood, 14 per cent), building materials (12 per cent), medical and hygiene requisites (9 per cent) and household goods (furniture, mats, bedding) comprised the bulk of the remainder.

The majority of items (62 per cent) were bought, but the importance of purchasing varied according to locale. In Kambia (the smallest urban centre), 62 per cent of items were gathered; in the capital, Freetown, this figure drops to 10 per cent. The relative importance of purchase and collection varies by category of item, and is also quite strongly gendered. Building materials, food items and medical supplies are 63 per cent, 54 per cent and 53 per cent gathered, but 88 per cent and 93 per cent of kitchen and household items are purchased. This then translates into a gender difference. Except perhaps in Freetown, young men hunt and often do quite a lot of construction and repair work on their dwellings. Women's kitchen and household items, in contrast, are mainly purchased from a craft specialist. Women accounted for 57 per cent of all bought items, but men accounted for 57 per cent of all collected items. This may tally with a later finding that young men tend to prefer draconian 'protective' legislation to halt the decline in supplies of forest products whereas young women favour technological options for increasing the output of essential supplies, when asked what they would do to halt the damage caused by deforestation.

Overall, it was reported that, for 56 per cent of items, procurement had become more difficult over time, whereas in 44 per cent of cases there was said to be no difference, or items had become more readily available. Price escalation was given as the major cause of difficulty in 14 per cent of cases, and deforestation was directly cited in another 9 per cent of cases. Uncontrolled bush fires were cited by 76 interviewees, nearly all (91 per cent) belonging to the Kambia sample. Thirteen interviewees (six in Bo and seven in Freetown) specifically mentioned the rebel incursion as a cause of supply difficulties, because people were now too afraid to venture far into the bush without military protection. But overall, fewer interviewees complained that bush products were harder to acquire in Freetown (43 per cent) than in Bo (57 per cent) and Kambia (69 per cent). This seems to be directly related to the fact that 90 per cent of NTFPs in Freetown are acquired through market channels. Although some informants were worried about price trends, in a period of steep inflation and falling real wages, others detected the benefit of recent improvements in fuel supply and transportation following the 1992 coup.

Experience of the forest

What direct knowledge of forests do young Sierra Leoneans possess? How well-based in experience are their ideas about deforestation and its social significance?

Over two-thirds of the sample (68 per cent) claimed to have visited a forest, and were able to provide a date and location. Women – 50 per cent of the sample overall – were not far behind the men, accounting for 48 per cent of all such visits. Over three-quarters of all interviewees in Kambia had visited a forest, but the figure was high (66 per cent) for Freetown interviewees as well. Bo slightly lags the other two centres, with only 64 per cent of interviewees having visited a forest. This is perhaps surprising in a place where forest-capped hill-tops can still be glimpsed from within the town. Age made a slight difference, with the under-20s (as might be expected) somewhat less likely to have visited a forest (60 per cent of all under-20s) than older interviewees. The small group (33) of those born and interviewed in Freetown were least likely to have direct knowledge of a forest (45 per cent). This figure is still quite high, nevertheless, and reflects the fact that the protected forests of the Peninsula mountains are within easy reach of the city.

The more highly educated are among the *most likely* to have direct experience of forests (74 per cent of all interviewees with secondary or higher education). A surprisingly large proportion of the sample (25 per cent) had made such a visit for the sake of seeing the forest, and with no direct practical motive, and two-thirds of these visitors had secondary or higher education. Some had made their visits as part of an organized field-trip from school, but others were responding to a whim or personal, or a friend's, intellectual enthusiasm. Some were drawn by the hope of seeing wild animals. Others wanted to learn about the different kinds of forest tree. One interviewee claimed his visit was made 'to see how life began'. There is no evidence, therefore, that modernity drives a wedge between young Sierra Leoneans and their forest roots. Forests are an important and cherished part of their intellectual heritage.

Many interviewees, of course, had more directly practical reasons for their visits; 11 per cent had gone into forests on hunting expeditions (including six women). Society initiation or forest burial accounted for another 7 per cent of visits. But the single largest category, apart from curiosity, was the 21 per cent who had experienced forest conditions in the course of gathering firewood. Women cited this as their single most important reason for visiting forests (61 per cent of all interviewees). Seven interviewees had experienced life in a real rainforest for the first time as a result of the rebel incursion; as one interviewee put it, they had been forced to flee through the forest 'to escape rebel bondage'.

In all, 334 interviewees thought there were clear differences between 'forest' and 'bush', and proceeded to describe them with considerable accuracy. Most interviewees noted obvious features such as the size and type of trees, and other vegetation features distinguishing a true rainforest from 'farm bush'. Several noted that elephant grass and 'bush razor' (*Scleria barteri*) are signs of secondary disturbance. Some remarked that wild fruits and palm trees are much more numerous in bush than in forest. Many saw 'wild', 'large', 'strange', 'bad' and 'tricky' animals as a distinguishing feature of forest, and associated small animals such as 'cutting grass' (the cane rat, *Thryonomys swinderianus*) with bush (cane rat numbers depend on grassy wetland areas for their dry-season survival). One interviewee correctly noted that snakes were more common in bush than in high forest. Interviewees frequently noted that high forest was relatively clear at ground level, and visibility was good, whereas bush was impenetrable thicket; the point was often made that 'you can run through forest, but not through bush'. Forest was frequently characterized as 'cool', 'moist', and 'dark', whereas bush was more open to sunlight, hotter, and drier. Bush soils were 'drier than forest soils', and one 'O' level candidate, perhaps reflecting a well-taught geography lesson, remarked that while canopy leaves held moisture, in bush 'rain runs on the ground'. A number of interviewees, all in Kambia and Bo, were left with the impression that the forest is a lonely and dangerous place, with grave sites, evil spirits, and many large trees behind which wicked persons might lurk. Bush, by contrast, was open and friendly, with frequent signs of human occupance. One young woman in Freetown noted that middens were among these markers.

As a way of assessing informants' understanding of some of the biological changes associated with deforestation, interviewees were then asked what plants and animals could be found only in high forest. 336 respondents made a total of 1517 suggestions.

The elephant dominated the list (55 per cent of all respondents), but chimpanzees, leopards, and various species of monkeys were each cited by a quarter of the sample. Harnessed antelope, bush hog and buffalo were also mentioned frequently. Specific reptiles, snakes and birds mentioned included tortoise, pangolin, monitor lizard, python, baboon viper, and various birds of prey. Where plants were cited, they tended to be useful species associated with secondary forests rather than closed canopy rainforest. This is true of silk cotton, the tree mentioned most often (15 per cent of respondents). Fruit trees and other items which the young frequently forage in the bush were commonly cited (for example, bush yams and *Dialium guineensis* [*blak tombla* in Krio]).

About 20 per cent of responses could be considered 'dubious'. These mainly concerned large animals (lions, tigers, bears, foxes, zebras, horses, and even a kangaroo or two). Despite the country's name (literally 'Lion Mountains'), the lion is no forest creature, though lions may once have been present in the northern, savanna, part of the country. Lion skin does turn up from time to time in ritual objects in rural forested areas of Sierra Leone (in the Gola forest I was once shown a fine warrior's jacket made of strips of red cloth alternating with leopard and lion-skin). Whether all the responses classed as 'dubious' were really evidence of ignorance is open to some doubt, because of complications concerning the terms in common use for animals in Sierra Leone and Liberia. Liberians re-applied a number of North American names to animals found locally (most notably 'alligator' for Nile crocodile. The informant who noted that the 'elk' was only found in high forest was quite correct, since he meant the large antelope *Boocerus* (this animal has no common name in English – reference books refer to it as '*bongo*'). Similar problems occur with 'tiger' (*taiga* in Krio) since this is quite widely used by West African English-speaking creoles to refer to any large cat (including leopard, specifically *lɛpet* in Krio).

Can we detect any specific social patterns in these dubious responses? The dubious responses concerning plants were mainly confined to the 27 informants who thought oil palms and *yemani* (*Gmelina arborea*) were high-forest species. Oil palm is a light-dependent species common only in secondary bush, and *yemani* is an introduced quick-growing timber and fuelwood tree, common in roadside plantations laid down in the colonial period. In the main, women made the mistake about palms, while men were confused about *yemani* (but total numbers were very small in both cases). Over two-thirds of dubious responses concerning these two plants originated with young people who have received post-primary education.

Turning to the much larger category of dubious responses concerning forest animals (92 per cent of all such responses), there were no distributional differences of note according to gender, level of schooling, religion, or location. Nor is this conclusion changed by removing the 'lions' and 'tigers'. These account for 75 per cent of all animals in the dubious category, and, as noted above, may not be 'dubious' at all. This is a surprising result, since we might (for example) have expected 'bookish' responses (kangaroos and zebras) to be more concentrated among the formally educated.

From the evidence above it would appear that most young Sierra Leoneans have realistic, and reasonably accurate, knowledge of forest environments, and some of the biological changes taking place within these environments, based largely on direct experience. The type of experience varies with schooling and gender, and changes in character as patterns of urban-rural interaction also change. Incidental contact with the forest (helping parents on the farm, for example), will continue to decline with schooling and urbanization, but there is evidence that young people now organize deliberate visits to compensate for lost informal opportunities. This fits well with their ideas that forests are part of their modern national heritage, not just relics from the past. In line with this, there is little evidence that the attitudes of the urban, educated groups are noticeably different – more impoverished in content or less realistic about changes – to the attitudes of other groups within Sierra Leonean society today. This is an encouraging starting point for those anxious to develop conservation education programmes involving the institutional resources of the state. There is, apparently, little danger that pushing for the modernization of the state would risk cutting off young Sierra Leoneans from their roots.

Forests and the future

Despite the experience of war, a coup, and continuing economic difficulties, the majority of the young people we interviewed were remarkably optimistic about the future. Asked to say whether, and why, they thought their own lives would be different (better or worse) in 10 years' time, 91 per cent of the sample were prepared to commit themselves to a definite view. Of this proportion, 86 per cent were confident things would be better. This confidence was evenly distributed across the genders and age groups. Of the 14 per cent predicting no change or a worsening of personal circumstances, three-quarters of responses came from those with only primary education or no formal education at all. The reasons for confidence, not unexpectedly, mainly related to plans being made or already undertaken, concerning, for example, specific educational activities or commercial ventures. The largest single ground for hope (20 per cent of responses) was the age-related expectation of achieving financial independence (to have an income, to be in charge of one's destiny, not being under or 'behind' a parent or sponsor). Some informants (12 per cent of responses) were confident life would be better because of their own ability, capacity for effort, self-reliance, and determination to survive and prosper, come what may. Others (9 per cent of responses) couched their optimism in religious terms (they would succeed through prayer, ancestral blessing, the power of God, etc). But quite a few were quite specific about the route to self-improvement, and cited specific career plans or business ventures. Independent business activity was the largest single category of projected activity (18 per cent of responses, but with females outnumbering males 2 : 1). Men were to the fore in seeing agriculture as their route to success, and also among the small group of interviewees (5 per cent) who believed that politics in Sierra Leone was on the mend (some citing the 1992 coup, specifically, as grounds for increased optimism about the future).

Interviewees were then asked explicitly about their career plans. The professions (31 per cent) and business (29 per cent) vied for first place. There was a 50 : 50 gender split among those aiming for professional employment (though girls tended to aim lower than boys, with the latter typically hoping to become doctors and lawyers, while girls had in mind nursing or teaching). Females (67 per cent) were dominant in the group espousing business ambitions (these ambitions varied from petty trade to international commodity dealing). Agriculture, especially plantation work and market gardening, accounted for 20 per cent of responses. Less than a third of the agricultural responses came from women. Artisanal activities featured relatively rarely (only 7 per cent of responses). The single most notable feature of the entire set of responses was the lack of interest in diamond mining, the mainstay of the Sierra Leone economy and source of much political conflict. Only two respondents (one female) *intended* to make mining their choice of employment. In practice, many young men are sucked into diamond mining, but, seemingly, few Sierra Leoneans see it having a long-term, stable future.

The survey then enquired whether interviewees thought that forests in Sierra Leone were increasing, decreasing, or remaining stable, and whether this would have any direct bearing on the interviewee's own future. Definite views were entertained by 90 per cent of the sample; 81 per cent thought that forests were decreasing, 9 per cent that there was no significant change, and 12 per cent that they were increasing. In general, in explaining their viewpoint, this last group tended to argue that young people had left farming for the city, and that the rebel war had further emptied forested districts, so they expected (given the strong recuperative powers of the bush) that they would encounter much more forest in future. This kind of response was somewhat commoner among older age groups (20–29 year olds), and less common among the teenagers.

Altogether, 308 informants gave a total of 515 explanations for what they believed to be a decrease in forest cover. Farming was thought to be the single most important factor (28 per cent of responses). The second largest set of responses, somewhat surprisingly, cited building, the expansion of settlements, and road building (21 per cent). Uncontrolled logging and mining accounted for a further 10 per cent and 7 per cent, respectively. Of those citing mining as a factor in deforestation, 70 per cent were males. A number gave graphic and presumably first-hand descriptions of the kinds of damage caused by uncontrolled diamond mining in a forest reserve. Others had been more impressed by a film made for BBC Television, but widely available on video in Sierra Leone, of the environmental damage caused by international bauxite and rutile (a titanium oxide found in quartz) mining operations in southern Sierra Leone. Informants were often very well-informed about, and gave chapter and verse for, specific abuses by loggers and miners. This aspect of youth culture in Sierra

Leone (the idea that young people are watching the activities of the older generation and keeping score) is well summed up by the chorus of a political song composed by the band Blind Musical Flames, and released not long after the 1992 military coup: *'lɛ dɛm lɛf wi noo, dɛm fil sɛ wi no no'* ('let them clear off, they think we don't know [what's been going on]').

Of those who thought the forest to be decreasing, 85 per cent believed it would affect them directly, and gave a total of 515 examples, comprising a rich tapestry of all the reasons conservationists might give for preserving tropical rainforest. The great majority of reasons were directly practical – loss of non-timber forest products (9 per cent), shortage of timber (7 per cent), reduced agricultural productivity (19 per cent), lack of further opportunities for opening up new farms (4 per cent), shortage of firewood (6 per cent), shortage of medicinal herbs (3 per cent). But there was also concern for the environment in general, and a particular focus on climate. In all, 25 per cent of responses (the largest single group) expressed concern for the connection between deforestation and climatic change, and their fears that the country would be afflicted by drought, that temperatures would rise, that bush fires would become more prevalent, and that Sierra Leone would become as hot and unpleasant as Guinea in the dry season. About 10 per cent of responses concerned the loss of animals – some interviewees were specifically worried by loss of access to bushmeat, but others regretted that they might never now have the chance to see rare animals like elephants for themselves. Three mentioned extinction as a bad thing in itself. A small number of interviewees were concerned by the macroeconomic consequences of forest loss (citing reduced government revenues and extra pressure on foreign exchange reserves to acquire substitute items). Seven respondents specifically regretted that the next generation would no longer enjoy forest benefits, perhaps feeling in some way the present generation had failed in its duty of stewardship. Four interviewees mentioned the potential threat posed by forest loss to the confidentiality of secret societies. Nine informants (eight in Bo) were concerned that the depletion of forests would further reduce the number of potential refuges in which villagers might hide from evil people like the rebels.

Deforestation and war

The guerrilla campaign begun by the rebel Revolutionary United Front in eastern Sierra Leone in 1991 was fought in some of the most heavily forested parts of Sierra Leone and, after the failure of initial attempts to capture one or other of the main towns in provincial Sierra Leone, military action was dominated by the tactic of the ambush. Bush survival skills were emphasized in the training of RUF conscripts/recruits. Displaced populations from the war zone also had an intense experience of the forest, escaping through secluded forest by-ways, and sometimes hiding from the troops on both sides for weeks on end. Villagers were required by government forces to clear plantations and bushes close to settlements, and roadside forests (many left as shade for travellers from the nineteenth century) in order to create free-fire zones and reduce risks of ambush. The war, then, has both heightened fears of dangers in the forest (both mystical and practical), and accelerated the process of local deforestation.

In the interviews, respondents were asked to comment on the proposition 'rebels hide in forests, so the government should clear all remaining forests to make the area safe'. Asked to rank responses on a five-point scale, from 'strongly agree' to 'strongly disagree', some interviewees took time to clarify their choice in additional, often quite lengthy, comments. The same statement was one of the items used to spark conversation for informal, taped, group discussions.

There was a 90 per cent response rate to this item, and the results are symmetrically distributed (31 per cent of respondents opting to 'strongly agree', and 31 per cent to 'strongly disagree'). Only 3 per cent of interviewees opted for the neutral middle point (a testimony to the vividness of the experiences described above), with 25 per cent favouring the 'agree somewhat' option and 10 per cent favouring 'disagree somewhat'. Women tended to be more in favour of the 'strongly agree' option than men). Strong agreement with the 'enforced deforestation' option as a way to make the countryside safe was more marked among women than men (39 per cent of all women's responses, but only 22 per cent of men's responses). As might be expected, the pattern reverses at the other end of the scale, with more men 'strongly disagreeing' (25 per cent women, 37 per cent men). There were no marked variations in support for the proposition according to age or location, the latter perhaps slightly surprising given the greater remoteness of Freetown and Kambia from the war. It should be noted, however, that the pre-war social 'mix' in eastern Sierra Leone was great due to diamond-mining, and there are many households in Freetown and Kambia housing displaced relatives. Age made a slight difference, with the youngest age group (perhaps less fully aware of the longer-term economic implications than their elders) slightly more bullish about clean-felling the war zone to end the war.

Education was the single biggest factor in determining the pattern of responses. Those with no formal education or only primary education were twice as likely to 'strongly agree' with the proposition as interviewees with post-primary education. The pattern holds good over all three research locations, in forested Bo, savanna-transition Kambia, and urbanized Freetown. This result and the gender difference noted above, are important, in that they stand in marked contrast to earlier evidence suggesting rather high levels of common knowledge and experience concerning the forest, irrespective of gender, religion or educational background. Nothing has served to differentiate the experience of deforestation among Sierra Leoneans more than the RUF rebellion.

Two points can be made. The first is that the war has mainly affected rural areas and, as in any such war, it is the rural poor (many now displaced in towns like Bo, Kambia, and Freetown) who have suffered the most. They have suffered not only the loss of family and property, but also of social amity. The RUF arrived apparently having learned some of the lessons of Renamo guerrilla destabilization in Mozambique – how to spread social dissension, for example, by embroiling young conscripts in violence against their own families (Renamo may have acquired this knowledge from guerrilla-training sources within the Rhodesian and South African military). One technique now regularly deployed by factions in both Liberia and Sierra Leone is to seek to exacerbate underlying social tensions by selectively burning the houses of Muslims or Christians in any village they attack. When the rebels withdraw into the forest and the community attempts to regroup, neighbours will tend to draw unwarranted conclusions about who among their number was in league with the invaders, and why. This results in ongoing civil strife which the armed factions later turn to their strategic advantage. Small wonder, then, in conditions of heightened tension and incipient social collapse, that the rural poor (and women, perhaps more heavily engaged in social networking and fully aware of what it takes to sustain co-operation) are so keen to let in as much light as possible on the scene, and see where their enemies are coming from. Deforestation is a wholly understandable response to those whose priority is the protection of the social fabric of rural society.

The more highly educated and, in contrast, males more intensely engaged with the cash economy, see with considerable clarity that forests offer income, and that their own futures are tied up with this future source of economic strength. Cutting down forest as a short-term security measure offers few attractions. Many of those who commented spontaneously were at pains to stress that deforestation was strategically short-sighted. Whereas women and the less educated, in touch with the needs of rural society, prioritized the need 'to make people safe', 'to protect lives', 'to ensure that these evil thugs have nowhere to hide', men, and the more highly educated, tended to make points like 'rebels don't just hide in forests, they are in the towns as well', 'the war will be over one day, but we will still need forests for income', and 'cutting down forests for security will lead to environmental insecurity'.

One older man even brought up 'star wars' technology to support his case, arguing that satellites had already solved the problem of working out where, and who, the rebels were. This reminded me of a fine cartoon I had once seen adorning the wooden shutter of a village mud-built house close to the Liberia border in 1978. One of the decorations through which young men in the village typically exhibit their modernity, this cartoon showed a helicopter hovering low over the village, carefully observing events on the ground, as two village women went about their daily business of pounding the rice for household meal in their *mata odo* (this is an item of forest produce without which no household can function, even in the city). The cartoon embodied, at a glance, an aspect of globalization – linking 'the bush' with 'outer space' – that is part of the cultural context guiding development in Sierra Leone. Many Sierra Leoneans remain, perhaps justifiably, confident that just as diamonds, semi-automatic rifles, and satellite telecommunications have contributed to their present woes, the answers will come from a similar blending of internal and external innovation and initiatives, a process characterized by Hannerz (1987) as 'cultural creolization'.

What is to be done?

Two-thirds of the interviewees believed that forests in Sierra Leone are diminishing, and had concrete ideas about what to do to reverse the trend. They provided 614 suggestions (39 per cent from women). The majority involved either regulation (41 per cent) – strengthening and implementing the law on forest exploitation, delimiting forest reserves, fining those who abused resources and caused environmental damage; or technical solutions (42 per cent) – scientific management of reserves, development of sustainable agriculture, through research into better crops and farming systems and use of fertilizer and, (above all), through reafforestation (26 per cent of all suggestions). Parren and van der Graaf (1995), cutting against the grain of enthusiasm for 'tree planting schemes' in development circles (and especially among NGOs), argue strongly in favour of 'scientific management' of natural rain forest as being, in general, a superior option to tree plantation in West Africa. But Sierra Leone has little natural forest left to manage, and local perceptions may, in this case, be pretty much on target.

Tree planting is a 'commonsense' solution, and fits well with local experience of not clearing forest, but modifying and enriching it with 'plantation crops'. A small-scale farmer around Gola, with forest to convert, never considers clear-felling the forest for cocoa or coffee plantation, but first opens up and thins the canopy with selective felling, and introduces a scattering of seedlings to see how they do (Davies and Richards, 1991). In a couple of years, the farmer returns to assess progress, and then decides whether it is worth investing more labour to fell some of the smaller trees likely to compete with the coffee or cocoa seedlings. Large trees will be left, especially economic trees such as kola, and species good for timber, to provide shade, and a source of additional income (the timber will be earmarked for felling only in another 15–20 years, when the plantation has passed its peak). Once derided by development experts, who wanted to encourage high-productivity plantations established in straight lines, this type of low-intensity, slow, step-by-step, modification of the forest environment has a number of clear environmental advantages, as well as providing steady, if modest, returns to the farm household. Although it falls between two stools (admired as little by conservationists as by developers), this 'hybrid' between Northern conceptions of a 'proper' plantation, and natural secondary vegetation, may prove to be a good ('creolizing') template for further technological elaboration.

Somewhat differing from the gender distinction noted in relation to forest and war, women, it is interesting to note, tended to favour technical solutions (and the tree-planting option in particular) more than men. Men proposed 59 per cent of all regulatory and control options, and women 57 per cent of all technical solutions. Since women provided fewer suggestions overall (39 per cent) than men (although they are equally represented in the sample) the difference is even more marked than these percentages seem to suggest. There is also a rather interesting regional slant to the figures: technical solutions tended to be favoured, among all informants, more in Bo (48 per cent of all suggestions from Bo) than in Kambia (37 per cent of suggestions from Kambia), and Freetown (35 per cent of all suggestion from Kambia), the pattern then running in reverse for regulatory options (Freetown 48 per cent, Kambia 44 per cent and Bo 34 per cent). Perhaps there is greater confidence in Freetown in the capacity of the state to enact and implement the draconian measures these young informants often had in mind.

Education and persuasion accounted for 9 per cent of suggestions, and surprisingly few informants (3 per cent) thought in terms of community-based solutions (whether management of common property resources, or locally-generated technical solutions). This will come as bad news to conservation agencies pinning their hopes on local civil engagement by 'stake-holders' on the margins of forest reserves (an engagement that may actually be counter-productive to the interests of the wider society, but favoured because it offers the prospect of mobilizing the local community to 'police' the forest against 'outsiders', and so provides – in theory – effective conservation 'on the cheap'). Even fewer attended to the question of economic incentives or overall government policy on the environment (although the few suggestions made were generally highly apposite, for example, the importance of price incentives as a stimulus to more sustainable agriculture, and the need for the government to decide upon and publish an overall strategy document for the environment in Sierra Leone). Broadly speaking, young Sierra Leoneans are pinning their main hope on the possibility of strong government, increased respect for the law, and technical solutions for sustainable resource management, perhaps mainly outside reserved forests.

This picture is borne out by their comments on who should be responsible for implementing these suggestions. As many as *half* of all the 584 suggestions made involved 'government' or organizations of the state (mainly technical departments of 'line' ministries, or, in some cases, schools and research institutions). In keeping with the emphasis on technical solutions, much responsibility would lie with experts. There was a strong feeling that national expertise needed to be built up as an urgent priority in environmental resource management (this, doubtless, is a feeling linked to the educational ambitions of many of the interviewees, and some interviewees reiterated career ambitions at this point); but there was also a strong emphasis on the need for international inputs, and a real awareness that Sierra Leone could not 'go it alone' on environmental issues. Supporters of 'community conservation' may be somewhat reassured to note that quite a good number of regulatory options were assigned, as responsibilities, to local authorities (6 per cent), and the institutions of civil society (31 per cent), such as farmers' groups and bush-owning lineages. Strikingly, many informants included themselves at this point, emphasizing that the onus for the future was not on 'traditional' groups, but on 'Sierra Leoneans', 'the people', 'citizens' and, above all, 'us'.

The evidence from the survey, outlined above, shows that on balance young people in Sierra Leone have a sound grasp of current environmental changes and the problems that these might cause, and clear and cogent ideas about possible solutions. There are some variations by background and locale, but not so large as to suggest the impossibility of forging future, broad-based consensus concerning environmental issues. Despite a long-drawn-out war in which over 20,000 people have died and many hundreds of thousands have been rendered displaced and homeless, younger Sierra Leoneans are remarkably positive about the future. While not underestimating the need and potential for civil action, young people of all backgrounds have a strong conviction that the state will be the major player in any concerted attack on environmental problems. There is an interesting gender difference, however, in the stress given to regulatory and technical action. Young men tend to stress regulatory action, young women technical solutions. For both genders, however, the legacy of 'cultural creolization' remains strong, and is a potentially viable basis for forging locally based solutions to new environmental dilemmas.

11 Indigenous knowledge of trees and forests in non-European societies

KLAUS SEELAND

NOWADAYS, CROSS-CULTURAL RESEARCH is no more only an exceptional research agenda of academic social anthropology, but is a multicultural encounter in environments that matter to many societies – not just their inhabitants. The condition of the great territories of the earth, such as the polar regions, the rainforests, and the great lakes of mainland Asia, is recognized as important for the maintenance of a tolerable climate world-wide. When the physical surroundings of one or more cultures, inhabiting the same region, become relevant to people living far away, a general interest in what is culture, and how different cultures compare is awakened. This raises methodological questions.

First there is the question of the common ground. Cultures make common-sense comparisons among themselves. People of one culture usually perceive other cultures in relation to their own interests and achievements. A scientific theory of cross-cultural comparison is necessary, however, when investigating how local and non-local knowledge meet at a level of configurations of phenomena. We assume that there is a difference in scope and depth as to how far what can be called 'knowledge of forests', is perceived as globally relevant to *all* cultures and societies. Different world-views and traditions, at different stages of economic and technological development, reflect what the terms 'forest', and 'knowledge of forests', mean to those who share a common culture. This is more than technical knowledge – botanical knowledge, or hunting skills, wood-harvesting know-how or what to do with non-timber products. It means more than having a grasp of the disciplines classified under the Northern tradition of forestry sciences; it is an applied social science approach.

Local knowledge about forest-related phenomena makes sense, both for local forest dwellers, and for those who appreciate the cultural wisdom, and its skilful socio-cultural performance from a perspective of scientific interest, environmental concern, and bearing responsibility for a renewable resource that matters to the future of mankind. Indigenous knowledge of forests unites aspects of nature and culture which are of both local and global concern. What comparisons can be made between cultures which share a practical or theoretical interest in forest knowledge? Why, for example, are Western social scientists curious about what indigenous forest dwellers know about and do with their forest? Is there a common ground for cross-cultural comparison between both environmental perceptions, other than Western global concern on a rather detailed level?

Indigenous knowledge as a phenomenon complex

Knowledge may be called indigenous if it originates from, and is bound to, local experiences, and takes its local 'world' perhaps not as the only one in existence, but as the most relevant. It is an authentic appropriation of being. The environment is not an environment in a technical sense, but a world. The opinion that there is a locally meaningful world characterizes an indigenous world-view. 'Indigenous' or 'local knowledge of forests' as we shall refer to it, is a holistic view of what is revealed to human perception through, and as, forest life. The term indigenous means something that originates locally, and is performed by a community or society in this specific place. It emerges as peoples' perceptions and experiences in an environment, a continuous process of observation and interpretation in relation to the locally acknowledged, everyday rationalities and transcendental powers. The context of local social performances makes sense for people who share a common rural habitat and language. Indigenous knowledge is human life-experience in a distinct natural and cultural amalgamation, within a unique local and contemporary setting.

In a traditional society, the local context is taken as the universal frame in which knowledge matters. This context is formed from physical facts, social interactions among people in the surroundings they perceive as their world, and of the spirituality connected with this space. Indigenous knowledge is perceived in, and represents, a particular context at a certain stage of the perceiver's consciousness that grows in the local world.

The question of what forests are, therefore, should not be considered in the sense of the natural sciences, but as an overall cultural notion, in the sense of a local world. Forests are a configuration of living beings who constitute their own surroundings of particular plant societies, mankind, and animal species. Configurations of different, yet related, forms of life tend to perpetuate themselves in the forms of specific successions, that characteristically occur in biotic configurations – commonly denominated as forests. Knowledge about forests is multifold, therefore, and ranges from individual experience with particular aspects of flora and fauna, to forest lore and ascriptions to it as, for example, the dwelling place of ancestors, demons, and benevolent and malevolent spirits. Forests have a spiritual aspect in every culture. This spirituality is the more vivid, the more traditional a community's lifestyle. Transcendental notions matter predominantly in this setting, where wilderness and growth are combined with decay. Growth and decay are united here, unlike in the social world, where the living are separated from the dead.

Among forest dwellers, indigenous knowledge about forests represents the principle of 'sociality,' as social life is reflected in its natural surroundings. The constitution of social life is generated by social activities, cultural layout and perceptions, religious beliefs and personal experience of the environment, as well as a collective knowledge that is passed down through generations. Settlement and spatial organization of a forest-dwelling community is done taking the space available for social interaction into consideration, and determine suitable dwelling-place. The appropriateness of the dwelling-place is decided in accordance with the community's territorial and cosmological perception. A comparatively safe and ritually auspicious settlement, for example, has to be paralleled by local potential to provide the means for a community's subsistence. This applies to sedentary as well as to nomadic or semi-nomadic groups. Social life within a forested area depends on the potential of resources that can be operationalized by a community within the process by performing a local identity.

Apart from the locale, the history is also relevant to a community's identity. Both influence how local resources are used within a culture. Nature, in the shape of fertile surroundings, and people's abilities to build a sustainable society through social institutions permeate each other to a very great extent. The amalgamation of both local natural resources and their mobilization through social cognition and institutions at distinct local levels is what culture means. The order in which nature is recognized, then transformed into a social order to which it becomes the basis of rituals and symbols, where culture and nature become exchangeable terms, is the process of classification. Classification processes aim to 'create' phenomena by deciding whether, in any given culture, they are commonly understood as 'natural' or 'cultural'. When phenomena 'come into being' in such a way, they become relevant elements of the world-view of those who recognize them somehow. Whatever is perceived is culture, and remains 'nature' only in a sense which is adapted as a culturally agreed term. What 'nature as such' could be remains obscure, apart from its denomination as culture. If we agree to perceive the denomination and classification of any phenomena as culture, the term nature then applies to all phenomena which are believed to grow, exist and decay according to their own species' scripts, with little, or no, or only indirect human interference, and ultimately unknown to him.

In Western everyday communication – even in most contemporary scientific perceptions – nature and culture are treated as equally known or unknown phenomena irrespective of the logic of their degree of reality. Indigenous knowledge is much more closely bound to a particular context. The context is the focus of all the knowledge at a person's disposal at the very moment he or she is exposed to a situation in which knowledge is called upon to be applied within this context. What indigenous people 'know' is difficult to evaluate in general. Knowledge varies between individuals, and their particular perceptions of a situation decides upon what aspect of one person's knowledge is asked for in a specific situation. Knowledge is not so much a distinct and confirmed set of what one person definitely knows or claims to know or not to know, but it is the context that decides what is perceived as knowledge and, thus assumed to be applicable. The term 'context' stands for events that happen in a locality at a time. It is a process of calling something into being under the circumstances in which human beings participate in a natural and similar cultural setting. What indigenous people know is drawn from their experience of appropriating nature as culture. The highly aggregated complex of forests represents a world of mankind, plants, and wildlife, a natural world that has evolved as culture. This *complex* constitutes contexts where knowledge results from the processes of these appropriations.

Core problems of cross-cultural research

One of the basic questions of comparative research is to what extent, if at all, can phenomena be compared? In the particular context of knowledge about forests, natural phenomena appear, if they appear at all, in the shape of socially relevant phenomena. Thus, any process of physical perception is a social act of interpretation of what is perceived and appropriated by adaptation into a context called culture. When nature is selectively perceived as relevant – after becoming an aspect of a social context – it gains a cultural meaning which is a significant dimension for its social performance. The process of appropriation represents the specific mode by which one can discriminate things as elements of the natural surroundings that guide the act of selection and transformation through interpretation. A socially relevant interpretation of what is a perceivable thing is only possible against an ontological background of a classificatory process of a community as a process of the social formation of knowledgeable people and users who benefit from their acquired knowledge.

There can be no discourse on sociality as such between cultures which does not reflect the process in which nature is appropriated. The level of comparison evolves from the necessity to exchange notions and perceptions about what the processes are that ascribe significance to what is to be perceived at all, and why.

Intercultural communication about the possibility of cross-cultural comparison is a phenomenon of modern societies and their rationalizations about possible and, finally, socially agreed ways to make use of their surroundings and, in principle, the question of the constitution of culture. Within the context of modernity, there is a discourse on these differences in appropriation. The process of appropriation itself, however, is not disputed, because it is the very principle of a self-constitution of culture. Berlin (1992, p.5), for example, pinpoints the basic cognitive problem of modern ethnobiological research: 'Why do human societies classify nature in the way they do?' Likewise, he could have asked: 'Why do human communities constitute themselves as cultures?'

The prefix 'ethno' in names of all these scientific disciplines examining particular elements of non-European cultures, such as ethnozoology and ethnolinguistics proves that scientific theory does treat these cultures as distinct from the mainstream subjects. This perception has a built-in cultural relativism, as all aspects of different cultures can be compared through their respective ethnosciences, and these refer, ultimately, to the framework of the Northern scientific paradigm of how non-Northern cultures are to be perceived – through ethnology, and cultural or social anthropology and their respective subjects.

Ethnobiology is also a rare and outstanding exemption from this pattern. It purports to be a combination of anthropology and biology with sometimes rather broad variations (Berlin, 1992, p.3f), but it is actually far more than that. Strictly speaking, it is a *proto-science*, although, so far, this seems to be little recognized by ethnobiologists. The main argument for ethnobiology being a proto-science is that it is more than just an enquiry into the ways human communities *relate* to plants and animals and do or do not use them. The processes of cognition and classification are based on cosmological, spiritual, and philosophical notions and assumptions, which refer to the constitution and confirmation of cultural core-terms. The commonly shared world-view of a community is, thus, reflected in this cosmogonic process which, on the surface, appears to be a classificatory process of botanical or animal genera.

This can be seen most clearly with regard to the number of known species that, in the mid-1980s, amounted to nearly *1.4 mio.*, while the number of species to be found in rainforests all over the globe were estimated at approximately *30mio.* (Wilson, 1988:5); the *unknown* flora and fauna to be found in rainforests is estimated to be more than 20 times that figure. The deplorable loss of some of the known species, therefore, might be outweighed by far by 'discovering new' species. But, known species are 'culture,' and obviously matter more to concerned people, particularly in economically developed countries. This would represent the comparativist's view, because she takes all globally available data into account. From a relativist's point of view, the loss of species is unimportant, because all ethnoscientific knowledge is locally bound, and limited to the species that are found in this part of the globe, and which only ever takes a limited number of these into account.

A comparative perspective is only a possibility for modern societies who, unlike traditional societies, have thrown off the culturally binding perception that only their natural surroundings are of any real relevance.

Polysemy and the methodology of the context

A modern natural science approach necessarily has a comprehensive vision with which to detect, sooner or later, all species on earth, and to proceed with their systematic classification according to a scientific pattern which is claimed to be valid for *all* species, irrespective of their cultural appropriation. From this perspective there are, strictly speaking, no ethnobiological *data*, because they would be either botanical data or anthropological data, but, in fact they are merged into an ethnobiological *paradigm*. Within this paradigm, taxonomic terms might be, and often are, polysemous and might be difficult to categorized within a scientific theory of classification (Ellen, 1993, pp.215–26). It is the process of research itself that produces data, whereas the context of cultural appropriation does not necessarily distinguish between plants, animals, or an ancestor's spirit that may appear to local people as a plant, animal, or both (Vitebsky, 1993, pp.53–141).

Ethnobiological configurations are neither authentic accounts from the emic point of view of the culture concerned, nor simply one-dimensional scientific data. The ethnobiological paradigm represents the evolution of a distinct culture, because it has to take into account all forms of life which are experienced as an interconnected whole by those who share the culture's mode of perception. As there are no ethnobiological *data*, there are no species to be found *in* a forest. The question is, how do people from a particular area recognize and become familiar with their surroundings? What is revealed to them, in what way, and how do they embark on a process of comparing what they know with what they do not know?

An ethnobiological inquiry into a people's world has to find out how and what has led this group to convert its surroundings into a sphere of culture. Such an inquiry goes far beyond the reconstruction of the process of classification of different species. Humans tend to compare these similarities which function as a bridge between known phenomena and phenomena to be known. Discriminating distinctions thus evolve from comparing new items with those already identified.[1] Whether imagination or experience has cognitive priority in man's primordial acquisition of knowledge is disputed. It is widely accepted, however, that metaphorization is identical in this process. It is the metaphor[2] that charges a previously unknown thing – spotted as a new object of interest amidst a partly ordered environment – with attributes that will place it within one's own culture. Paul Ricoeur claims, for example, that common, everyday language is a 'sunken metaphor', which cannot or can only rarely be traced back to the origins of the meanings of any ordinary words. In this way, forest communities perceive and order a good proportion of their culture out of their dominant forest environment. By employing a metaphor, one can give a previously unknown thing a name that is already used for one or more existing items. Its application out of context broadens the scope of what is potentially to be known by transferring a term into another context.[3]

A context is a configuration of the interrelating dimensions of nature and culture at the material, as well as at the immaterial, level. It can be taken as a focus of plants, animals, and human imagination and interventions that shapes an area's environmental setting. This method of contextual configurations was used in the research project on indigenous knowledge on forests in Orissa (Seeland, Patnaik et al, 1995)[4]. Basically one accepts that a culture is composed of contexts which are interconnected, and thus can be interpreted with the help of the hermeneutic methodology. The hermeneutic circle as the core imaginative pattern of this methodology – where all possible contexts are lying on this circle – is equally connected with its centre. These contexts refer to each other through their interconnectedness, and represent different and multifold forms of beings, like flora and fauna influenced by human management in an ontological framework of Being. Honey-bees, for example, unite the contexts of flora and fauna by collecting the plant's nectar and transforming it into a much desired food.

The names of certain types of forest is another example. To the Kuttia Kondh, a tribe of central Orissa, forests are patches of land containing various plant species, large and small trees including shrubs, bushes and creepers, and different types of beasts that make the jungle a dangerous wilderness. They believe that the forest is a place, divided into three levels: Earth (*Tana*), Over Earth (*Tana Kueti*), and Under Earth (*Tana Daeti*). Plants occupy only one place (*i.e.* earth) while animals are found in all three. Although plants survive on 'earth', their roots get into the 'under earth' and their branches and twigs scrape the 'over earth' (the sky), thereby giving shelter to animals.

Any patch of land with a lot of trees and animals, therefore, is seen by tribal people, as a forest. They define the wilderness (*Boti ne Ajine*) of the forest in numerous ways. The large number of timber plantations surrounded by bushes are also defined as forest; a plantation is a forest if it is multi-storeyed, and contains large trees with coiling tree creepers.

The places where sunlight (*Ujada*) does not infiltrate, because of the concentration of canopies of huge trees, are known to the Kuttia Kondh as 'real' wild forest. For them, the sun (*Weda*) is the most powerful being in the whole universe. They believe that trees compete to grow highest towards the sky (*Wani*) and that trees in the forest are more important than animals. The reason for this is that they believe strongly that the earth was once barren; there were very few animals and the first human beings who emerged from the earth hunted to stay alive. The Kuttia Kondh's primordial song (*Kui gaani*) details all these elements – their cosmogonic myth: Without trees the earth was not luscious. Then the idea of planting trees came to the supreme lady of the earth (*Nerandali*); and the supreme lady requested the supreme man (*Betamangera*) to do something. As a result, the first tree was born near '*Sapangada*', the mythical earth hole.

The myth further states that the first species of plants came out of the species of the trees, and that the trees evolved from the dead body of a sambar (Cervus Unicolor). The species that evolved near '*Sapangada*' were later known as *Sati Kambani* and *Pditi Kambani*. Here, *Sati* means born of the earth, and *pdite* means coming out of the female genitalia.

Types of forest in the perception of the Kuttia Khonds of Burlubaru

The tribal people divide the forests in Burlabaru (Phulbani District/Orissa) into five different types: *Kambani*, *Bati*, *Umda*, *Tuleni*, and *Katani*; a classification based mainly on the way the trees are arranged as forest.

Kambani (forest)

Kambani is a *Kui* name which derives from a particular species' set of trees. The *Kambani* usually consists predominantly of species like *Shorea robusta*, *Pterocarpus marsupium*, *Bombax ceiba*, *Eugenia jambolana*, *Mangifera indica*, *Ficus benghalensis*, and *Ficus religiosa*. *Kambani* literally means 'trees of equal height'. The top of a single tree is called '*Sarene*', while the top of a group of trees is called '*Sarena*'. In a Kambani, certain tree species have a common form of canopy. According to the *Kui gaani* these trees tend to touch the sky; but are prevented from doing so by the supreme lady, Nerandali. The myth says that when Nerandali and her people came on earth for the first time, the sky and the earth were one. To separate them, they pushed heaven up and, in the process, created a space which sheltered them. But afterwards, when these trees rose towards the sky, people feared that they might cover the sun, the primary source of life on earth. There was also a fear of the sky coming back through the trees and uniting with earth again. Moreover, Nerandali feared that the creepers at the tree-tops could pull down the sky and make earth and sky one unit again. To prevent unlimited growth therefore, Nerandali created birds to check it. But this was not enough, so she created squirrels and white ants, as the former can wreck the shoots and buds of the tree-tops, and the latter can infest the over-grown roots of the trees. Now the trees could no longer grow too tall. The Kuttia Kondh consider these animals to be the 'designers' of the *Kambani*. All these things took place near *Sapangada* where, according to the Kondhs, the first forest was created with the help of Nerandali. The name of this forest is *Sati Kambani*.

Usually, the Kondh's dwellings are found in the hilly forest areas. They rarely dwell in the plains or lowland forest area, for they strongly believe that the trees belonging to the hilly areas *(Kambani)* are of immense intrinsic value. These large, tall trees *(Dera mara)*, along with some undergrowth *(Lika mara)* and the creepers *(Tula)* constitute the vegetation of the hill top forest. This includes a variety of species like *Shorea robusta (Sargi mara)*, *Terminalia tomentosa (Mardi mara)*, *Ficus benghalensis (Bade mara)*, *Ficus scandens (Pipoda mara)*, *Acacia pinnata (Sikari tula)*, and *Bauhinia vahlii (Paeri tulla)* which are all self-germinating. The hill-top areas usually consist of dry soil *(Bachit vira)* and rocks *(Balinga)* on which only tree species such as *Ficus benghalensis* can grow because of their tremendous self-generating power. Although the undergrowth and the shrubs are not to be found here, creepers like *Bauhinia vahlii* and *Acacia pinnata* – along with a wild grass called *'Babe' (Eulaliopsis binata)* – can be found.

These combinations of natural vegetation on the hill top are interesting from the Kuttia Kondh's point of view. They regard their hill god *(Donger Penu)* as solely responsible for the distribution of such vegetation, and believe that the *Penu* (the supreme god of the forest) decides upon the plantation according to the locality. He chooses the tall trees as his abode, and he prefers the hill-tops for two major reasons. One is so he has a clear view of the sorrows and sufferings, or vices and virtues of the villagers who dwell at the foot of the hill. The other reason is so he can enjoy the first touch of the virgin rain. He uses the creepers to move around the different places inside the forest to meet the other *Penus* on matters regarding the welfare of the tribal people. He allows grass to grow at the base of the trees to make the forest floor softer so that celestial beings can roam around freely.

Regarding the fauna of the *Kambani*, the *sambar (Maju)* is very common, as it cannot survive in the dense forest. The other major animals in the area are the tiger *(Kdani)*, bear *(Ali)*, elephant *(Hati)*, wild boar *(Braha)*, four-horned antelope *(Kateri)* and fowls *(Kambat kaju)*.

Bati (forest)

The term *Bati* has several meanings. *Bati* is the most common name for forest. It is also a term of respect for bushy vegetation, including undergrowth, shrubs, creepers, and herbs. In the hill-forests, *Bati* lies between the foot-hills and hill-slope areas. The Kuttia Khondh consider *Bati* to be the primary state of forest. From a scientific point of view it is taken for granted that the growth of a forest is never static but always dynamic; this concept is not shared by the Kuttia Kondh. According to them, the branches of the trees *(Kena)* inside the *Bati*, which spread through the forest, reserve space for small plants to grow *(Ningine)*. *Bati* is believed, therefore, to constitute vegetation over a particular period of time.

This perception confirms that *Bati* grows better in a soft soil *(Dea vira)*, because on such a soil all types of plant species grow easily and swiftly. Furthermore, the rainwater from the hill-top runs off easily to the base of the hills, also facilitating the growth of trees. *Bati* benefits from even more water than *Kambani* for, even if the rainfall in both places is equal, *Bati* receives the surplus water from the hill-tops. The fertility of *Bati* is also enhanced by many fast-growing species, which after atrophying, add to the fertility of the soil.

Animal life inside the *Bati* deserves special mention, for the variety is formidable. It includes snakes *(Srachu)*, pythons *(Masi)*, monitor lizards *(Boda)*, porcupines *(Saju)*, and pangolins *(Jerandi)*, and many different birds.

Umda (grove)

This term is used to describe a patch of forest surrounded by rocky or barren land. It is common on hill-tops with a rocky floor or huge stone surroundings. *Umda* vegetation is generally composed of *Ficus benghalensis*, *Ficus religiosa* and *Ficus scandens*, (which are dominant by nature) along with *Terminalia tomentosa*, *Chara*, *Shorea robusta*, *Pterocarpus marsupium* and *Acacia pinnata*. *Umdas* in other non-rocky surroundings normally consist of a wide variety of small trees and plant species *(Ladenga)*.

Tuleni (graveyard forest)

Tuleni is the part of the forest used by the Kuttia Kondhs exclusively for the cremation of the dead; and is not entered by visitors. The collection of firewood and any tree-felling is totally prohibited, and this encompasses resin, mushrooms, tubers, herbs, or any sort of edible product. Villagers are careful not to pluck a leaf or flower or to break a brush-stick inside *Tuleni*. They believe that collecting anything from *Tuleni* means taking the food of the spirits of their ancestors. These taboos are believed to have existed since the Kuttia Kondh first settled here and gradually, certain myths built up around these virgin patches of wilderness. Among the different plant species found in *Tuleni*, the sal tree *(Shorea robusta)* is given special status as it is believed to be the dwelling-place of *Dukeli Penu* (main god of *Tuleni*). As a result, sal trees were left virtually untouched for many years. Even certain medicinal plants considered as highly effective in curing certain diseases are never touched in *Tuleni*. In exceptional cases, the medicine man, if permitted by the *Dukeli Penu*, can use certain herbs and roots. On the day of a funeral, the village priest *(Jani)* has to break a brush-stick which is offered to the corpse. Then, with 'permission' from the dead person's spirit, others can break brush-sticks. *Tuleni* firewood is used only for cremation purposes; firewood from other areas is forbidden to be used inside *Tuleni*. A dead person is considered to be a forest-dweller and is given the name *Kambanate*.

Consequently, these forbidden places are a source of fear to the villagers. Besides trees and plants, a large variety of animals such as deer, mouse-deer, porcupine, sambar and wild boar are to be found in these forests. Hunting inside

Tuleni, although not prohibited, rarely happens and, if at all, is only done by a group, during the day. Nobody dares to enter *Tuleni* alone for fear of ghosts and spirits, who may kill by infecting the visitor with a rare disease. During the cremation ceremony the village attendants pray to *Dukeli Penu* who provides them with sufficient game when hunting, which takes place during the mourning period *(Dasah)*, generally between the third and seventh day after death. This celebration of group hunting is a crucial rite after every death. It is believed strongly that if *Dukeli Penu* is satisfied with their prayers, the hunting expedition will not be in vain. Normally, the villagers do not shift the site of *Tuleni* for, they believe, by doing so they would disturb the spirits of their ancestors. Only certain events, such as plant-disease epidemics, the proliferation of certain orchids *(Gochchi)*, or forest fire – (which kills the sal trees) – force them to abandon the *Tuleni*. In these circumstances, a new patch of forest (in this case, the villagers of Burlubaru have chosen Ratadinella), is chosen as the replacement *Tuleni*. The leasing of forest patches to outsiders by government departments is the other factor which forces them to abandon the *Tuleni*; to do so, they must get the permission of *Dukeli Penu*.

Katani (hilly forest)

Katani denotes wild vegetation and from it the terms *Bati*, *Kambani* and *Umda* derive. Very often, this term is used to describe anything that is wild; *Katani* is not confined to any specific variety of vegetation, natural resource, or animal. *Katani* is a 'four-storey forest'. The ground floor consists of wild grass *(Randa)*, the first floor beds of herbs and small bushes. The *Bati* and the *Kambani* are the third and fourth floor, respectively.

Usually the Kuttia Kondh dwell in the cleared patches of woodland, surrounded by hills and forest. The entire hill range is covered by a vast number of plants. This aggregation of plants in the hill-forest is also loosely termed as *Katani*. Different parts of the hill-forest are characterized by different types of plant and animal.

The Hills of Dera Salla and Siramdeu

There is a large hill next to Bamanadeu hill, west of Burlubaru village, known as Dera Salla. Literally, Dera Salla means 'big shed'. There are many large caves in this hill. The forest near these mountains is not used, because it is covered by trees of the ficus species. The majority are *Ficus benghalensis, (Bademara), Ficus religiosa (Sorupipadi)*, and *Ficus scandens (Pipadi)*. The banyan tree *(Bademara)* is always regarded as the home of the different *Penus*, such as *Maunli Penu, Kama Penu, Mardi Penu, Adabai Penu*, and *Satari Penu*. The Kuttia Kondh believe strongly that, if a ficus is injured even slightly, the goddess living there will be angered, and a major epidemic such as smallpox or chicken-pox, and other misfortunes will follow and extinguish the entire tribe. Thus this forest is not only spared, but people are forbidden to use it. *Maunli Penu* and *Adabai Penu* are demonic goddesses, notorious for giving people stomach trouble, and causing various horrendous diseases.

Burlubaru is surrounded by hills: Gunjigata lies to the east, Bangeri to the south, Bamanadeu to the west, and Ladiguru to the north. The Siramdeu hill near Bamanadeu is regarded as the supreme *(Majhi)* of the gods *(Soru Penu)* because he is the decision-maker. No one except the Bangura caste *(Gachi)*, who offered the first homage to the *Penu*, is allowed to go there. Their worship is known to the Kondh as *Bangura Dakina*. It is offered to the god once every 15 to 20 years. It is believed that the *Jani*, the Kuttia Kondh's priest, who presides over the ritual, dies shortly after the ceremony. This prevailing fear is shared by the entire tribe. Usually, a *Jani* of the Bangura caste does not visit Siramdeu unless his son, or a man from the same caste, is elected as his successor. The evidence to support such a belief comes from the case of Balujani of Burlubaru, who died immediately after performing the worshipping ritual of Siramdeu *Penu*.

Knowledge – metaphors in interconnected contexts?

These examples make the connection between their names for forests, hills, and animals, and the cosmogonic myth of the Kuttia Khondh obvious. Gods, priests, death rituals and worship are interwoven with flora, fauna, and the physical – as well as the ritual or spiritual landscape. Any tree is a god *(Mara Penu)* as are the hills. The landscape *(Dharni)*, in general, is an entirely deified configuration of spiritual space which is represented by a particular god *(Penu)*. 'Thus *penu* defines the whole, the whole being the mystery to the Kuttia Kondh understanding. The whole or the collective body is termed as *'Grudu'* by Kuttia Kondhs. So nature is understood in a metaphorical way through *penu*.' (Seeland, Patnaik *et al.*, (1995) vol.1:195f.). *Penu* is the key, as well as the core-term, to many a context that reflects the Kuttia Kondh culture from various perspectives. Indigenous knowledge *(Budhi)* combines all aspects of the Kuttia Kondh culture by taking all aspects into account and constituting a context. What more there is to be learned about environmental issues becomes a derivation of what is already known about some aspects of this environment in the shape of a culture established from this very environment.[5] There is a metaphoric transfer, either of the spiritual world to the material, or a recognition of the similarities between already known and newly perceived phenomena which are, in this way, appropriated as culture. A prototype example for a metaphoric transfer is, for example, the naming of flora, fauna and landscape sites according to a particular cosmogonic myth where the coming of things into being is described in a text, but simultaneously reflected in the physical and socio-cultural context of a material reality. As stated above, a context is calling up knowledge, while its function can be seen as extended, in the sense that it creates 'new' knowledge through the transfer of metaphors.

Argued from an ontological point of view, knowledge and the polysemous meaning of terms, which link different parts of the Kuttias' world, constitute holistic contexts. In principle, the whole fabric of Kuttia Kondh culture is present in a constituting context that is connected with other contexts through the power of analogy and similarity that works in metaphoric language.[6] Knowledge as a transfer of metaphors thus becomes a 'self-contained tautology' (Barrett 1979:89) in the positive sense of the term that constantly refers to itself in varying contextual frames of reference.

Conclusion

The question of what can be compared between cultures, and what the peculiarities of cross-cultural comparison are, as far as forests in a cultural perspective are concerned, leads to more fundamental considerations about the nature of man's perception of complex phenomena. These phenomena are recognized and ordered according to local ways of appropriation. Nature is appropriated, according to a distinct indigenous pattern, to constitute a local culture. Providing there is increasing public awareness within economically developed countries of the need for the sustainable management of the world's large forest areas, and other renewable and exhaustible resources, the principle of locality is transcended by a concern, if not a commitment, for the survival of the earth's natural and cultural environments.

The dynamics of a transfiguration of nature into culture, by perceiving the former according to the distinct tradition of the latter, leads to the appropriation of natural phenomena or species through the use of metaphors. While nature is perceived in an acquisitive cultural perspective, the 'known nature' is appropriated as culture, once it has become indigenous local knowledge. Nature is to be called whatever the remainder of, as yet unknown, living species, minerals, or forms of energy there may be.

Natural phenomena are not engaged, if there are no contexts for human beings – either local dwellers or interested foreigners to lead them to an improved cultural status. Every enquiry into the secrets of nature is reflected in culture, or it can be said, *is* culture.

The international interest in forests is itself an intercultural attempt to extend one's outlook on world phenomena which one believes to be personally relevant. This extension, is not a superficial phenomenon, however, once nature in any part of the world has become one's own culture. The appropriation of a world that transcends the local environment through one's interest in the appropriation of nature and culture anywhere on earth, is a step towards cross-cultural acquisition of experience. This process may be called a post-modern phenomenon, the public opinion in the North becomes that of 'world locals' who perceive, for example, the tropical rainforests to be meaningful, and are as concerned about them as if they were living in the immediate vicinity. Yet there is one major difference between the post-modern and the traditional perception of what forests can be.

Kuttia Kondh's denomination of forests, in which they connect their gods, the hills, animals, their ancestral spirits, and their metaphoric language, shows that their concern for their world is holistic, or cosmological. This is reflected in the fact that, for them, a forest is a highly aggregated context where beings perform their respective forms of being, united by the sense these beings make in a culture.

Cross-cultural comparison of indigenous knowledge on forests may lead to a better understanding of cultures. One possible way of achieving this could be to take an interest in the differences in the particular way in which a culture is constituted, that cause it to appropriate nature in the form of forest. Perhaps the Kuttia Kondh's world will tumble once devoid of forest. Whether occidental cultures could carry on in future worlds without forests is open to debate. The public culture of the North, however, has gained an essential dimension in its global concern to investigate what nature and the world of forests can mean to those communities, whose cultures still reflect a 'local' rather than a global life.

What a society knows about forests is a reflection of its culture. The appeal of researching people's knowledge of forests in any culture is the opportunity to understand other cultures through investigating nature, and thus developing a concern for it. A prerequisite for evolving this perspective is that industrialized societies cease to perceive the state of the global environment only as an ever-increasing mass of problems. To learn from tribal indigenous knowledge on forests means to proceed with research on how yet unknown aspects of nature will become tomorrow's culture. In many a culture, man, forests, and trees do share a common fate.

Environmental problems reflect the state of political strife, in which various sections of a society are involved according to their respective interests and political bargaining power. Particularly controversial are usufructuary rights and benefits connected to resource use. If these depend on forest resources – belonging to areas of national interest and importance, these controversies indicate a lack of political consensus on the role of the state in distributing national wealth. This lack of consensus, for example, between ethnic groups and the social mainstream, is highlighted by the struggle over the appropriation of resources between interest groups, who emphasize conservation and the survival of the poor and marginal sections of society, and those who favour the economic development interests of the richer sectors of a society.

The recent history of the expropriation of tribal societies in post-colonial nations is, for the most part, a depressing account of environmental colonialism, where ethnic sections of young, developing nations are pauperized, expelled from their territories, and sometimes vanish along with the forests where they used to live. Tribal societies still, to a large extent live lives exposed to the power of ruthless nature, and at the mercy of the hierarchies of administrators in modernizing societies who aim to achieve urban, middle-class standards for countries in which the overwhelming majority of people are rural peasants. The knowledge of forest dwellers or poor peasants thus becomes the legacy of a cultural heritage and tradition that shaped the face of the forests, and the source of some of today's cultures.

Concern for ecology and the environment reflects the commitment of a world community that considers itself aware of the linkages between knowledge and conservation. Ecology and sustainable management of the environment are but other terms for the common future of all people of the globe in which diversity and pluralism are favoured over monoculturalism. But, national and international politics indicate that the struggle for survival, and control over the use of resources inside and outside a country's boundaries, is perennial. The dispute over what is perceived to be a resource for society as a whole, and what is left at the disposal of those ethnic groups who claim ancestral rights over it, is a social contest. The role of indigenous knowledge has to be seen in the perspective of this contest, because it cannot transcend it. It is up to a society's political will to acknowledge and safeguard the value of the country's cultural heritage, not as a goal in itself, but for the sake of having common, future options. Forest management as the contribution of tribal people to a national environmental policy may be an opportunity to share social responsibility for the country's forests and resources.

12 Forests and trees in the world of two Tamang villages in central Nepal: observations with special reference to the role of Tamang women in forest management

BETTINA MAAG

ON ENTERING THE Himalayan region one can hardly overlook the ubiquitous terraced hills and the vast number of lopped trees which give away the intensive interaction between man and nature. Thus, in focusing on environmental problems, such as forest degradation, one is compelled to include the human aspect: issues regarding biomass consumption, fodder cycles, or forest productivity can only be fully understood if we take a look at the man-forest relation in its entirety.

Since the 1980s the loss of forest cover has provoked far-reaching soil and water supply instability. This has led to hundreds of villages being exposed to environmental hazards such as landslides, floods, and a shortage of resources. In the hill region, in particular, the activities of the increasing population, such as collecting firewood, making charcoal, and timber harvesting are believed to have contributed substantially to forest degradation. And yet, local management practices can be easily adapted to high ecological fragility, as shown in many other places where dense forest patches and plenty of field trees can be found.

Local forest use also needs to be seen within the local, social and political orders and ownership patterns. Tamang men are considered the main actors of trade and village politics and are, in this sense, linked with forest management. Meanwhile, as previous research has shown (Gurung, 1987, Pandey, 1987, Shrestha, 1988), women are frequent users and manipulators of natural resources (Pradhan and Rankin, 1988) – forest products.

This chapter is based on studies made during a stay in two villages in central Nepal. Both villages are ethnically relatively homogeneous – with the majority of the inhabitants Tamang. The first village studied – here referred to as Sunnamsa – lies to the north-east of Kathmandu in the Sindhupalchowk district. The second village, Djavanamsa, lies at the edge of the Mahabharat Lekh range to the south-east of Kathmandu and is situated in the Lalitpur district. The prosperity of the two villages differs in terms of natural resources and economic wealth.

The Tamang, an ethnic group belonging to the Tibeto-Burman language group, primarily live as farmers, subsisting on the cultivation of maize, millet, paddy, wheat, and potatoes, and animal husbandry. They live in hamlets scattered along the mountain ranges and hills around the Kathmandu valley at an altitude of about 1200 to 1900m above sea level. Their dialects and traditional rites vary between western and eastern groups. The patrilineal clan and the family are the central social units in Tamang community. Life and social order are based, to a large extent, on egalitarian principles. The religious culture of the Tamang is rooted in tribal cults and shamanism. Through continuous contact with the Tibetan highlands as well as strong links with other originally Tibetan groups, Lamaism, the Tibetan form of Buddhism, has become the core of

Tamang culture. Lamaism has not taken on the form of monastery life, however, probably because it never received 'sufficient economical and political backing' (Höfer, 1971). Along with the process of Sanskritization, the Tamang were gradually incorporated into the Hindu caste system at a very low level. Today almost all villages are ethnically mixed. The Tamang remain, therefore, under the influence of different religious and cultural traditions.

Economic and Cultural Values of Forests and Trees

The role of trees in the subsistence economy of the Tamang

The subsistence economy of Tamang farmers depends in many ways on natural resources. Firewood and charcoal serve as the main energy sources, and animals are fed with leaves, grass, and the remains of the harvest. Manure mixed with compost is used to fertilize the soil. Timber is taken for the framework of the local houses; the walls are traditionally made of manure and red soil. Since many of these basic materials for agriculture and household purposes derive from forest and field trees, it is not surprising that a Tamang, when asked about the use of the forest, will immediately answer 'the forest gives us good timber, fuelwood and fodder.'

Indeed, a wide spectrum of tree species found in the Tamang region is used to satisfy various local needs. Almost every species is in some way incorporated in the farming system. The Appendix shows the economic uses and some of the ecological significance of the tree species of Sunnamsa village.

Tree species which can be used for several purposes are of particular interest. Unfortunately this is only rarely the case. The conclusion that the Tamang attach particular value to multi-purpose trees and thus protect them more carefully is not necessarily true. By living with the Tamang, one begins to understand that certain phenomena related to the forest and trees reach beyond the material perception and stand in a larger, transcendental context. A tree or a group of trees, for example, can gain special respect because of its location or its significance in the sensibility of a cult. Other trees are each valued for only one outstanding quality: dry twigs of *Dhupi*, (*Juniperus wallichiana*), for example, are used in various purification rituals.

Natural setting and forest cover of the two villages

The hamlets of Sunnamsa are scattered on the steep hillside of a narrow river valley. The slope covers more than 1500m of altitude between the valley bottom and the highest settlements on the mountain ridge. This topography, combined with violent summer monsoon rains accelerate soil erosion on the open land. Due to early efforts in forest conservation, the people of Sunnamsa still live in an environment in which the 900ha woodlands cover nearly two-thirds of the village area, and numerous field trees can be found on cultivated land. Surveys highlighted more than 60 different tree and shrub species. The abundance of nearby fodder and firewood sources means that the villagers do not need to go far from their homes.

The landscape can be described as a gradual transition from forest area to cultivated land. Forests and fields are linked by small woods, field trees and riparian vegetation. Dense sal (*Shorea robusta*) forests are located on the steep slopes of the lower areas (900–1400m a.s.l.), close to the river. In higher reaches where slopes are less steep, the forest becomes less dense and is dominated by *Katus* (*Castanopsis sp.*) and *Chilaune* (*Schima wallichii*). Alongside larger streams, this forest community reaches altitudes of 1800m a.s.l. where it gradually gives way to oak forests, dominated by *Baajh* (*Quercus incana* and *Quercus lanuginosa*), *Khasru* (*Quercus semecarpifolia*), *Laliguras* (*Rhododendron arboreum*), and *Angeri* (*Lyonia ovalifolia*). Around higher settlements, at exposed and unstable sites, species of pine (*Pinus sp.*) predominate. Some of them have been planted, others germinate naturally.

Alongside small streams – which can still swell to torrents during the monsoons – there are corridors of forest land and riparian vegetation, dominated by the pioneer species *Utis* (*Alnus nepalensis*) and *Chilaune* (*Schima wallichii*). The streams and their vegetation often provide a natural boundary between two settlements. Small groups of houses are generally situated along the border of the fields close to a stream. In the gardens, and along paths, there are numerous fruit and fodder trees, most of which have been planted by their owners.

The open land is usually terraced and interspersed with numerous trees, which are mostly situated along terraced fields, on the terrace-walls themselves, or in steep lots. About half of the trees have been planted, the rest have grown naturally but are maintained by the community. The natural setting of Sunnamsa depicts the virtually undisturbed, natural surroundings of a typical Tamang village.

In contrast to Sunnamsa, the natural resources of Djavanamsa are overexploited. The bulk of the 500ha forest land is degraded to shrubland with bushes and trees under 2m high, and the open land is seriously affected by erosion. The remaining woodland is dominated by shrubs and trees of *Khasru* (*Quercus semecarpifolia*), *Baajh* (*Quercus incana* and *Quercus lanuginosa*), *Bangse* (*Quercus lamellosa*), *Chutro* (*Berberis asiatica*), *Phalat* (*Quercus glauca*), and *Kafal* (*Myrica esculenta*). Trees with suitable fodder, such as thicker oaks, are found only at a great distance from the settlements, near the top of the mountain range. Most people have to go there daily during the dry season to collect fodder, firewood, and leaf-litter. Several patches of private forest look strikingly denser, and contain thicker and higher timber and fodder trees. In addition, some areas of pine trees have been afforested by the government ranger's office.

The state of the forest in Djavanamsa needs to be seen in relation to political and demographic development. In the last few decades, Djavanamsa's population has increased continuously. This has led to a rising demand for arable land which, in turn, resulted in widespread deforestation. The population density is 10.6 persons per hectare of cultivated land, which is twice as high as in Sunnamsa. Another important aspect is its proximity to the capital Kathmandu, which has a good market for charcoal and timber. Because of its location, the commercial exploitation of such goods has always flourished. In the first part of this century, the forests were used by the Rana regime as an important source of timber and charcoal. Later on, several local families as well as traders from other regions, were involved in the profitable business of making charcoal and selling timber.

Significance of forest

The forest's natural capacity for regeneration serves as a continuous and cost-free source of energy, and as a reserve of useful products and materials. Wood is used for fuel and timber, coal for metal refinement, leaves and grass serve as fodder and compost; fruit, mushrooms and medicinal plants are harvested and preserved. The trunks of older trees are particularly appreciated as timber.

Furthermore, the forest can be seen as a potential reserve of arable land. Nevertheless, the extension of agricultural land into forest areas has become rather unpopular as forest protection has advanced. The intensification of agricultural practices on existing fields, such as the application of chemical fertilizers, is preferred.

As the Tamang mostly live on very steep slopes of narrow valleys, the heavy seasonal monsoons result in an extremely fragile, ecological situation. Erosion and landslides are very common in the region, except in wooded areas, where the soil is, to some extent, stabilized. Forests can even persist on types of soil which are too steep or insufficiently fertile for agricultural use, and forms an area rich in resources. Furthermore, the forest has a favourable influence on the water balance and local climate; in deforested regions, the springs are said to dry up more often in the dry season.

Going beyond these environmental implications, finding access to the cultural relationships between the Tamang and their forests was far more difficult.The following account, therefore, gives only fragments of a much more complex sphere of interrelationships. Traditionally, the forest was an important hunting-ground. Hunting was in the men's domain and contributed much to their prestige. To ensure hunting success, the deities of the wild animals were preserved with symbolic gifts:

> '*Dabla Mabon* is at the same time *kulgi la* of the Mamba clan and the deity of the wild animals. *Dabla Mabon*, armed with bow and arrow, roams in the forest and, since he is the Lord of the game, every successful hunter owes him a sacrifice.' (Höfer, 1971:18)

Hunting has lost its importance, however, since being prohibited by the government.

In villages which are still deeply rooted in animistic cults, and where there are also other religious influences, the forest is viewed as a realm of innumerable ghosts and powerful demons. 'Shinto (ghost) and other beings are said to adhere in and around the forested domains' (Holmberg, 1980:128f.). They may leave the forest domain but will then meet their counterparts – the guardian gods of the settlements, for example. In order to defend against attacks by such demons, a small altar stands in the middle of the path passing through the forest in Sunnamsa. Leaves, fruits, and mushrooms are placed on this altar, in the hope that the gods will be benign. Attacks from wild animals are also attributed to the power of such spirits. In Djavanamsa, attacks from wild animals seem to be less of a problem: most people said that there were no longer any bears in the forest, and that tigers and leopards rarely leave the dense forest, which is far away from the village.

Natural spiritual beings roaming in the forests seem to belong either to the underworld or somewhere between the worldly beings and the heavens. In Sunnamsa, one particular phenomenon of this kind is the *Ban Jhakri* (B.J.). This being is said to live on particular trees or conspicuous natural formations such as cliffs or waterfalls in the forest. In the villagers' descriptions its appearance often takes on human traits:

○ B.J. is a little man with a beard who always wears a cap and sometimes holds a golden gong.

○ B.J. is about one metre tall, with long hair and feet pointing backwards.
○ B.J. is a gnome who can suddenly appear and disappear.
○ B.J. is a little man with a cap – sometimes he carries a light, sometimes he can be seen wearing several little lamps. He can make himself invisible. (Maag 1992:29)

Steinemann (1987:139) describes the *Ban Jhakri* in her book on the Tamang:

'*The bompo* locate the savage shamans (*N. ban jhakri*), which are very similar to witches, in the forest. The most famous *ban jhakri*, *Suna jhakri*, the 'golden' shaman is, by definition, a ruling shaman over the savage spirits of the forest, which try to capture the souls of the apprentice shamans. These can only become real shamans if they succeed in taming these spirits. The principal manifestation of these untamed spirits on the apprentices, i.e. an uncontrolled trance and uttering of speechlike sounds, is performed through an intermediary dumb shaman (N. lata jhakri). For the Tamang *Suna jhakri* is a match to the first shaman *Dunjur Bon*. He is the chief of a group of demons (N. *bir*)which have been exorcised through the rituals perfomed by the *bompo*.' Translation: Ch. Giesch

According to the Tamang of Sunnamsa and Djavanamsa, the powers of the *Ban Jhakri* are not only limited to the wooded areas but can also extend into fields and hamlets. Like many demonic beings, *Ban Jhakri* has an ambivalent character: on the one hand, its powers can cause humans or animals to lose control of themselves, fall ill or become insane. On the other hand, it possesses great strengths and is regarded as the spiritual mentor of the *Jhakris*.[1] I was also told by the grandfather of my host family that he would offer something for *Ban Jhakri* at the beginning of the harvest season to appease him and prevent him from foraging the harvest.

The Lamas of Sunnamsa mentioned the forest as a place of silence and primordial powers: Lama monks are brought to the forest to meditate before their initiation ritual. Because of their symbolic contact with their (personal) god, they have no fear of wild animals.

Private ownership of woods
All the private-forest lots I saw were situated either between cultivated land and common or state forest, or along the banks of rivers. These forests are often well-protected, and comprise a remarkable diversity of trees.

Two forests apparently belonged to a clan which attached particular religious significance to their lots. In the middle of one of these forest patches, there was an altar on which the clan deities were offered sacrifices and offerings. These worshipped gods derive from tribal tradition and are responsible for soil fertility, protection against demons and natural forces, the clan's prosperity, and social coherence. In most cases, they belong to the group of the *La*-gods, which manifests itself in manifold ways. Some are peculiar to a certain clan, others are attributed to certain territories, and land formations, such as springs or caves, and are, thus, respected by the entire village. The traditional respect the Tamang show for these locations is marked by the presence of numerous, massive old trees.

Significance of single trees
The Tamang generally have a more direct relationship to individual trees than to the forest as a whole. These trees can host spirits or are perceived as a

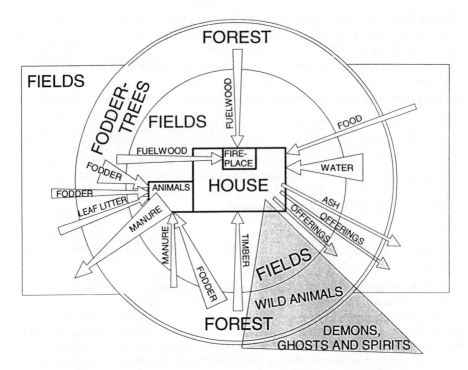

Figure 1: *Extended view of the ecosystem's forest-agriculture-settlements*

particularly religious place. Some Tamang farmers compared the life of a tree with that of a human being. The cutting of a tree-top was at one time linked with the beheading of a person. On another occasion, it was compared to the loss of sons or daughters.

Garden trees
Traditional Tamang houses have small gardens with vegetables and herbs which supplement the staple foods of maize, millet, rice and wheat. Fruit trees are also planted and raised with special care, as they provide a welcome addition to the daily meals. Furthermore, their fruits serve as offerings and symbols of fertility in several Buddhist and tribal rites such as the 'rites of passage' or practices of shamanism. The trees themselves, or their immediate surroundings, are often referred to as the residence of deities:

'The house has its natural extension in the garden that provides the basic vegetables and fruits. This garden is rectangular in shape and has a centre. Rocks, caves, extraordinarily formed trees or land are considered the abode of the deities *lu* and *can*, whereas the erect stones are the altar of *Bhimsen*. The cave which is the altar of *lu* lies generally in the shade of a tree, on which a *can* god dwells.' (Steinemann 1987:135)

Trees in agricultural fields
The cultivated land is interspersed with numerous trees which provide important farm products such as fodder, fuel-wood, and leaf-litter. They further protect the

fields from erosion, and provide workers with shade from the scorching sun. Field trees also have their disadvantages, however, such as the competition for nutrients and light with the main crop, so on small private plots we find fewer field trees; in order to optimize the crop yields, the owners would rather walk further to the forest than cultivate field trees. Nevertheless, the propagation of field trees has brought remarkable advantages for the majority of families in Sunnamsa.

In Djavanamsa, I was shown some religious trees marked by a *Dunga*, a holy stone. At these sites, the clan unites once a year to worship its deities. I was told by another Tamang that these trees personify a Buddhist god, and were planted by ancestors two or three generations ago.

Tamang religion and perceptions of nature

In order to gain a better understanding of the immaterial aspects of perception we shall first look at the human relationship with nature in the three cultural and religious traditions by which the Tamang are influenced. In Nepal, contact with different religions and peoples has led to a distinct syncretism of Hindu, Buddhist and animistic elements. It is difficult, therefore, to determine to what extent the villages concerned have been influenced by any of these beliefs.

In Sunnamsa, perhaps the more traditional Tamang village, I observed rites which indicate intense interaction with ancestral cults and deities. They derive from the animistic view of life and from the practices of shamanism. Many of these practices take place within the family and require no colourful temples or special locations. The sacred symbols are found in the immediate natural surroundings. Water ghosts, for example, are said to abide in springs, and are appeased there with small gifts. In the animistic culture, nature is inhabited by innumerable deities, spirits and demons in a more direct sense than in Hindu tradition:

'For an animist one aspect of the natural resource actually is the deity, whereas in a process of Sanskritization it only represents the deity or its divine aspects.' (Seeland, 1994).

All trees, wild animals and particular parts of the landscape are penetrated with the spirit of this immaterial world and, therefore, can influence mankind for better or worse. Likewise, the growth of vegetation, natural calamities, or attacks by wild animals are attributed to spirits and deities. The concordance between the human spheres and the realm of nature depends on these beings. The shamans, as mediators, strive to preserve coherence between mankind and spiritual beings. Human intervention, such as the exploitation of the forest, is also seen within this cosmic order:

'Savage deities dwell in the nearby forests that are predominantly visited by carpenters. When a *sikarmi* fells a tree, he sacrifices a cock to the *can* deity before which could dwell there.' Translation: Ch. Giesch (Steinemann 1987:139)

Rites to appease natural forces and ensure the well-being of the village or family are mainly conducted by the shaman, who is said to be able to make direct contact with the spirits of nature. Meanwhile, it is the Lama's task to conduct the ceremonies which mark the beginning or end of a particular stage of life.

Lamaism is the Tibetan form of Buddhism. It focuses on the evolution and individual development of mankind, treating the concepts of nature as secondary. In the studied region, Lamaism is largely influenced by the local cults:

'At its most uncompromising level, Buddhism denies the reality of the world of phenomena. Nature as perceived by ordinary mortals is therefore construed more as an obstacle than a help on the path to deliverance. (. . .) The final, composite picture of man's place in the universe as developed in Tibet and passed from there to the Buddhist Himalayas, where local cults added their own contribution, is one of great richness and complexity. If there could be said to exist a single notion which encapsulates all these various streams, it is perhaps the conception of the natural world as a 'vessel' (snod) and of sentient beings as its 'contents' (bcud, literally 'essence'). Thus the primary function of the universe is to enclose, accommodate and nurture the beings who reside there at its core. It is not a truly anthropocentric view of the universe because the term 'sentient being' includes not just man but all six forms of existence of which man is only one.' (Aris, 1990, p.90f)

On the other hand, each and every form of life in Buddhism – animals as well as plants – is treated with particular respect and care. A Lama may not slaughter animals, nor should he cut trees. Plants enjoy great respect for their medicinal value. In honour of Buddha, who was enlightened under a tree, many young monks in Sunnamsa meditate in the forest in an effort to encounter God. In this context, it is not surprising that Lamas vehemently encourage the protection of forests. The cutting of trees in protected areas is viewed as a religious offence/sacrilege for which an interview with the Lama is required. Buddhist belief is still very much present in the community of Sunnamsa. Numerous Lamas live there and a second temple is being built. In contrast, Djavanamsa has no Lamas, and there is only one religious Buddhist site.

The Hindu view of life largely builds on the path of reincarnation – Samsara – and its redemption, Nirvana. Redemption can only be found in fulfilling Karma, which involves rites of purity and ascetism, and total indifference towards transitoriness. Nature and the living sphere are part of everyday needs, in a passive sense.

'There is no supreme right of man to interfere with karma in the Hindu world-view or with the realm of the gods in the animist world-view. It is an inherent principle of dharma to act as a man, when being a man. Consequently it is a transgression of dharma to act as a man, when being a man. God Visnu is the preserver of all existent beings, and it is not the dharma of man to act like a god, to decide which part of nature should be cared for and which part should be regarded as an economic resource.' (Seeland, 1986, p.194)

At the same time, certain elements in nature, such as water and fire or solitary trees and particular animals, are of great religious significance. It is a religious duty to protect them. In this sense, the religious principles have a positive ecological impact contributing to an environmental awareness.

Signs of Hindu influence are more obvious in the region of Djavanamsa. The most conspicuous religious site is a temple dedicated to the Hindu god Shiva, where annual festivals are also attended by Tamang. In spite of a number of common practices, I believe the influence of Hindu customs on the Tamang should not be overrated. To the Tamang, the assimilation of Hindu customs often serves as a possibility of self-assertion in a society dominated by Hinduism. The absence of Buddhist temples and Lamas in Djavanamsa could simply be a matter of poverty and political influence or control. Typically, those Tamang who try to improve the political influence of the Tamang declare themselves

Buddhists. In Sunnamsa, where only a minority of the population is Indo-Aryan, Hindu customs practised by Tamang seem to be limited to activities related to trade and political contact with Hindus.

The question arises as to what extent these religions have an impact on the relationship between the people and their environment. Comparing the ecological situation of Djavanamsa with that of Sunnamsa, one is inclined to attribute the unsatisfactory conditions in Djavanamsa to the predominance of non-traditional religions. To interpret human behaviour in a religious context can be misleading, however, if it is not seen in conjunction with geographical, social and political differences between the two villages.

Whatever the influence of the different religions and customs may be, the Tamang world-view cannot be reduced to a material level. Moreover, I learned to recognize the forest as a place of great significance for the Tamang people. The forests takes over where the familiar sphere of the village and cultivated land ends. Tamang do not feel at home in the forest. Typically, the forest is not the centre of the Tamang view of the world, although it does make up an important part of it and is, in many ways, interwoven with the cosmic and social equilibrium. Villagers can be fearful of the forest and, at the same time, highly aware of their dependence on it.

Social dimensions in forest management

Social and political order are intimately linked with local forest management. Changes in ownership, for example, can have a crucial impact on social balance and local practices. Another important social dimension of forest management is the gender-specific division of labour, decision-making and perception of the forest. Beyond this, a changing environment can have distinct impacts on the spheres of women and men.

Ownership and social balance

In the villages I surveyed, the forest was originally considered to be common property. Apart from some peripheral regions and private areas owned by families or clans, the forest belonged to the community as a whole, and was not divided into lots. In Djavanamsa, however, it was claimed by the Rana Regime in or around 1920, which put many restrictions on the villagers' rights to use the forest. With the Forest Nationalization Act of 1957, all forest land in Nepal became state property. Later on, in the 'era of community forestry', some land was returned to the local population.

Today, all upper parts of the forest of Sunnamsa legally still belong to the government, whereas the area close to the river has been declared community property. As they are a long distance from government offices, the woodlands of Sunnamsa have never been under strict state control. The forest has mainly been managed by locals, on egalitarian principles. A forest was thus seen as a common good, and has gained strong protection. For example, when a house was built or improved, each villager had the right to extract a certain number of tree trunks from the community forest. These trunks were chosen and marked by village officials and then given free for felling.

It can be assumed that, within an originally egalitarian property system, the forest was not over-exploited. The annexation of the forest by the state has undoubtedly had far-reaching implications for the Tamang, because their expropriation also leads to social imbalances in many places. Taking the example of Djavanamsa, where most of the forest was under the control of the Ranas for a long time, and today still belongs to the government, one can assume that the use of forest is no longer based on social control. There are families who still respect the forest as common property and mutually decide on its common usage. Others have abandoned this tradition and extract whatever they can since the forest is owned by an authority, whose legitimization they do not recognize as justified. This leads to social tension, since the entire community suffers from the unchecked economic depletion and only few profit from the exploitation. When local families require timber, they have to either take it from the wood reserves of the neighbouring villages, or purchase it from villagers with private lots, because it is no longer available in the surrounding forest areas.

Gender and forest in Tamang society

The division of labour by gender can generally be summarized in the way that men mostly operate at the periphery of the subsistence economy and are the formal representatives to the outside world, whereas women are responsible for domestic matters. These include the education and care of the children, tending to the house, farm and garden, cooking, and entertaining guests, as well as taking care of the family's daily needs. Women are, furthermore, indispensable as labourers in the fields, where men take the main responsibility.

Gender relations in forest management

As Table 1 shows, occupations relating to the use of forests and trees, and which concern household supplies tend to be delegated to women, whereas activities of forest management in a strict sense (plans for tree-protection, tree-felling, propagation of trees, etc.) are, in general, carried out by men. Women are substantially involved in forest development by lopping trees and gathering fuelwood and leaf litter. Traditionally, men are mainly involved in propagating and harvesting timber and cutting fuelwood; they also hunt in the forest.

Male activities in the forest are irregular, whereas women's gathering work is a daily routine. Women thus spend more time in the forest than men, and are highly aware of the changes in quality of the collected products. They are particularly affected by the degradation of the forest areas as the increasing distances between settlements and the forest border mean an additional daily workload, and the shortage of products demands more time spent gathering them. Most of the women's work takes place in the peripheral parts of the forest, whereas the men's occupations – such as hunting and charcoal-making – take them further into the woods. The men's concerns about forest degradation, therefore focus on the availability of thick trunks and the presence of game.

The abundance and diversity of accessible hardwood largely determines the quality of timber. For every part of a typical Tamang building a particular tree species is preferred. A house built with hardy and valuable wood shows prosperity, and contributes to a certain personal prestige. In this sense, forest protection can be seen as an economic investment, a man domain, nearly all activities related to trade, sales and barter are arranged by men.

The rules and long-term plans of forest use are also generally determined by men, who are responsible for decisions at the village level. The job of forest watchman has always been given to Tamang men in these villages. In

Table 1: Gender-specific division of forest and trees – labour related

Occupation	Carried out by	Comments
Animal husbandry		Fodder: twigs with leaves,
Feeding of livestock:	Women	grass from the wood and
Collecting fodder	Women	from their own trees; daily
Carrying fodder	Women	business
Fuelwood		Fuelwood logs, dead
Cutting	Men	wood, dry twigs from
Gathering	Women	weeds and their own trees
Carrying	Women and men	Daily/weekly jobs
Tending fire	Oldest woman	
Worship of stove-diety	Oldest woman	
Timber production		
Choice and marking	Men (village representatives and consumers):	Once or twice a year; – in the community forest
	Proprietor:	– of private trees
Forest dieties-'*puja*'	Shamans	
Felling	Men	
Utilization	Men (consumers, carpenters, wood-carvers	
Sale	Men	
Coal-making	Men	Sunnamsa: on agreement between Tamang and Kami, for villagers' usage Djavanamsa: illegal and also for sale to Patan
Utilization of bamboo	Men	Bamboo products; fences,
Bamboo processing	Men, oldest women	mats, baskets, waterpipes,
Marketing	Men	etc.
Gathering fruit and berries	Men and women	Rare activity, seasonal
Gathering medicinal herbs	Shamans	
Gathering mushrooms	Men and women	Seasonal
Marketing	Men	
Hunting	Men	Hunting permission
'*Puja*' for blessing	Men, shamans	required from village chief
Preparation of game	Men and women	
Forest management		Sunnamsa:
Assembly	Men	assembly once a year or
Supervising guard	Men	as required
Security concepts	Men	Djavanamsa: assembly
Afforestation	Men (women)?	under supervision or organizations
Nursery	Men (women only temporary)	Nurseries: set up by organizations
Private trees		
Planting	Men	
Inauguration 'puja'	Men	
Watering, tending	Women (men)	As required
Use	Women and men	Seasonal: daily

Djavanamsa, several men have founded a forest group, which intends to improve protection of the remaining woodlands. Likewise, decision-making concerning forest development projects in Sunnamsa is under the supervision of local men.

The maintenance and improvement of forest areas can only be sustained if they are protected from intruding livestock. This is the reason behind the introduction of stall-feeding in many places. In this context, the women – as tenders of the cattle — indirectly take over another responsibility relevant to forest preservation.

An interesting question is which gender-specific activities may lead to over-exploitation of forest resources? The women's activities include collecting products and lopping trees – tasks which do not necessarily conflict with sustainable management. Women do not feel, therefore, that they are destroying the forest. Their gathering is seen primarily as a contribution to the material subsistence of the family. Wood is only rarely sold in the local markets. With skilled and careful tree-lopping, for example, women can ensure the survival of the trees from which they harvest fodder. Tree-felling, slash-and-burn practices, and the production of charcoal are conducted by men; the economic benefits of which are often spent on alcohol and gambling. The felled trees do not regenerate; the spots burned from charcoal-making remain bare, and trigger soil erosion. These 'male' activities often provoke proclamations for reforestation in public discussions.

Tamang women as sustainers of social balance
After discussions in Djavanamsa, I realized that the situation of natural degradation results in women having to face specific hardships. Many propagated efforts to reduce the pressure on forest land require a particular commitment by women. Beyond this additional labour, they are affected more directly than men by the social imbalance which results indirectly from the shortage of resources. A Tamang woman has an important linking role in the social network. She maintains the contact between children and men, and between the sphere of the household and agriculture. After marriage she is admitted to another clan which, from that time, is under mutual obligation to the bride's maternal family. By the continuing promotion of contacts with the maternal family, the responsibility of match-making, and efforts in fulfilling social and religious obligations, women play an important role in society. Further activities in this context are welcoming guests and contacts with other women in the community. I noticed a strong feeling of solidarity and co-operation among women (particularly at work). In the forest, for example, the use of the nearer forest areas was left for the elderly women. All the women exchange information on the choice of fodder trees. Tamang women are probably well accustomed to team-work. In the traditional labour-exchange system, members of different families work together in small teams, sometimes even for other castes and ethnic groups. Even in fulfilling their various household duties women collaborate and are rarely seen alone at work.

The concept of unity and equality is especially relevant in Tamang society. Running the family household, which I consider to be the main duty in the life of a Tamang woman, can only be sustained in a stable and peaceful family. The coherence of the family is determined to a large extent by the mother, who spends most of her life within this close community. As a young married wife she has to prove herself to her husband's family, and to settle in to new and unfamiliar surroundings. Although the raising and education of children is not as time-consuming as some of her other duties, they require great skill and diligence and are a mother's most important responsibilities. On the one hand, the prosperity and continuity of the family depends on the next generation, on the other hand, a mother's personal security and status is closely linked to that of her children. Daughters relieve her of a lot of work, which she would be unable to accomplish on her own. Sons ensure the continuity of the patrilocal family and, hence, her old age. Women have stronger bonds with their children than their husbands. This leads, perhaps, to more long-term thoughts on their future outlook – a dimension which is crucial for the sustainable use of the forest. They feel the importance of preserving the forest for future generations.

The Tamang woman is not only a real, but also a symbolic guardian of the family's well-being and happiness, as shown by March (1979) in the example of the Tsen: 'a special kind of divinity which is inherited by women from women, [. . .] which can bring good fortune and prosperity on the one hand and harm and misfortune on the other'. Women bear the symbols of destruction and fertility at the same time. Many Tamang women are suspected of witchcraft and are rejected by the community for this reason. Women are often considered to bring good luck but also illness. They are perceived to be more receptive to spiritual powers and have to protect themselves accordingly. In my opinion, these aspects contribute to the great care Tamang women show in fulfilling their religious and family responsibilities. And, as the guardians of provisions and valuables, they have much control and influence over the household's prosperity.

Another reason for their stronger interest in social stability could be the fact that women stay in the village throughout the whole year and thus experience its development more intimately than men. Men leave the village to seek work and income in the army, or in other villages or towns, especially if they are no longer able to earn their living from agriculture.

Women, however, have no social tradition allowing them to be directly influential at the village level, where many of the decisions concerning forestry practices are made. Only if men spend much time outside the village do women gain control over certain aspects of the village organization. I am convinced that women have their ways of exercising influence over their husbands within the family. Their social status and egalitarian opinions reflect this in many ways. The question is, do women have any influence, in this indirect way, on village decisions, which ultimately have a strong impact on their daily work?

The significance of the forest for Tamang women

The forest provides the basis of life

Forests provide many basic materials for agriculture and the household. The stove, for example, needs to be continuously supplied with fuelwood. Far from being merely a cooking-place, it is a central point of communication, a source of warmth, and a place of great religious significance. The woman who is responsible for the stove will always keep enough fuelwood nearby. Likewise, animal husbandry, another important woman's domain, depends largely on fodder, which may need to be collected in the forest. It is not surprising that, when asked about the purpose and significance of forests, the 'qualities of giving' come first to mind.

Apart from the direct material provisions, forest and trees contribute in many indirect ways to the means of livelihood, and social security or status. The richer and more diverse the resources from the forest and trees, the more time is left for other activities, such as duties in and about the house. Since household activities and the care of children should not be neglected, the gathering of forest goods is often delegated to the daughters. A woman who spends much of her time gathering forest resources has less opportunity to earn an income from carpet weaving and paid field labour. Even if such wages formally belong to the family, the Tamang woman gains some personal benefit: new clothes and jewellery – things which contribute to her social status and prestige.

Carrying water is another woman's task. Hence, a woman is considered fortunate if she lives near a perennial spring, such as those which are often found in the woodland or its surroundings. Many Tamang relate closely the existence of water resources to the presence of forests. As mentioned above, it was often pointed out that wells in wooded areas do not dry out in the winter season.

Successful animal husbandry is extremely important to Tamang women. Apart from jewellery, clothing and food, livestock is to be used by the daughters as dowry. Land ownership and the house go to their brothers. Taking good care of her animals and raising their offspring again demands fodder from the forest and trees in the fields. In general, only a part of the fodder demand can be supplied from private cultivated lands, especially in the case of poor landowners. In addition to agricultural residues, grass is cut in the forest during the summer months and particularly in the dry season, twigs are lopped from trees. Further fuelwood is needed to cook *kudo*, a broth of wheat and left-overs, which is fed to the cattle. The husbandry of small animals also symbolizes immaterial security. These animals are often sacrificed to the deities of the family, clan or village, thus contributing to the maintenance of the community's social and cosmic equilibrium.

The availability of fuelwood can influence the choice of staple food. In many villages, maize and millet broth is cooked to save both fuelwood and time . While maize is appreciated in the mornings – which seems particularly appropriate as it is very nourishing – cooked rice is definitely preferred, and more prestigious, for other meals.

The forest as a place of demons and wild animals
The denser and darker the forest, the greater is the perceived danger of attacks from wild animals on livestock and human beings. Many women are afraid to go into the forest alone; they avoid dense parts, and fetch fuelwood and fodder from peripheral areas whenever possible. This fear is ambivalent, as the fear of a tiger, for example, expresses at the same time a certain respect. Demons and ancestral spirits are beings which are considered to be a part of life and demand the people's awe and obedience. In the perception of Tamang village society, women are generally said to be susceptible, due to pregnancy or menstruation, to evil spirits and demons.

The forest as a place of encounter
Early in the morning, women leave together to work in the forest. On their way they find time to exchange news, whereas on the way back, one can only hear the heavy breathing under the weight of the full baskets. As they work the women encourage and help each other. Although this kind of work is strenuous, the mutual effort seems to be of great value in the lives of these women. Young women and girls, in particular, who spend all day weaving carpets, complain that they have little opportunity to meet companions. The common path to the forest leads to daily contacts which bring a certain symbolic solidarity as the women carry their 'common burden'. Working in the forest also provides an opportunity for contacts and discussions between young girls and boys. Boys and young men often cut the fuelwood, while girls and young women collect and bundle the

wood and clip the fodder trees. Young women who do not return from the forest on time are vulnerable to village gossip.

The role of accessibility and quality of forest resources
In the present state of forest degradation, more and more time is invested in collecting fodder and fuelwood. Women are particularly affected by this when stall-feeding is practised as a measure of forest protection. In addition to fuelwood, women now have to carry fodder from the forest:

> Oftentimes it is not only deforestation that is responsible for the unavailability of supplies, but, ironically afforestation and protection programmes that close off previously used grazing lands. This forces women to stall-feed their animals – a practice which is more labour-intensive unless fodder sources are close by. (Denholm, 1989)

While children often tend the cattle, adult women are responsible for feeding the cattle in the stalls. For men, who build and maintain the stalls, the additional labour is not as demanding. In Djavanamsa, a large part of the forest-land no longer exists, or is degraded to shrub-land. Dense patches of trees of good fodder quality can only be found far away from the settlements. During the dry season, women have to go there every day and this requires nearly half a day's work. In Sunnamsa, households own between 15 and 60 trees of 25 different species. The villagers often cut fodder on the way back from working in the fields. This stock of private trees reduces the pressure on the forest area remarkably, and the women are freed from collection-work far from the homestead. They are often highly motivated, therefore, to propagate fodder trees on cultivated land.

Women are also very aware of the different fodder qualities of the trees. They can provide detailed information about which leaves are appreciated by which animal or produce high milk yields. Certain leaves are never fed to pregnant animals (for example *Payo, Prunus cerasoides*). The popularity of fodder trees further depends on the extent of its canopy and the number of yields per year. Susceptibility to disease and its capacity for natural regeneration are other criteria for determining the choice of species when trees are propagated. Trees bearing edible fruits or leaves are popular as they add to the daily meals and fruits offered in religious ceremonies. Dishes are made from the leaves of certain trees (*Shorea robusta, Ficus cunia*) which are taken outdoors or used at festival meals. Other tree leaves are used as tobacco.

Likewise, the quality of accessible fuelwood is of great importance for women. The various kinds of fuelwood differ considerably in terms of quality: some kinds of wood are appreciated for their slow burning. Further criteria are less smoke and the quality of the ashes, which are used for dish-washing. A number of women also mentioned the aspect of ease of cutting or gathering. Fuelwood of the *Pinus* species, for example, is easy to gather because the dry twigs fall from the branches. The amount of dry wood on the forest ground largely determines the efficiency of gathering. In a cleared forest with a high percentage of young trees, green wood, which needs to be dried before it can be burned, has to be collected as fuelwood, and demands greater effort.

Gender-specific perception/awareness of environmental changes
When and how are the changes in the state of the forest perceived? As daily users of the forest, women experience the changes in diversity, regenerative

capacity, and quality of fodder and fuelwood species more directly. They are aware of the continuously increasing distance of the forest from the settlement. In discussions with Tamang women of different generations, I was told that these changes had been noticed many years ago. A true concern and the desire to change the situation arises only when the scarcity of resources leads to an unbearable workload. While the women in Sunnamsa never really complained about intolerable hardships in the gathering of forest produce, the forest degradation and its consequences are a daily issue in the conversations of women in Djavanamsa. An increase in forest area, however, can also be perceived negatively, as the number of wild animals would increase, which may cause more fear. Indeed, in Sunnamsa, many women declared that 'a lot of forest means a lot of wild animals, which means increasing danger for men and livestock.'

Men are particularly aware of the changes concerning timber; the lack of massive trunks suitable for building houses can provide the motivation to protect forest grounds. This kind of protection often implies limited access to minor forest products, and can temporarily increase the workload of women even more. Men are also aware of the decreasing number of game in their hunting grounds.

Conclusion

The interrelationship between forest and people has many dimensions. Ecological, economical, cultural and social aspects all influence the local perception of forest and natural resource management.

To summarize, the importance of forests and trees at a material level lies in the diversity of basic products and energy supply which are part of the economic foundation of a Tamang household. Furthermore, the Tamang are aware of ecological functions concerning water, the household, and soil stability. The material uses of trees and forest are clearly linked to cultural values. In both villages I gained the impression that solitary trees in particular are ascribed high cultural and religious value, be it as the abode of a spirit in the animistic view of the world, or as sacred symbols of the Buddhist and Hindu religions.

In Sunnamsa, where the village is still deeply rooted in animistic cults, the forest is a realm of many spirits and demons. Just as human beings use and intrude in the forest, it can extend its spheres of action into human settlements in the shape of its inhabitants (demons, wild animals, etc.). In order to maintain harmony with the beings which are responsible for these evils, periodic sacrifices, offerings, and rituals are necessary. The well-being of the village can only be sustained in accordance with these supernatural forces. Where this cosmic equilibrium is lost, human beings are exposed to evil spirits (often deceased relatives), demons and natural calamities. In the same sense the harvest of natural goods needs to be legitimized from time to time by special ceremonies of thanksgiving. In Djavanamsa, where the natural forest areas are degraded to shrubland, the spirits and wild animals of the forest are said to have retreated to the denser forest land far away from the villages.

If the forest and trees are seen as a part, or rather as a vehicle of the cosmic forces, does deforestation then imply an immense cultural loss? And how much could this influence the extent of forest use? The possibilities of the Tamang to appease demons and spirits through ritual sacrifice gives the Tamang a certain right to change forest land into cultivated land. It would be interesting to find out whether dense patches of forest land in the hamlet surroundings are primarily understood as special territories with sacred significance for the village or for certain clans, and are, therefore, worth being protected.

Forest management implies co-operation. Collaboration between the decision-oriented domain of the men and the realization which is supported by both sexes needs to be adequately represented in the local social order. Only on the basis of social coherence can new practices be established. Thus one may state that Tamang women have played a background role in decisions made about the traditional management of forests. This does not mean, however, that their influence is less important; it seems that their continuous efforts in the forest and the resulting perception influence important decisions indirectly. Through their daily activities, women can contribute to a large extent to the protection of forests. Measures of protection or reforestation will only be successful if women accept the additional burden and agree the rules concerning the daily use of the trees in the forest.

At the same time, we must consider that although women are not directly involved in the destruction, they are affected in many ways by the resulting conditions. Traditionally, women have tried to compensate for the resulting problems and difficulties by putting in even more effort. They have neither found innovative solutions, nor sought confrontation at the community level because they do not have the time to do so and there is no culturally acknowledged forum for the exchange of views between men and women. Such an arrangement has, so far, not been given priority as Tamang women have always managed to fulfil their traditional duties with some assistance from the men. Under the increasing burden brought about by the scarcity of resources, however, questions concerning a new orientation of the village structure arise. I assume that the contribution of women to decision-making in the village could be just as valuable to the sustainability of the society as their linking role in the traditional, familiar setting has been so far. The women's capacity for teamwork, their remarkable sense for sustaining social coherence in the community, and their concern for future generations could also be of great value, particularly for tomorrow's forest management.

Appendix to Chapter 12   Tree names, their economic uses, and the ecological significance of Sunnamsa village

Name of Tree			Use/remarks
Nepalese name	**Scientific name**	**Tamang name**	
Aap	*Mangifera indica*		Fruit tree Gives shade, hardens soil
Aaru	*Prunus persica*	*Kale*	Fruit tree, (firewood) grows rarely on this soil Requires a lot of fertilizer Gives shade – competition for crops
Aarubakhardaa	*Prunus domestica*		Fruit tree
Amala	*Emblica officinalis*	*Ambel*	Fruit tree, vitamin C used for 'achar'
Amba	*Psidium guajava*	*Gyagar-amba*	Fruit tree
Angeri	*Lyona ovalifolia (Paeris ovalifolia)*	*Dompsing*	Firewood, charcoal Stump sprouts
Baajh, Banjh sano	*Quercus incana*	*Berkup*	Fodder, firewood, furniture Windows, doors
Baajh, Banjh thulo	*Quercus lanuginosa*	*Berkup*	Fodder, firewood
Badahar	*Artocarpus lakocha*	*Badar*	Fodder (best), firewood, stumps sprout quickly Gives shade
Bakena	*Melia azedarach*	*Baksia*	Fodder, firewood, compost, bedding, timber Fruit for stomach troubles Stump sprouts
Bar	*Ficus bengalensis*	*Bara*	Holy tree

Bhaas	*Dendrocalamus hamiltonii*	*Kryn*	Leaves for fodder Sticks for lighting fire Baskets, *nanglo*, roofs Bamboo-roots Troublesome in the fields
Bhalai	*(Semecarpus anarcardium)*		Slightly poisonous (skin irritation)
Bhalayo	*Rhus succedanea*	*Grusing*	Firewood
-?-		*Bhlengsing*	Fruit, fodder
Bogate/Bhogate	*Citrus maxima*		Fruit tree
-?-		*Bulungkising*	Firewood (mostly full of white insects)
Chaap	*Calistenom virnalis*	-?-	Grows only on the other side of the mountain
Chilaune	*Schima wallichii*	*Kyaasing*	Good firewood Good timber (house, stable, plough) Compost, bedding, gives shade Insects eat leaves Stumps may sprout quickly
Chiuri	*Bassia butyraceae*	*Singmar*	Timber, fruit A little fodder and firewood
Chutro	*Berberis asiatica*	*Chutre*	Fruit with spines
Dhayaro	*Woodfordia floribunda*	*Yatika*	Fodder for goats Firewood, timber
Dhupi	*Juniperus wallichiana*		The *Jhakhris* use it for incense
Epil	-?-		Three seasons for fodder Wood, seed edible
Gangaru/ Ghangaru	*Pyracantha crenulata*	*Changaru*	Firewood Spines

Harro	Terminalia sp.	Arla	Fruit used as cough medicine
Jamuno, Jamburra	Syzygium sp.		Fodder, timber
Kagati	-?-		Fruit tree
Kaphal	Myrica esculenta	Karpassi	Fruit tree
Katus/Kotus Dhale	Castanopsis indica	Koru	Firewood, fodder
Kera	Musa paradisiaca		Fruit tree
Khasru	Quercus semecarpifolia	Khasur	Firewood Fodder
Khanayo		Fruit: Kosing	Fruit (modest quantity) Gives shade Competition for crops Stump sprouts
Khanyu	Ficus cunia	Kangkhai	Good fodder
Koiralo	Bauhinia variegata	Ambu	Fodder Fruit, flower edible as vegetable
Kutmero	Litsea polyantha	Kutmiro	Good fodder, firewood, compost Gives a lot of shade Poor crops under the tree
Kyamuna	Syzygium cerasoides	Kyamuno fruit: Rendong	Furniture Firewood Compost, bedding, fruit Stump sprouts Competition for crops
Laliguras	Rhododendron arboreum	Padhaa dong	National flower Firewood Fruit, flowers
Lankuri, Laakuri	Fraxinus floribunda	Lahuri-dong	Timber
Lapsi	Choreospondias axillaris	Kaiang	Fruit tree Timber, carving Good charcoal

Masala	Eucalyptus sp.		Firewood, furniture Gives shade along paths Not indigenous Fast growing
Mayal, Mayel	Pyrus paschia	Paana	Firewood
Mayala			Fodder for goats Fruit (dry) Stump sprouts
Musre	Tribuloides		Bedding, timber, coal Small fruits Leaves: barnroofs, cigarettes Stumps sprout slowly
-?-		Nagadamsing	Fodder, fruit, bush
-?-		Nakote	Timber Small tree Stump sprouts
Naspati	Pyrus communis		Fruit tree
Nemaro			Leaves used as plates Female fruit edible
Nigalo/Ningalo	Arundaria intermedia	Maa	Fodder Baskets, mats, barnroofs, fences A lot of roots – hardens soil
Nimaro, Jemara	Ficus roxburghii	Mago	Fodder, firewood
Payu	Prunus cerasoides	Birru	Timber, fodder Firewood Stump sprouts
-?-		Nanifal	Some firewood
Phalat, Falant	Quercus glauca	Sulsing	Timber (plough, tools) Fodder, firewood Stump sprouts (only young plants)
Pipal	Ficus religiosa		Holy tree Status prevents this good fodder being used

Saaj, Saj	Terminalia sp.	Pharsing	Timber, furniture Fodder, firewood Stumps sprout quickly
Sal	Shorea robusta	Sagu	Best timber (highly water-resistant) Fodder, firewood Good charcoal Insects like leaves Leaves for cigarettes and plates Stumps sprout quickly
Sallo	Pinus sp.	Thanksing	Firewood, timber Gives shade, crops suffer Hardens soil Stumps sprout quickly
Sethikath	Myrsina capitellata	Tarsing	Firewood, small tree Stump sprouts
Simal	Bombax sp.	Kagha	Good fodder Seeds with cotton wool Used for pillows, timber, furniture
Singada	-?-		Firewood, fodder
Singara			Soft timber, fruit Stumps sprout slowly
Siris, Sirris	Albizzia sp.	Teba, Teve	Firewood, fodder
-?-		Singfanti	Timber, furniture Fruit; big tree Stumps sprout slowly
Suntala	Citrus nobilis		Fruit tree Needs a lot of manure
-?-		Syungan	Fodder, firewood Small tree Stump sprouts

Tatelo	*Ororylon indicium* *Oroxylum indicium*		Big seeds: used at celebrations Big tree
Tuni, Tooni	*Cedrus toona*		Firewood
Utis, Uttis	*Alnus nepalensis*	*Kyansing*	Good firewood Good, soft timber Compost, bedding Gives shade, crops grow poorly and collapse underneath Insects eat leaves Stump sprouts

Notes on contributors

James Fairhead (Dr.) is a social anthropologist and Research Fellow of the School of Oriental and African Studies, University of London. He has worked extensively in Africa on the social construction of ecological knowledge, especially in Rwanda and Zaire.

Barun Gurung (Dr.) is a Bhutanese anthropologist who has conducted research on the indigenous knowledge and cultural aspects of tribal groups in North-eastern Nepal, to analyse links between cultural knowledge and natural resource management, particularly related to biodiversity and conservation. He is co-ordinating a Mountain Network for Indigenous Knowledge to build local capacities for ethnobotanical research for cultural preservation and community development in five areas in the Himalayan region.

Andrew W. Ingles was a forestry adviser and deputy team leader of the Nepal-Australia Community Forestry Project for several years. He wrote a diploma thesis on the management of religious forests in Nepal. At present, he is working at the Australian National University, Canberra.

Mihir Kumar Jena is a research scholar working in the research team 'Man and Forest' of the Institute of Oriental and Orissan Studies in Cuttack, India. He is a professional botanist writing a dissertation on the ethno-botany of some Orissan tribal groups.

John Knight (Dr.) was a Junior Research Fellow at Wadham College Oxford and is now teaching at the International Institute for Asian Studies in Leiden, the Netherlands. He is the author of a number of articles on rural Japan and is currently working on a book about Japanese mountain villages.

Melissa Leach (Dr.) is a social anthropologist and a Fellow of the Institute of Development Studies at the University of Sussex. She specializes in environmental aspects of rural development and gender issues in resource management, mainly in West Africa: She is the author of *Rainforest Relations: Gender and resource use among the Mende of Gola, Sierra Leone* (1994, Edinburgh University Press).

Bettina Maag is an Environmental Scientist with a university degree from ETH. Study of Environmental Sciences at the Swiss Federal Institute of Technology, Zurich 1991/92. Field study in Nepal as a Junior Fellow of the International Centre for Integrated Mountain Development (ICIMOD) Kathmandu.

Robert Parkin (Dr.) is a British social anthropologist, one of whose interests is the tribal groups of central India. He has recently finished a book on the work of the French sociologist of religion, Robert Hertz. He has taught at the universities of Berlin and Cracow, and is currently planning research on Silesia.

Kamala Kumari Patnaik (Mrs.) (Prof., Dr.) is a retired professor of botany. Until 1994, she taught botany at Rawenshaw College, Cuttack, and did research on the medicinal use of plants in some parts of Orissa, India.

Paul Richards (Prof., Dr.) teaches anthropology at University College, London, and is Chair of the Working Group on Technology and Agrarian Development at Wageningen Agricultural University. He has carried out long-term field work in forested regions of Nigeria (1968–77) and Sierra Leone (1977–95). His latest book, *Fighting for the Rain Forest: War, youth and environment in Sierra Leone*, was published in 1995, Oxford.

Laura Rival (Dr.) was educated in France (Paris XIII 1979), in Canada (University of British Colombia, B.A. Soc.Anth. & Linguistics 1986), and in England (University of London, Ph.D. Soc.Anth. 1992). She has taught in Ecuador at FLACSO (Facultad Latino-Americana de Ciencias Sociales) in 1990, 1991 and 1994, and has held appointments in Social Anthropology at the University of Manchester (Lecturer 1992–1993) and at The London School of Economics and Political Science (Lecturer 1992–1993). She was the first Research Fellow of the newly established Oxford Centre for the Environment, Ethics and Society, based at Mansfield College, University of Oxford. She is currently a lecturer in anthropology at the University of Kent.

She carried out research in the Andes (1987). Her doctoral research was among the Huaorani Indians (1989 1990, 1991). Her work focuses on the processes of modernization and national development in Amazonia, and she has written on the impact of the petroleum industry on indigenous people in the Amazon region of Ecuador. More recently, she has been engaged in a comparative study of indigenous conceptualizations of the rain forest. She is presently reviewing her doctoral dissertation for publication.

Dietrich Schmidt-Vogt (Dr.) was born in 1954 in Munich and has studied geography and anglistics at the Universities of Saskatoon (Canada), and Freiburg and Heidelberg (Germany). His main field of investigation is the role of man in the modification of forest ecosystems in the mountainous regions of South and South-east Asia. He obtained his doctorate with a study of the influence of traditional forms of forest use on montane and sub-alpine forests in Nepal, and has recently finished a habilitation thesis on swidden farming and vegetation change in northern Thailand. Dietrich Schmidt-Vogt holds a position as 'Wissenschaftlicher Assistent' at the Geography Department of the South Asia Institute, University of Heidelberg.

Klaus Seeland (PD, Dr., M.A.), born 1952 is at present reader in Sociology and Forest Resource Economics at the Chair of Forest Policy and Forest Economics, Swiss Federal Institute of Technology (Zurich/Switzerland), in Sociology at the University of Konstanz (Germany) and Vice Chairman of 'Economic and Social Aspects of Forests in Developing Countries', at the International Union of Forestry Research Organizations (IUFRO). He has done research in Nepal, Pakistan and India for both short and long periods from 1978 on. His area of research is South Asia, covering indigenous knowledge and environmental management through efforts of the local population.

Notes

Chapter 2

1 This chapter draws on fieldwork and analysis by Dominique Millimouno and Marie Kamano. The research was funded by ESCOR, the Overseas Development Administration's Economic and Social Committee for Overseas Research, which we gratefully thank; opinions represented here are, however, the authors', not necessarily those of the ODA. Many thanks are also due to the villagers in Kissidougou Prefecture and to our Guinean collaborators: Projet Dévéloppement Rurale Intégré de Kissidougou (DERIK), the Direction Nationale des Forêts et de la Chasse (DNFC), and the Direction Nationale de Recherche Scientifique (DNRS). A slightly altered version of this chapter also appears in L. Rival (ed) *The Social Life of Trees*, Berg Press.

2 Kissia is the preferred and correct plural term for the people who speak Kissie, a language categorized within the Mel group of West Atlantic languages. Kuranko is a dialect of Mandinka, part of the Mande language group.

Chapter 4

1 Ue (1984) refers to such resistance on the Kii Peninsula. For the shrine-merger deaths, see Hardacre (1989).

2 The theme also emerges in literature. In *The Phoenix Tree* (*Aogiri*), Kizaki Satoko (1990) tells the story of an old woman dying with cancer. The old woman identifies with the tall, erect phoenix tree close to the house, a tree she planted many years ago. As she struggles with her illness, the presence of the tree comforts her. The associations of the tree are complex, however, for it was planted where an ancient cedar tree once stood. The old woman had cut down this tree, against the will of an old man living nearby who warned her that it was a sacred tree and that she risked being cursed as a result! There are two possible interpretations. The first is that the planting of the phoenix tree compensates for the felling of the cedar tree. The second is that the old woman, in her last days, is finally suffering the consequences of her earlier actions.

3 For sources of the Shingu tree requiem, see Ue (1987), Shingūshishi Hensan Iinkai (1972) and Kida (1984).

4 For the *tatari* of chickens, cows and horses, see Ibaraki (1993), Chapple (1993) and Ōishi (1990); for the *tatari* of dogs and cats, see Watanabe (1986), Suzuki (1982), Ōishi (1990), Kobayashi (1994) and Matsutani (1994b).

5 The *ireisai* is the Shinto equivalent of the Buddhist *kuyō*.

6 For references and discussions of such *kuyō*, see Asquith (1986) for laboratory animals; Nakamaki (1992) for birds; Sakamoto (1957) for needles; and Umehara (1988) and Reader (1991).

7 Bloch has detected this motif in his analysis of the myths of a variety of different cultures. There are 'certain types of myth which stress the indistinguishable aspects of all living things' and emphasize 'the continuity between plants, humans and animals, which are all seen as mutually helpful siblings' (Bloch, 1992).

Chapter 5

1 My work at Ban Tun was part of a comparative study of plant succession on the swidden fields of different ethnic groups in northern Thailand, who practise different forms of swidden farming: Lawa, Akha.

2 Field research was funded by the Alexander von Humboldt Foundation and supported by Dr Thawatchai Santisuk, Director of the Forest Herbarium, Royal Forest Dept., Bangkok, which is gratefully acknowledged. A comprehensive treatise on swidden farming and vegetation change in northern Thailand is forthcoming.

138

Chapter 6

1 This description is of the traditional situation: under pressure of modern conditions, descent has become bilateral or patrilineal, and the traditional marriage system has disappeared. The standard account on the Nayar has long been Fuller (1976), but see also Dumont (1964) and, for a succinct description, Good (1991).

2 The *tali* is a token tied round the neck of the bride at weddings in many south Indian castes, normally by someone other than the husband.

3 Nambudiris eldest sons could also enter such relationships, but not with women whose *tali* they had tied.

4 Crooke gives as the reason for the rite the girl's father's inability to find her a husband, but it seems likely that its purpose is similar to that described by Bailey (1957) and Dube (1953) and is, therefore, generally applicable.

5 No attempt will be made to discuss its rich detail here, save for one quite significant point: the explanation Good received for why a boy was not used was that this would make it a real wedding (Good, 1991). Here too, it seems, arrangements are made to avoid ritual danger for the girl and her family without diminishing her chances of a full married life.

6 *I.e.* the generation of the grandparents. The parental generation is +1, that of children and grandchildren -1 and -2 respectively; ego's own is defined as 0 (zero). From the perspective of ego's generation, +1 and -1 are adjacent generations, +2 and -2 alternate or alternating generations.

7 There are, of course, variants: for example, the Sora do not associate naming with reincarnation (Vitebsky, 1993). McDougal's ethnography on the Juang (1963, 1964) provides perhaps the best account of the general structure of opposition between alternating and adjacent generations. In addition to my own previous syntheses of these data (Parkin 1988, 1992), Obeyesekere (1968, 1980) is relevant on the contrasts between Hinduism and what might be called a generalized version of the tribal ideology, not only in India.

8 Hodson was obviously inspired by similar material from Australia linking reincarnation, naming and tree burial (1921b, after Spencer and Gillen). We can agree with his feeling that, in India, the use of stones in death ritual, as megaliths, is different, since they seem to be associated with the personalized soul.

Chapter 7

1 Andrew W. Ingles works for the Nepal-Australia Community Forestry Project, PO Box 208, Kathmandu, Nepal.

Chapter 8

1 These stereotypes (which undoubtedly pre-date the Conquest and may have their roots in the ethnic divisions between those who participated in the pre-Columbian long-distance trade in salt and metal, and those who did not) are too often uncritically adopted by anthropologists working with acculturated riverine populations, who come to consider forest dwellers, like the Huaorani, as devolved, marginalized people with no culture of their own (see Gow, 1993 for a striking example).

2 Some versions talk of *Quenihuè* (eagle), others of *Abarè* (condor). It is a bird of prey which eats *both* raw and rotten meat.

3 One can easily imagine the vine which ties the tree to the sky as a kind of umbilical cord which not only holds the tree straight – a role that cannot be fulfilled adequately by the Amazonian soil – but also nourishes it. Moreover, it is worth noting that the father buries his newborn's umbilical cord and placenta at the foot of an emergent tree.

4 A number of themes, characteristic of Europe and Asia, are entirely absent from Huaorani beliefs. In Germanic beliefs, the cosmic tree is linked to a god or king who sacrifices himself to enhance his power and knowledge. He hangs himself from the

tree, dies and is reborn. Human sacrifices to trees replace this original self-sacrifice. In Ancient Crete, Minos, the king-priest, whose name means 'lord, protector and saviour', is the master of time and fertility during his limited reign (then his strength weakens, his vitality is too low to remain in office). The tree of life in Mesopotamia and India brings fertility by linking death with life. The birds visiting its branches are the souls of the dead. As Jacques Brosse (1989) argues, the fig tree under which Buddha meditates can also be classified as a cosmic tree, and so can the tree of Genesis (and the cross on which Christ died: it grew into a tree on Mount Golgotha). In China, we find another type of cosmic tree, the *Kine-mou*, the tree of the absolute beginning.

5 Fluff used as wadding, *kapok* eases the passage of darts along the grooved stave of blowguns.

6 It is not uncommon to find 60m-high specimens, with a 3m basal diameter, and a 40m-wide circumference/girth (Villajero 1952:80).

7 From *tey*, 'hard', and *ahuè*, 'wood', literally means 'hard wood'.

8 Local agronomists have told me that 65 per cent of the Quechua population along the Napo river plant the peach-palm; an outstanding figure compared to the modest 0.6 per cent to 3.5 per cent for other palms.

9 Balslev and Barford (1987), following Moore (1973), have found 239 species of *Bactris gasipaes*, 14 of which have been described under the old genus *Guilielma*, but there are still disagreements on the taxonomy, in particular as to whether *Guilielma* is a subspecies of the genus *Bactris*, or a separate genus.

10 Clement calls 'management' all practices that can be categorized as a milder form of care – perhaps less intentional – than cultivation, and concludes that it is possible to observe a 'continuum from wild and used, to cultivated, to domesticated', and that such a continuum 'refers not only to human interaction with the plant to obtain its economic product, but also to the plant's genetic response to this interaction (progressive changes in gene frequencies), leading finally to full domestication' (Clement, 1992, p.71).

11 See Sponsel (1986) for a concise summary. The extreme naturalism of some cultural ecologists is well-illustrated by the following statement: 'That the indigenous populations of South America may have developed mechanisms which prevented them degrading their environments is a tribute not so much to their rationality as to their responsiveness to signals and cues in the environment comparable to that possessed by other animal populations', cited in S. Nugent (1981, p.65).

Chapter 9

1 KK=Kui, E=English, O=Oriya.

Chapter 10

1 This chapter is a somewhat enlarged and revised version of material to be found in Chapter Eight of the author's book, *Fighting For the Rain Forest: War, youth and resources in Sierra Leone*, Oxford: James Curry for the International African Institute, 1996, and is reproduced with permission of the publisher.

Chapter 11

1 See the compilation in Berlin (1992): 31ff. that gives a good overview on the general principles used in contemporary ethnobiological research.

2 The Greek verb *metaphorein* stands for a transfer of meaning into a different and, what is at first glance, an alien context.

3 In such a way the term 'Indian' as applied to the native inhabitants of both Americas and at a later stage to those of the Indian sub-continent; the former group were then called 'American Indians' or 'Red Indians'. In another example, the 'red oak' that was found in New England by European settlers was a metaphoric appropriation of what

appeared similar to the oak species they knew from their homelands. B. Berlin refers to this category as 'secondary lexemes' (1992, p.17).

4 I am particularly grateful to M.K. Jena, P. Pathi and S.C. Behera for their excellent field-work.

5 The history of inventions refers to new technical assets mostly with archaic names: electricity, automobile, telephone, television etc. A newly discovered chemical element, for example was named after a planet which in turn, was named after a Roman deity – 'Mercury'.

6 In the Kuttia Kondh ceremony offering sacrifices to the god of the landscape *(Dharni Penu)* there are linguistic similarities between the core terms of the sacrifice: *Neri* (blood) – *Neda* (middle [of the hill]), and *Nella* (swidden plots). Blood (human or animal) is offered to please the god of the middle hill to allow the clearing of a forest patch for practising swidden agriculture (see Seeland, Patnaik *et al.*, 1995, vol.1, p.311f).

Appendix to Chapter 12

1 Nepalese word for '*Bompos*': Shamans who are capable of transmigration of souls or of performing ancient cults.

Bibliography

Acharya, H.P. (1984), 'Management of Forest Resources in Nepal: A case study of Madan Pokhara Village Panchayat'. MPS thesis, Cornell University, USA.

Adam, J.G. (1948), Les reliques boisées et les essences des savanes dans la zone préforestière en Guinée française, *Bulletin of the Société Botanique Française* 98, pp.22–6.

Anderson, A. and D. Posey (1989), 'Management of a tropical scrub savanna by the Gorotire Kayapo of Brazil'. In *Resource Management in Amazonia: Indigenous and folk strategies*, D. Posey and W. Balée (eds.). Advances in Economic Botany 7, pp.159–73.

Anonymous (1987), 'Forest Management Plan for Sano Ban (Pande Gaon)'. Unpublished English translation, Kathmandu, NAFP.

Aris, M. (1990), *Man and Nature in the Buddhist Himalaya,* Himalayan Environment and Culture, Shimla Indian Institute of Advanced Study, India.

Asquith, P. (1986), 'The Monkey Memorial Service of Japanese Primatologists'. In *Japanese Culture and Behaviour. Selected Readings.* T.S. Lebra and W.P. Lebra (ed.), pp.29–32, Honolulu, University of Hawaii Press.

Aubréville, A. (1949), *Climats, Forêts et Desertification de l'Afrique Tropicale.* Paris, Société d'Editions Géographiques, Maritimes et Coloniales.

Bahl, K.N. (1979), 'Afforestation: Where have we gone wrong?' In *Man and Forest*, Krishna Murti Gupta and Desh Bandhu (eds.), pp.170–77, Delhi, Jain.

Bahuguna, S. (1986), 'Chipko – The Peoples' Movement to Protect Forests', *Cultural Survival Quarterly*, Vol. 10, No. 3, pp. 27–30.

——(1988), 'Chipko Movement: The Role of the Local Communities in Upland Conservation'. *Tiger Paper*, XV, No. 4, pp. 5–7, Bangkok, RAPA, FAO.

Bailey, F.G. (1957), *Caste and the Economic Frontier: A Village in Highland Orissa,* Manchester, Manchester University Press.

Bajracharya, D. (1983), 'Fuel, food or forest? Dilemmas in a Nepali village'. *World Development* 11, No. 12, pp. 1057–1074.

Balée, W. (1988), Indigenous Adaptation to Amazonian Palm Forests. *Principes* 32, 2, pp. 47–54.

——(1989) 'The Culture of Amazonian Forests'. In *Resource Management in Amazonia: Indigenous and Folk strategies,* Advances in Economic Botany 7, D.Posey and W.Balée (eds.), pp. 1–21.

——(1992), People of the Fallow: A Historical Ecology of Foraging in Lowland South America'. In *Conservation of Neotropical Forests: Working from Traditional Resource Use*, K. Redford and C. Padoch (ed.) pp. 35–57, New York, Columbia University Press.

——(1993) 'Indigenous transformation of Amazonian forests: An example from Maranhão', Brazil. *L'Homme* 126–28 XXXIII, 2–4, pp. 235–258.

Balick, M.J. (1979), 'Amazon oil palms of promise: a survey', *Economic Botany* 33, 1, pp. 11–28.

Balslev, H. and A. Barford (1987), 'Ecuadorian palms. An overview'. *Opera Botanica* 92, pp. 17–35.

Banwari (1992), *Pancavati. Indian approach to environment,* A. Vohra (trans.). Delhi, Shri Vinayaka Publ.

Barrett, William (1979), *The Illusion of Technique. A Search for the meaning of life in a technological age.* London, Kimber.

Berlin, B. (1973), 'The relation of folk systematics to biological classification and nomenclature'. *Annual Review of Ecology and Systematics*, 4, pp. 259–271.

——(1978), 'Ethnobiological classification', in *Cognition and Categorization*, E. Rosch and B.B. Lloyd (ed.), pp. 9–26, New York, Lawrence Erlbaum Associates.

——(1992), *Ethnobiological Classification: Principles of categorization of plants and animals in traditional societies.* Princeton, Princeton University Press.

Berlin, B., Breedlove, D. and P. Raven (1973), 'General principles of classification and nomenclature in folk biology. *American Anthropologist* 75. pp. 214–242.

Berreman, G.D. (1972), *Hindus of the Himalayas: Ethnography and change.* Berkeley, University of California Press.

Berry, S. (1989), 'Social institutions and access to resources'. *Africa* 59, 1, pp. 41–5.

Bhandari, J.S. and S.M. Channa (1992), 'Forests and tribals: A macro-level perspective'. *Mainstream* 30, 49.

Bird-David, N. (1990), 'The giving environment: Another perspective on the economic system of gatherer-hunters. *Current Anthropology* 31, pp. 189–196.

——(1992) 'Beyond "the Original Affluent Society" ' ': A culturalist transformation'. *Current Anthropology* 33, pp.25–47.

Bista, D.B. (1987), *People of Nepal*, Kathmandu, Ratna Pustak Bhandar.

Bjønness, I. (1986), 'Mountain hazard perception and risk-avoiding strategies among the Sherpas of Khumbu Himal, Nepal'. *Mountain Research and Development* Vol. 6, No. 4, pp. 277–292.

Blaikie, P. (1985), *The political economy of soil erosion in developing countries*. Longman Development Studies, New York, Wiley.

Bloch, M. (1992), *Prey into Hunter: The politics of religious experience*. Cambridge, Cambridge University Press.

Bodley, J.H. and F.C. Benson (1979), 'Cultural ecology of Amazonian palms' in *WSU Laboratory of Anthropology, Reports of investigation* No. 56. University of Michigan.

Bouez, S. (1985), 'Réciprocité et hiérarchie: L'Alliance chez les Hos et les Santal de l'Inde'. Paris, Société d'Ethnographie.

Biokensha, D., Warren, D.M. and O. Werner (ed.) (1980), *Indigenous Knowledge Systems and Development*. University Press of America.

Brosse, J. (1989), *Mythologie des Arbres*. Paris, Plon.

Brown, Cecil H. (1976), 'Some General Principles of Biological and Non-Biological Folk Classifications'. *American Ethnologist*, 3: 73–85.

Burley, J. and P. von Carlowitz (1984), 'Multipurpose Tree Germplasm'. Proceedings, Recommendations and Documents of a Planning Workshop to Discuss International Cooperation. Nairobi, International Council for Research in Agroforestry.

Cavalcante, V. (1977), 'Edible palm fruit of the Brazilian Amazon', *Principes 21*, pp. 91–102.

Cartmill, M. (1993), *A View to a Death in the Morning: Hunting and Nature through History*. Cambridge, Mass, Harvard University Press.

CATIE-FAO (1983), 'Informe de la reunion de consulta sobre las palmeras poco Utilizadas de America Tropical'. Costa-Rica, mimeograph in Oxford Forestry Institute.

Chambers, R., Pacey, A. and L. A. Thrupp (1989), *Farmer First: Farmer innovation and agricultural research*, London, IT Publications.

Chandrakanth, M.G., Gilless J.K., Gowramma V. and M.G. Nagaraja (1990), 'Temple forests in India's forest development'. In *Agroforestry Systems* 11: 199–211.

Chapple, C.K. (1993), *Non-Violence to Animals, Earth and Self in Asian Traditions*, New York, SUNY.

Chase, A.K. (1989), 'Domestication and Domiculture in Northern Australia: a social perspective' in *Foraging and Farming. The evolution of plant exploitation*, D.R. Harris and G.C. Hillman (ed.). London, Unwin Hyman.

Chaudhuri, H.N. Rai; Pal, D.C. and C. R. Tarafdar (1975), 'Less-known uses of some plants from the tribal areas of Orissa', *Bull. Bot. Surv. India.*, Vol. 17, Nos. 1–4, pp. 132–136.

Chevalier, A. (1933). *Les bois sacrés des Noirs de l'Afrique tropicale comme sanctuaires de la nature*. C. R. Société de Biogéographie, pp. 37.

Chiba, T. (1975), *Shuryō Denchō (Hunting Legends)*, Tokyo, Hosei Daigaku Shuppankyoku.

——(1977), *Shuryō denchō kenkyū (Research on Hunting Legends)*. Tokyo, Fūkan Shobō.

——(1995), *Ōkami wa naze kieta ka (Why Did the Wolf Disappear?)*. Tokyo, Shinjinbutsu Ōraisha.

Childe, V.G. (1936), *Man makes Himself*. London, Watts.

Clad, J.C. (1985), 'Conservation and indigenous peoples: a study of convergent interests' in *Culture and Conservation*, McNeely, J. and D. Pitt (ed.) pp. 45–62, London, Sydney, Croom Helm.

Clement, C.R. (1988), 'Domestication of the Pejibaye (*Bactris gasipaes*): Past and present'. *Advanced Economic Botany* 6, pp.155–174.

——(1992) 'Domesticated palms', *Principes* 36, 2, pp. 70–78.

Clement, R.C. and J. Mora Urpi (1987) 'Pejibaye Palm: Multi-Use Potential for the Lowland Humid Tropics', *Economic Botany* 41, 2, pp. 302–311.

Commission Européenne (ed.) (1994), 'Situation des populations indigènes des forêts dense humides', Rapport rédigé sous la direction de S. Bahuchet et P. de Maret. Luxembourg, Office des publications officielles des Communautés européennes.

Condominas, G. (1990), *From Lawa to Mon, from Saa' to Thai: Historical and anthropological aspects of South-east Asian social spaces*. Canberra, Australian National University.

Conklin, H. (1957), 'A report on an integral system of shifting cultivation in the Philippines'. *Hanunoo Agroculture*, Rome, FAO.

Cox T. (1989), 'Divine Support in Langtang and Khumbu', *Himal* Vol. 2, No. 3, pp. 26–27.

Credner, W. (1935), *Siam – das Land der Tai*. Stuttgart, Engelhorns Nachf.

Croll, E. and D. Parkin (1992), 'Cultural understandings of the environment' in *Bush Base: Forest Farm: Culture, environment and development*. Croll, E. and D. Parkin (ed.), pp. 11–38. London, Routledge.

Crone, G.R. (1937), *The Voyages of Cadamosto*. London, Hakluyt.

Crooke, W. (1906), *Things Indian*. London, John Murray.

D'Azevedo, W.L. (1962), 'Some historical problems in the delineation of a Central-West Atlantic Region'. *Annals, New York Academy of Sciences* 96, pp. 513–538.

Das Gupta, P.K. (1984), *Life and Culture of Matrilineal Tribes of Meghalaya*. Delhi, Inter-India Publications.

Davies, A.G. and P. Richards (1991), 'Rain Forest in Mende Life: Resources and subsistence strategies in rural communities around the Gola North Forest Reserve (Sierra Leone)'. Report to the UK Overseas Development Administration, Department of Anthropology, London, University College.

Deep, D.K. (1982), *The Nepal Festivals*. Kathmandu, Ratna Pustak Bhandar.

Denholm, Jeannette (1989), 'Reaching out to Forest Users: Strategies for involving women'. Kathmandu, ICIMOD.

Descola, P. (1996), 'Constructing Natures: Symbolic ecology and social practice'. In *Nature and Society: Anthropological Perspectives*. P. Descola and G. Palsson (ed.), London and New York, Routledge.

DeWisser, M.W. (1908), 'The Fox and the Badger in Japanese Folklore'. *Transactions of the Asiatic Society of Japan*, Vol. 36: 1–159.

——(1935), *Ancient Buddhism in Japan*. Leiden, E. J. Brill.

Dhungel, B.P. (1987), 'Socio-cultural and legal arrangements for grazing on public land'. Natural Resource Management Paper Series No. 11. Kathmandu, HMG-USAID-GTZ-IDRC-FORD-WINROCK PROJECT.

Dixit, K.M. (1989), 'An obsession with tourism', *Himal* Vol. 2, No. 3, pp. 3–12.

Dove, M.R. and A.L. Rao (1986), 'Common Resource Management in Pakistan: Garrett Hardin in the Junglat'. Paper prepared for AKRSP/ICIMOD/EAPI Workshop on 'Institutional Development for Local Management of Rural Resources', 18–25 April 1986, Gilgit, Kathmandu, ICIMOD.

Dube, S.C. (1953), 'Token pre-puberty marriages in Middle India'. *Man*, 53, pp. 18–19.

Dumont, L. (1964), 'Marriage in India, the Present State of the Question II. Marriage and Status, Nayar and Newar', *Contributions to Indian Sociology* 7, pp. 80–98.

——(1972), *Homo Hierarchicus: The caste system and its implications*. London, Paladin.

——(1983), *Affinity as a Value: Marriage alliance in South India, with comparative essays on Australia*. Chicago and London, The University of Chicago Press.

Earhart, H.B. (1970), *A Religious Study of the Mount Haguro Sect of Shugendo*. Tokyo, Sophia University Press.

Eden, M. (1990), *Ecology and Land Management in Amazonia*. London, Belhaven Press.

Ellen, Roy (1989), [1982]: *Environment, Subsistence and System: The ecology of small-scale social formations*. Cambridge, Cambridge University Press.

——(1993), *The Cultural Relations of Classification. An analysis of Nualu animal categories from central Seram*. Cambridge, Cambridge University Press.

Ellen, Roy F. and D. Reason (ed.) (1979), *Classification in their Social Context*. London, Academic Press.

Falconer, J. (1990), 'The major significance of "minor" forest products: The local use and value of forests in the West African humid zone', *Community Forestry Note*. 6. Rome, FAO.

Fisher, R.J. (1988a), 'Local organizations in forest management', in *Directions for Community Forest Management in Nepal*: Seminar series at the Institute of Forestry, Pokhara September 1988, pp. 20–36. Kathmandu, NAFP.

——(1988b), 'The ecology of doubt: An anthropological study of agrarian systems in Western Rajasthan, Department of Anthropology, University of Sydney'. PhD Thesis.

——(1989), 'Indigenous systems of common property management in Nepal'. Working Paper No. 18, Nepal Australia Forestry Project, Kathmandu, Nepal.

Fisher, R.J., Singh, H.B., Pandey, D.R. and H. Lang (1989), 'The management of forest resources in rural development: A case study of Sindhu Palchok and Kabhre Palanchok Districts of Nepal'. *Mountain Populations and Institutions*, Discussion Paper No. 1. Kathmandu, ICIMOD.

Fox, J.M. (1984), 'Firewood consumption in a Nepali village'. *Environmental Management* Vol. 8, No. 3, pp. 243–250.

Fuller, C. (1976), *The Nayars Today*. Cambridge, Cambridge University Press.

Fürer-Haimendorf, C. von (1975), *Himalayan Traders: Life in highland Nepal*. New Delhi, Time Books International.

——(1981), 'Social structure and spatial mobility among the Thakalis of Western Nepal in Asian Highland Societies' in *Anthropological Perspective*, pp. 1–19, Christoph von Fürer Haimendorf (ed.). New Delhi, Stirling Publishers.

Furley, P., Proctor, J. and J. Ratter (ed.) (1992), *The Nature and Dynamics of Forest-Savanna boundaries*. London, Chapman & Hall.

Gadgil, M. (1987), 'Diversity: Cultural and biological'. *Tree* Vol. 2, No. 12, pp. 369–373. Cambridge, Research Publications.

Gilmour, D.A. (1988), 'Field Report: Palchok Panchayat 29–12–88'. Kathmandu, NAFP, unpublished report.

——(1989), 'Forest Resources and Indigenous Management in Nepal'. East-West Environment and Policy Institute, Working Paper 17, East-West Center, Honolulu.

Good, A. (1991), *The Female Bridegroom. A comparative study of life-crisis rituals in South India and Sri Lanka*. Oxford, Clarendon Press.

Gow, P. (1993), 'Gringos and wild Indians: Images of history in Western Amazonian cultures', *L' Homme* 126–128, pp. 327–348.

Grandstaff, T.B. (1980), 'Shifting cultivation in Northern Thailand: Possibilities for development'. Tokyo, UNO.

Greenwold, S.M. (1981), 'Caste. A moral structure and a social system of control' in *Culture and Morality: Essays in honour of Christoph von Fürer-Haimendorf*. A.C. Mayer (ed.), Delhi, Oxford University Press.

Gross, D.R. (1975), 'Protein capture and cultural development in the Amazon Basin'. *American Anthropology* 77, 3, pp. 526–49.

Guha, R. (1988), 'Forestry and social protest in British Kumaun, c. 1893–1921'. In *Whose Trees? Proprietary Dimensions of Forestry*, Louise Fortmann and John W. Bruce (ed.), pp. 284–296, Boulder, Colorado, Westview Press.

——(1989), *The Unquiet Woods: Ecological change and peasant resistance in the Himalaya*. Delhi, Oxford University Press.

Gurung Durga Kumari (1987), 'Women's Participation in Forestry: A case study of Akrang Village', Forestry Research Paper Series No. 10. Kathmandu, HMG-USAID-GTZ-IDRC-FORD-WINROCK PROJECT.

Guthrie, S. (1988), 'A Japanese New Religion: Risshō Kōsei-kai in a Mountain Hamlet'. Ann Arbor, Center for Japanese Studies, University of Michigan.

Gyawali, D. (1987), 'Development Dharma'. *Himal* Vol. 0, No. 0, pp. 17, Kathmandu, Himal Associates.

——(1989a), 'Water in Nepal'. Occasional Paper No. 8, East-West Environment and Policy Institute, Hawaii, East-West Center.

——(1989b), 'Nepal-Australia Forestry Project socio-economic monitoring and evaluation: Case study of Mathurapati-Phulbari Panchayat, Kavre Palanchok District'. Kathmandu, NAFP. Unpublished report.

Haines, H.H. (1921–1925), *Botany of Bihar and Orissa*. Vol. 1–3. London, Abelson & Co.

——(1924), *The Flora of Bihar and Orissa*. London, Abelson & Co.

Hannerz, U. (1987), 'The world in creolization'. *Africa* 57.

Hardacre, H. (1989), *Shintō and the State 1868–1988*. Princeton, University Press.

Harris, D.R. and G.C. Hillman (ed.) (1989), *Foraging and Farming: The evolution of plant exploitation*. London, Unwin Hyman.

Harris, M. (1984), 'Animal capture and Yanomamo warfare: Retrospect and new evidence. *Journal of Anthropological Resources*, 40, 1, pp. 183–201.

Harrison P. (1984), *Inside the Third World*. Harmondsworth, UK, Penguin.

Hayashi, H. (1980), *Yoshino no minzokushi (A Record of Yoshino Folklore)*. Tokyo, Bunka Shuppankyoku.

Hecht, S., Anderson A. and P. May (1988); 'The subsidy from nature: Shifting cultivation, successional palm forests, and rural development'. *Human Organization* 47, 1, pp. 25–35.

Hecht, S. and D. Posey (1989), 'Preliminary results on soil management techniques of the Kayapo Indians'. In *Resource Management in Amazonia: Indigenous and folk strategies*, Advances in Economic Botany 7, D. Posey and W. Balée (ed.), pp. 174–188.

Hida, I. (1972), *Yamagatari: daishizen no dōbutsutachi (Mountain Tales: Animals of nature)*. Tokyo, Bungei Shunjū.

Higuchi, K. (1979), *Shizen to nihonjin (Nature and the Japanese)*. Tokyo, Kodansha.

His Majesty's Government of Nepal (1988), 'Building on Success: The National Conservation Strategy for Nepal'. Kathmandu, Malla Press.

Hodson, T.C. (1921a), 'The doctrine of rebirth in various areas of India', *Man in India* 1, 2, pp. 1–17.

——(1921b), 'Tree marriage', *Man in India* 1, 3, pp. 202–221.

Höfer, Andràs (1971), 'Some Non-Buddhist Elements in Tamang religion', *Vasudha*, Vol. 14, no. 3, pp. 17–23.

Holmberg, D.H. (1990), 'Lama, Shamar, and Lambu' in *Tamany Religious Practice*. PhD Thesis, Cornell University.

Hopkins, B. (1992), 'Ecological processes at the forest savanna boundary'. In *Nature and Dynamics of Forest Savanna Boundaries*, Furley, P.A., Proctor, J., and J.A. Ratter (eds), London, Chapman & Hall, pp. 21–34.

Houis, M. (1958), 'Conte Koniagui: la fille orgueilleuse', *Notes Africaines*, 80, pp. 112–114.

Howes, M. (1980), The Uses of Indigenous Technical Knowledge in Development. In Brokensha, D., Warren, D.M. and Werner, O. (ed) *Indigenous Knowledge Systems and Development*. University Press of America.

Howes, M. and R. Chambers (1980), 'Indigenous Technical Knowledge: Analysis, implications and issues'. In *Indigenous Knowledge Systems and Development*. Brokensha, D., Warren, D.M. and O. Werner, (ed.),University Press of America.

Huber, J. (1909), 'Mattas e Madeiras Amazonicas'. Bol. Mus. Goeldi (Museu Paraense), *Hist. Nat. Ethnogr.* 6, pp. 91–225.

Ibaraki, A. (1993), *Nihon no minwa: ki no kuni hen (Folktales of Japan: The Ki Edition)*. Ōkaka, Nenshōsha.

Ichikawa, T. (1989), *Yama to ki to nihonjin: mori ni ikiru Kisobito no kurashi (Mountains, Trees and the Japanese: The forest-dwelling life of Kiso People)*. Tokyo, NHK Books.

Ingles, A.W. (1988), 'Field Report, Khanalthok Panchayat; Kabhre Palanchok. 8–18th March 1988'. Kathmandu, NAFP. Unpublished report.

——(1990), 'The management of religious forests in Nepal', Department of Forestry, Australian National University, Canberra, Australia. Graduate Diploma in Science thesis.

Irokawa, D. (1985), *The Culture of the Meiji Period*. (Translated by M. B. Jansen). Princeton, University Press.

Irvine, D. (1989), 'Succession management and resource distribution in an Amazonian rainforest'. In *Resource Management in Amazonia: Indigenous and folk strategies*. Advances in Economic Botany 7, D.Posey and W.Balée (ed.), pp. 223–237.

Ives, J.D. and B. Messerli (1989), *The Himalayan Dilemma: Reconciling development and conservation*. London, Routledge.

Jackson, W.J. (1987), 'Field Report: Daraune Pokhari Panchayat, Kabhre District 1–9th December 1987'. Kathmandu, NAFP. Unpublished report.

Jackson, W.J. and M.R. Maharjan (1988), 'Matching indigenous and sponsored systems of forest management – a case study from Kabhre Palanchok District' in *Directions for Community Forest Management in Nepal*, Seminar series at Institute of Forestry, Pokhara, September 1988, pp. 37–54, Kathmandu, NAFP.

Jackson, M. (1977), *The Kuranko: Dimensions of social reality in a West African society*. New York, St. Martin's Press.

Jain, S. (1984), 'Standing up for trees: Women's role in the Chipko Movement', *Unasylva* Vol. 36, No. 146, pp. 12–20. Rome, FAO.

Jain, S.K. (1979), 'Economic relationship between people and forest flora'. In *Man and Forest*,Krishna Murti Gupta and Desh Bandhu (ed.) pp. 288–293, Delhi, Jain.

Kalland, A. and B. Moeran (1992), *Japanese Whaling. End of an era?* London, Curzon Press.

Kaneko, H., Konishi, M., Sasaki, K. and T. Chiba (1992) *Nihonshi no Naka no Dōbutsu Jiten (A Dictionary of Animals in Japanese History)*. Tokyo, Tōkyōdo Shuppan.

Kauffmann, H.E. (1972), 'Some social and religious institutions of the Lawa (N.W. Thailand). Part I'. *Journal of the Siam Society* 60, 1, pp. 235–306.

——(1977), 'Some social and religious institutions of the Lawa (N.W. Thailand). Part II', *Journal of the Siam Society* 65, 1, pp. 181–226.

Kida, Y. (ed.) (1984), *Shingu Mokuzai Kyodo Kumiai Hyakunenshi (A One Hundred Year History of the Shingu Timber Association)*. Tokyo, Gyosei.

Kimura, S. and M. Tsutsui (1990), *Mori no seikatsu dorama 100 (One Hundred Tales of Forest Life)*. Tokyo, Nihon Ringyō KyōKai.

Kizaki, S. (1990), 'The Phoenix Tree' in *The Phoenix Tree and Other Stories*. (Translated by Carol A. Flath.) Tokyo, Kōdansha, pp. 143–242.

Kobayashi, M. (1994), 'Nekozuka' (Cat mound). In *Nihon mukashibanashi jiten (Dictionary of Japanese Old Tales)*, Inada, K., T. Ōshima, T. Kawabata, A. Fukuda, Y. Mihara (eds) Tokyo, Kobundo, 706–7.

Kolenda, Pauline (1984), 'Woman as tribute, woman as flower: Images of 'Woman' in weddings in North and South India, *American Ethnologist* 11, pp. 98–117.

Koyama, Y. (1992), *Kishū no matsuri to minzoku (Festivals and Folklore of Kishu)*. Tokyo, Kokuisho Kankōkai.

Kunstadter, P. (1978a), 'Ecological modification and adaptation: An ethnobotanical view of Lua' swiddeners in North-western Thailand'. In *The Nature and Status of Ethnobotany*, R. Ford (ed.), pp. 168–200, Ann Arbor, USA, Museum of Anthropology.

——(1978b), 'Subsistence agriculture economies of Lua' and Karen hill farmers, Mae Sariang District, North-western Thailand', in *Farmers in the forest*, P. Kunstadter *et al.* (eds.), Honolulu, East-West Center, pp. 74–133.

——(1983), 'Animism, Buddhism, and Christianity: religion in the life of Lua people of Pa Pae, North-western Thailand'. In *Highlanders of Thailand*. J. McKinnon and W. Bhrusasri (eds.), pp. 135–154. Kuala Lumpur, Oxford University Press.

Kunstadter, P., Chapman, E.C. and S. Sabhasri (eds.) (1978), *Farmers in the Forest: Economic development and marginal agriculture in Northern Thailand*. Honolulu, East-West Center.

Kunstadter, P., Sabhasri, S. and T. Smitinand (1978), 'Flora of a forest fallow-farming environment in North-western Thailand'. *Journal of the National Research Council* 10, 1, pp. 1–45.

LaFleur, W.R. (1983), *The Karma of Words: Buddhism and the literary arts in Medieval Japan*. Berkeley, University of California Press.

——(1989), 'Saigyo and the Buddhist value of nature'. In *Nature in Asian Traditions of Thought: Essays in environmental philosophy*. J. Baird Callicott and R.T. Ames (ed.). New York, SUNY, pp.183–209.

——(1992), *Liquid Life: Abortion and Buddhism in Japan*. Princeton, University Press.

Lathrap, D. (1968), 'The hunting economies of the tropical forest zone of South America: An attempt at historical perspective'. In *Man the Hunter*. R. Lee and I. de Vore (ed.), pp. 23–29, Chicago, Aldine.

——(1970), *The Upper Amazon*. New York, Praeger.

Leach, M. and J. Fairhead (1994), 'Ruined settlements and new gardens: A gendered history of soil ripening by Kuranko farmers of the West African savannas'. Paper presented at the conference on Gender and the Politics of Environmental Sustainability in Africa, Centre of African Studies, University of Edinburgh 25–26 May 1994.

Lévi-Strauss, C. (1950), 'The use of wild plants in tropical South America' in *Physical Anthropology, Linguistics and Cultural Geography of South American Indians*. J. Steward (ed.), HSAI. Vol. 6, Washington DC, Smithsonian Institute Press.

Maag, Bettina (1992), 'Interactions between Trees, Forests and the People of Two Tamang Villages in Nepal'. Zürich, ETH. Unpublished manuscript.

MacCormack, C. (1980), 'Proto-social to adult: a Sherbo transformation in *Nature, Culture and Gender*, MacCormack, C. and M. Strathern (ed.), Cambridge University Press.

MacFarlane, A. (1976), *Resources and Population: A study of the Gurungs of Nepal*. Cambridge, Cambridge University Press.

Mahat, T.B.S., Griffin, D.M. and K.R. Shepherd (1986), 'Human impact on some forests of the Middle Hills of Nepal: Part 2. Some major human impacts before 1950 on the forests of

Sindhu Palchok and Kabhre Palanchok', *Mountain Research and Development* Vol. 6, No.4, pp. 325–334.

——(1987) 'Human impact on some forests of the Middle Hills of Nepal: Part 3. Forests in the subsistence economy of Sindhu Palchok and Kabhre Palanchok'. *Mountain Research and Development* Vol. 7, No.1, pp. 53–70.

Majumdar, D.N. (1950), *The Affairs of a Tribe*. Lucknow, Universal Publishers.

Majupria, T.C. and D.P. Joshi (1988), *Religious and Useful Plants of Nepal and India*. India, Gupta M. Lashkar.

Makino, K. (1986), *Kyōju no minzokugakuS (The Folklore of Giant Trees)*. Toyko, Kōbunsha.

Mansberger, J.R. (1988), 'In search of the tree spirit: Evolution of the sacred tree Ficus religiosa'. In *Changing Tropical Forests*, J. Dargavel, K.E. Dixon and N. Semple (ed.), pp. 399–411, Canberra, CRES, ANU.

March, Kathryn S. (1979), *The Intermediacy of Women: Female gender symbolism and the social position of women among Tamangs and Sherpas of Highland Nepal*. Cornell University, New York.

Matsutani, M. (1994a), *Mōkurei, heibi (Tree Spirits and Snakes)*. Tokyo, Rippū Shobō.

——(1994b), *Ōkami, yamainu, neko (Wolves, Dogs and Cats)*. Tokyo, Rippū Shobō.

McDougal, C. (1963), *The Social Structure of the Hill Juang*. Ann Arbor, University Microfilms.

——(1964), 'Juang categories and joking relations'. *South-western Journal of Anthropology* 20, 4, pp. 319–345.

——(1979), *The Kulunge Rai: A study in kinship and marriage exchange*, Nepal, Ratna Pustak Bhandar.

McKinnon, J. and B. Vienne (ed.) (1989), *Hill Tribes Today*. Bangkok, White Lotus.

Meggers, B. (1971), *Amazonia: Man and culture in a counterfeit paradise*. Chicago, Aldine-Altherton.

Messerschmidt, D.A. (1986), 'People and Resources in Nepal: Customary Resource Management Systems of the Upper Kali Gandaki'. Proceedings of the Conference on Common Property Resource Management April 21–26, 1985. Washington DC, National Academy Press.

——(1987), 'Conservation and society in Nepal: Traditional forest management and innovative development'. In *Lands at Risk in the Third World: Local level perspectives*, Little P.D., Horowitz M.M. and A.E. Nyerges (ed.), pp. 373–397, Boulder, Westview Press.

——(1989a), 'The Hindu pilgrimage to Muktinath, Nepal: Part 1. Natural and supernatural attributes of the sacred field'. *Mountain Research and Development* Vol. 9, No. 2, pp. 89–104.

——(1989b), 'The Hindu pilgrimage to Muktinath, Nepal: Part 2. Vaishnava devotees and status reaffirmation'. *Mountain Research and Development* Vol. 9, No. 2, pp. 105–118.

Mishra, S.C. and A.K. Dubey (1992) 'Medicinal use of some commonly occurring plants by tribals of Mayurbhanj'. Department of Botany, Bhanja Bharati, Orissa.

Mooney, H.F. (1950), *Supplements to the Flora of Bihar and Orissa*. Ranchi.

Moore, D. (1993) 'Contesting terrain in Zimbabwe's Eastern Highlands: Political ecology and peasant resource struggles', *Economic Geography* 69, 3/4.

Moore, H.E. Jr. (1973), 'Palms in the tropical forest ecosystems'. In *Tropical Forest Ecosystems in Africa and South America: A comparative review*, B. Meggers *et al.* (ed.), Washington DC, Smithsonian Institute Press.

Mora Urpi, J. (1984), 'El Pejibaye (*Bactris gasipaes*): Origen, Biologia Floral y Manejo Agronómico'. In *Palmeras Poco Utilizadas de América Tropical*. FAO/CATIE (ed.), pp. 118–160, Turrialba, FAO/CATIE.

Mudgal, V. and D. C. Pal (1980), 'Medicinal plants used by tribals of Mayurbhanj (Orissa)'. *Bulletin of the Botanical Survey*, India, Vol. 22, Nos. 1–4, pp. 59–62.

Muratorio, B. (1991), *The Life and Times of Grandfather Alonso: Culture and history in the Upper Amazon*. New Brunswick, Rutgers University Press.

Nakamaki, Hirochika (1992), *Mukashi diamyō, im a kaisha (Feudal lords of long ago and companies of the present day)*. Tokyo, Tankōsha.

Nakamura, T. (1987), *Nihon Dōbutsu Minzokushi (Japanese Animal Folklore)*. Tokyo, Kaimeisha.

Nakano, K. (1978), 'An ecological study of swidden agriculture at a village in Northern Thailand', *South East Asian Studies* 16, 3, pp. 11–446.

Nakazawa, K. (1992), *Nihon no mori o sasaeru hitotachi (The People who Maintain Japan's Forest)*. Tokyo, Shōbunsha.

Naumann, N. (1963), 'Yama no Kami'. *Asian Folklore Studies*, Vol. 22; 133–366 [English summary pp. 341–349].

——(1974), 'Whale and fish cult in Japan: A basic feature of Ebisu worship'. *Asian Folklore Studies*, Vol. 33, no. 1, 1–15.

——(1994), *Yama no kami (The Mountain Spirit)*, (Translated from German by Nomura Shin'ichi and Hieda Yo'ichiro). Tokyo, Gongyōsha.

Nebuka, M. (1991), *Yama no jinsei. Matagi no mura kara (Mountain Life: The village of Matagi)*. Tokyo, Nihon Hoso Shuppatsu Kyokai.

Niamir, Maryam (1990), 'Community forestry, decision-making in natural resource management in arid and semi-arid Africa'. *Community Forestry Note 4*, Rome, FAO.

Nishitsunoi, M. (1958), *Nenjū gyōji jiten (Dictionary of Annual Events)*. Tokyo, Tokyōdō Shuppan.

Nugent, S. (1981) 'Amazonia: Ecosystem and Social system'. *Man* 16, 1, pp. 62–74.

O'Malley, L.S.S. (1932), *Indian Caste Customs*. Cambridge, Cambridge University Press.

Obeyesekere, Gananath (1968) 'Theodicy, sin and salvation in a sociology of Buddhism'. In *Dialectic in Practical Religion*. E.R. Leach (ed.), Cambridge, Cambridge University Press.

——(1980), 'The rebirth eschatology and its transformations. A contribution to the sociology of early Buddhism'. In *Karma and Rebirth in Classical Indian Traditions*, Wendy O'Flaherty, (ed.), Berkeley, University of California Press.

Odum, Eugene (1969), 'The Strategy of Ecosystem Development'. *Science* 164, pp. 262–9.

——(1983), *Basic Ecology*. New York, CBS College Publishing.

Ohnuki-Tierney, E. (1987), *The Monkey as Mirror: Symbolic transformations in Japanese history and ritual*. Princeton, University Press.

——(1990) 'Monkey as Metaphor? Transformations of a polytropic symbol in Japanese culture. *Man* Vol. 25, No. 1, pp. 89–107.

——(1993), *Rice as Self: Japanese identities through time*. Princeton, University Press.

Ōishi, R. (1990), *Zenkoku reinō shinreika meikan (Guide to Spiritualists Nationwide)*. Tokyo, Yōshobō.

Oyadomari, M. (1989), 'The rise and fall of the nature conservation movement in Japan in relation to some cultural values. *Environmental Management*, Vol. 13 no. 1, 22–33.

Pal, D.C. (1980), 'Observation of folklore about plants used in veterinary medicine in Bengal, Orissa and Bihar'. *Bulletin of the Botanical Survey India*. Vol. 22, Nos. 1–4, pp. 96–99.

Pal, D.C. and D.K. Banarjee (1971) *'Some less-known plant foods among the tribals of Andhra Pradesh and Orissa State*. Bulletin of the Botanical Survey India. Vol. 13, Nos. 3 and 4, pp. 221–3.

Pandey Shanta (1987), 'A methodology to study women in resource management and a case study of women in forest management in Dhading District, Nepal'. Kathmandu, ICIMOD.

Pant, Deepak Raj (1993), 'Religion, society and state in Nepal'. *Occasional Papers in Sociology and Anthropology* Volume 3, Kathmandu, Tribhuvan University, pp. 47–57.

Parkin, R. (1988), 'Reincarnation and alternating generation equivalence in middle India', *Journal of Anthropological Research*, 44, 1, pp. 1–20.

——(1992), *The Munda of Central India. An account of their social organization*. Delhi, Oxford University Press.

Parren, M.P.E. and N.R. van der Graaf (1995), 'The quest for national forest management' in Ghana, Côte d'Ivoire and Liberia Troperbos Series No. 13, Wageningen.

Paulme, D. (1950), 'Fautes sexuelles et 'premiers morts' dans une société africaine', *Journal de Psychologie Normal et Pathologique*, pp. 507–24.

Posey, D. (1983), 'Indigenous ecological knowledge and development in the Amazon'. In *The Dilemma of Amazonian Development*, E. Moran (ed.), pp. 225–57. Boulder, Westview Press.

——(1985), 'Indigenous management of tropical forest ecosystems: The case of the Kayapo Indians of the Brazilian Amazon'. *Agroforestry Systems* 3, pp.139–158.

Posey, D. and W. Balée (eds.) (1989), 'Resource Management in Amazonia: Indigenous and Folk Strategies'. *Advances in Economic Botany 7*.

Posey, Darrell A. *et al.* (1990), 'Ethnobiology: Implications and Applications'. Proceedings of the first international congress of ethnobiology. Belém, Museu Paranese, E. Goeldi.

Pradhan, Bina and Kathy Rankin (1988), 'Conceptual Perspectives on Women's Roles in Resource Management'. Centre for Women and Development. Draft.

Presler, H.H. (1970), 'Indian aborigine contributions to Hindu Ideas of Mukti liberation'. In *Types of Redemption*. J. Zwi Werblowsky and Jouco C. Bleeker (ed.), Leiden, E.J. Brill.

Reader, I. (1991), *Religion in Contemporary Japan*. London, MacMillan.

Regmi, M.C. (1978), *Land Tenure and Taxation in Nepal*. Bibliotheca Himalayica Series 1, Vol. 26. Kathmandu, Ratna Pustak Bhandar.

République de Guinée (1988), *Politique forestière et plan d'action*. Conakry.

Richards, P. (1985), *Indigenous Agricultural Revolution*. London, Hutchinson.

Rieffel, R. (1987), *Nepal Namaste*. Kathmandu, Sahayogi Press.

Riley, K.W., Gautam A.K., Singh-Dangol D.M. and Y.K. Karki (1989), 'Rapid Rural Appraisal Trek-hill crops: to Jumla, Dolpa and Mustang Districts, May 16–25 and June 1–6, 1989'. Travel Report No. 5/89, Hill Crops Improvement Programme, Kathmandu, NARCS, HMG.

Rival, L. (1992), 'Social transformations and the impact of formal schooling on the Huaorani of Amazonian Ecuador'. Unpublished PhD Thesis.

——(1993) 'The Growth of Family Trees: Understanding Huaorani Perceptions of the Forest'. *Man 28*, 4, pp. 635–52.

——(1994) 'Los indigenas Huaorani en la conciencia nacional: Alteridad representada y significada' in *Imagenes e Imagineros. Representaciones de los Indigenas Ecuatorianos*. B. Muratorio (ed.), Siglos XIX y XX., Quito, FLACSO.

——(in press) 'Domestication as a historical and symbolic process: Wild gardens and cultivated forests in the Ecuadorian Amazon'. In *Principles of Historical Ecology*, W. Balée (ed.), New York, Columbia University Press.

Rivière, C. (1969), 'Fétichisme et démystification: l'exemple guinéen. *Afrique Documents*, 102/3, pp. 131–168.

Robinson, P.J., (1987), 'The Dependence on crop production on trees and forest land'. In *Amelioration of Soil by Trees*. R. Prinsley and M.J. Swain (ed.), pp. 104–120, London, Commonwealth Science Council.

Roosevelt, A. (1989), 'Resource management in Amazonia before the Conquest: Beyond ethnographic projection' in *Resource Management in Amazonia: Indigenous and Folk strategies*, D. Posey and W. Balée (ed.), *Advances in Economic Botany 7*, pp. 30–62.

——(1993) 'The rise and fall of the Amazon chiefdoms'. *L'Homme* 126–8 XXXIII, 2–4, pp. 255–84.

Ross, E.B. (1978), 'Food Taboos, Diet, and Hunting Strategy: The adaptation to animals in Amazonian cultural ecology'. *Current Anthropology* 19, 1, pp. 1–36.

Ross, Harold M. (1973), *Baegu: Social and Ecological Organization in Malaita, Solomon Islands*. Urbana, University of Illinois Press.

Sabhasri, S. (1978), 'Effects of forest fallow cultivation on forest production and soil' in *Farmers in the forest*. P. Kunstadter *et al.* (eds.), pp.160–184, Honolulu, East-West Center.

Sahlins, M. (1976), *Culture and Practical Reason*. Chicago, University of Chicago Press.

Sahoo, A.K. (1986) 'Plant resources of Phulbani District (Orissa): Some suggestions to develop cottage industries in tribal localities', *Orissa Review*, Vol. 43, No. 3, pp. 5–10.

Sakamoto, T. (ed.) (1957), *Fuzoku Jiten (Dictionary of Manners)*. Tokyo, Tōkyōtō Shuppan.

Sakuma, J. (1985), *Shuryō no minzoku (The Folklore of Hunting)*. Tokyo, Iwasaki Bijutsusha.

Santisuk, T. (1988), 'An account of the vegetation of Northern Thailand'. *Geoeconomic Research* Vol. 5, Stuttgart, Steiner.

Saxena, H.O. and Dutta, P.K. (1975), 'Studies on the ethnobotany of Orissa'. *Bulletin of the Botanical Survey*, India Vol. 17, Nos. 1–4, pp. 124–31.

Schmidt-Vogt, D. (1988), 'High altitude forests in the Jungal Himal (Eastern Central Nepal): Forest types and human impact'. Heidelberg, Ruprecht Karls University. Unpublished Ph.D. Dissertation. Skeiner, 1990.

——(1991), 'Schwendbau und Pflanzensukzession in Nord-Thailand, *AvH-Magazin* 58, pp. 21–32.

Schnell, R. (1952), 'Contribution à une étude phyto-sociologique et phyto-géographique de l'Afrique Occidentale: Les groupements et les unités géo-botanique de la région guinéenne'. *Mémoires de l'I.F.A.N* 18, pp. 41–236, Dakar.

Schreir, H., Shah, P.B., Kennedy, G., Schmidt, M. and C. Dunlop (1989), 'Soils, sediments, erosion and fertility in Nepal. Evaluation of soil fertility and erosion with GIS techniques in the Jhiku Khola Watershed in Nepal'. Annual report. IDRC Co-operative Research Program, University of British Columbia.

Seeland, Klaus (1980), 'The use of bamboo in a Rai village'. *Journal of the Nepal Research Centre* Vol. 4, pp.175–87.

——(1986), 'Sacred world-view and ecology in Nepal'. In *Recent Research in Nepal,* Schriftenreihe Internationalese. Asienforum Vol. 3, pp.187–98, Cologne, Weltforum Verlag.

——(1994), 'Sanskritization and environmental perception among Tibeto-Burman speaking groups'. In *Himalaya: Past and Present.* Joshi, M.P., Fanger, A.C. and C.W. Brown (ed.), pp. 121–39, Vol. III, Almora, Shree Almora Book Depot.

Seeland, K., Patnaik, G. B., Patnaik, K.K., Das H.C., Jena, M.K., Pathi, P. and S.C. Behera (1995), 'Indigenous Knowledge on Forests. An enquiry into the worlds of Kuttia Khonds and Saoras of Orissa, India.' Two volumes, Unpublished manuscript.

Shepherd, Gary (1982), *Life among the Magars.* Kathmandu, Sahoyogi Press.

Shidei, T. (1985), *Shinrin (Forest).* Tokyo, Hōsei Daigaku Shuppankyoku.

Shingūshishi Hensan Iinkai (ed.) (1972), *Shingu Shishi (The History of Shingū City).* Shingū, Shiyakusho.

Shrestha, A.M. and R.B. Shrestha (1988), 'Species composition and distributional analysis of the vegetation of Suryabinayak forest area'. *Forestry: Journal of the Institute of Forestry, Nepal* No. 10, pp. 29–48, Pokhara, IOF.

Shrestha, Neeru (1988), 'Women as mountain environmental managers in Nepal'. Centre for Economic Development and Administration, Kathmandu, Tribhuvan University.

Shrestha, V.S. (1984), 'A caste study of the Surya Vinayak Religious Forest: Bhaktapur, Nepal'. Institute of Forestry, Tribhuvan University. Unpublished B.Sc. thesis, Nepal.

Singh, H. (1989a), 'Katunje Panchayat: Kabhre District, Chiurikholaban 30–31.1.89', Kathmandu, NAFP. Unpublished report.

——(1989b), 'Thulosiru Bari Panchayat: Ashineko Ban 28–29/3/89', Kathmandu, NAFP. Unpublished report.

Singh, M.M. (1989), 'Controlled Growth in Bhutan', *Himal* Vol. 2, No. 3, p.11, Kathmandu, Himal Associates.

Singh, N.N. (1983), 'Heritage conservation plan and objectives with interaction on tourism'. Third International PATA Tourism and Heritage Conference Kathmandu, Nepal, 1–4 November, 1983.

Singh, S. (1986), *Conserving India's Natural Heritage.* Dehra Dun, Natraj Publishers.

Smitinand, T. (1988), 'Weeds in shifting cultivation in Thailand' in *Weeds and the environment in the Tropics.* K. Noda and B.L. Mercado (ed.), pp. 79–99.

Spencer, R. (1966), *Shifting Cultivation in South-eastern Asia.* Berkeley, University of California Press.

Sponsel, L. (1986), 'Amazon Ecology and Adaptation', *Annual Review of Anthropology* 15, pp. 67–97.

Steinemann, Brigitte (1987), *Les Tamangs du Népal: Usages et religion, religion de L'Usage.* Paris, Edition Recherche sur les Civilisations.

Stracey, P.D. (1979), 'Some Stray Thoughts on "People and Forests": with no apologies'. In *Man and Forest,* Krishna Murti Gupta and Desh Bandhu (ed.), pp. 55–9, Delhi, Jain.

Sutō, I. (1991), *Yama no hyōteki: inoshishi to yamabito no seikatsushi (The Mountain Target: A record of the way of life of wild boars and mountain people).* Tokyo, Miraisha.

Suzuki, T. (1982), *Nihon zokushin jiten (Dictionary of Common Beliefs).* Tokyo, Kadogawa.

Tamang, D. (1990), 'Indigenous forest management systems in Nepal: A review'. Research Report Series No. 12, Nepal, Winrock.

Tanigawa, K. (1980), *Tanigawa Ken'ichi chōsakushū 1 (Collected Works of Tanigawa Ken'ichi,* Vol. 1). Tokyo, San'ichi Shobō.

Turnbull, C. (1961), *The Forest People.* London, Triad Paladin.

Tuzin, Donald F. (1980), *The Voice of the Tambaran. Truth and illusion in Ilahita Arapesh religion.* Berkeley, University of California Press.

Ucko, P.J. and G.W. Dimbleby (eds.) (1969), *The Domestication and Exploitation of Plants and Animals.* London, Duckworth.

Ue, T. (1980), *Yamabito no Ki. Ki no Kuni, Hatenashi Sanmyaku (Diary of a Mountain Person: The Hatenashi Mountain Range, tree country).* Tokyo, Chūko Shinsho.

——(1983), *Yamabito no Dōbutsushi (A Mountain Villager's Record of Animals).* Tokyo, Fukuinkan Shoten.

——(1984), *Yama no Ki no Hitorigoto (The Soliloquy of Mountain Trees).* Tokyo, Shinjuku Shobō.

——(1987), *Seishun o Kawa ni Ukabete. Ki to Ningen no Uchū II (Youth Afloat in the River: The universe of trees and men* Volume Two). Tokyo, Fukuinkan Shoten.

Umeda, E. (1992), *Kishūki no Kuni 'Kikiaruki' (Walking Around the Land of Kishū Trees).* Wakayama, Chūwa Insatsu.

Umehara, T. (1988), 'Nihonjin no 'Ano Yo' Kan', *Chūō Kōron* (May), pp.102–130.

Uphoff, N. (1986), *Local Institutional Development: An analytical sourcebook with cases from the Rural Development Committee.* Cornell University, Connecticut, Kumarian Press.

Upreti, R.P., Adhikari, K.N. and K.W. Riley (1989), 'Rapid Rural Appraisal Trek-hill crops: To Solukhumbu, Ramechhap and Dolakha Districts on March 10–17, 1989'. Travel Report 2/89 Hill Crops Improvement Programme, Kathmandu, NARCS, HMG.

Uprety, L.P. (1986), 'Fodder situation: An ecological-anthropological study of Machhegaon, Nepal'. Forestry Research Paper Series No. 5, Kathmandu, HMG-USAID-GTZ-IDRC-FORD-WINROCK PROJECT.

Villajero, A. (1952), *Asi Es la Selva.* Lima, Samarti and Cia.

Vitebsky, Piers (1993), *Dialogues with the Dead: The discussion of mortality among the Sora of eastern India.* Cambridge, Cambridge University Press.

Watanabe, S. (1986), *'Inuzuka' (Dog Mound). Nihon denki densetsu daijiten (Dictionary of Romantic Legends of Japan).* Tokyo, Kadogawa.

Whitmore, T.C. (1984), *Tropical Rain Forests of the Far East.* Oxford, Clarendon Press.

Whitten, N. (1985), *Sicuanga Runa: The other side of development in Amazonian Ecuador.* Urbana, University of Illinois Press.

Wilson, A. (1993), 'Sacred forests and the elders' in *The Law of the Mother: Protecting indigenous peoples in protected areas.* E. Kemf (ed.). San Francisco, Sierra Club.

Wilson, E.O. (1988), 'The current state of biodiversity' in *Biodiversity,* Wilson, E.O. and F.M. Peter (ed.), pp. 3–18. Washington DC, National Academy Press.

WKMK (Wakayama Ken Minwa no Kai) (ed.) (1981), *Kumano Hongū no Minwa (The Folktales of Kumano Hongū).* Gobō, Wakayama Ken Minwa no Kai.

Woodburn, J. (1982), 'Egalitarian Societies'. *Man* 17, pp. 431–51.

Yamano, T. (1989), *Ki no koe ga kikoeru (I Can Hear the Voices of the Trees).* Tokyo, Kōdansha.

Yanagita, K. (1970), *About Our Ancestors: The Japanese family system.* Tokyo, Japanese Society for the Promotion of Science, Ministry of Education.

Yen, A. (1974), 'Thematic patterns in Japanese folktales: A search for meanings'. *Asian Folklore Studies,* Vol. 33 No. 2, pp.1–36.

Yen, D.E. (1989), 'The domestication of environment' in *Foraging and Farming. The evolution of plant exploitation.* D.R. Harris and G.C. Hillman (eds.), London, Unwin Hyman.

Yoshigaitō, K. (1987), 'Kishū Ōkami no "Seitai" (The 'Ecology' of the Kishū Wolf)', *Kiba* No. 2, pp.3–4.

Yukawa, Y. (1988), 'Sato ni Chikazuku Yama. Shiba Mura Omae no Minzoku Henyō (Mountain Descends to the Village: The transformation of folkways in Omae, Shiba Village)'. *Kokuritsu Rekishi Minzoku Hakubutsukan Kenkyu Hokoku* Vol. 18, pp. 341–68.

——(1991), *Hen'yō suru sanson: minzoku saikō (Changing Mountain Villages: Reconsidering Folklore).* Tokyo, Nihon Editasukuru Shuppanbu.

Zinke, P.J., Sabhasri, S. and P. Kunstadter (1978), 'Soil fertility aspects of the Lua' forest fallow system of shifting cultivation' in *Farmers in the Forest.* P. Kunstadter *et al.* (ed.), pp.134–59, Honolulu, East-West Center.

Zvelebil, K.V. (1988), *The Irulas of the Blue Mountains.* New York, Maxwell School of Citizenship and Public Affairs.